CONFLICT MANAGEMENT

A Communication Skills Approach
Second Edition

Deborah Borisoff

David A. Victor

Allyn and Bacon
Boston • London • Toronto • Sydney • Tokyo • Singapore

Vice President and Editor-in-Chief,
Political Science and Communication: Paul A. Smith
Series Editorial Assistant: Kathy Rubino
Marketing Manager: Jeff Lasser
Composition/Prepress Buyer: Linda Cox
Manufacturing Buyer: Suzanne Lareau
Cover Administrator: Jenny Hart
Cover Designer: Suzanne Harbison
Productiom Coordinator: Susan McNally

Copyright 1998, 1989 by Allyn & Bacon
A Viacom Company
160 Gould Street
Needham Heights, MA 02194

Internet: www.abacon.com
America Online: keyword: College Online

Library of Congress Cataloging-in-Publication Data

Borisoff, Deborah.
  Conflict management : a communication skills approach / Deborah Borisoff, David A. Victor. —2nd ed.
    p.   cm.
  Includes bibliographical references and indexes.
  ISBN 0-205-27294-0
    1. Interpersonal conflict.   2. Conflict management.   3. Interpersonal communication.   I. Victor, David A., 1956-   .   II. Title.
HM136.B597 1997
303.6'9--dc21   97-22524
                                                                                    CIP

Printed in the United States of America
10 9 8 7 6 5 4 3   02 01 00

CONTENTS

Preface v

Introduction vi

1   The Nature of Conflict 1
Assessment 5
Acknowledgment 11
Attitude 13
Action 16
Analysis 19
Third-Party Intervention 19
Explaining: The Rhetoric of Apology 25

2   The Languages of Conflict Management: Oral Strategies
for a Supportive Communication Climate 37
Descriptive Speech 40
Problem Orientation 48
Spontaneity 51
Empathy 53
Equality 57
Provisionalism 68

3   The Languages of Conflict Management: Nonverbal Strategies
for a Supportive Communication Environment 75
What Is Nonverbal Communication? 77
Types of Direct Nonverbal Communication 78

Paralanguage 94
Nonverbal Communication Strategies for Conflict Management 97

4   Gender Differences: The Impact of Communication Style on Conflict Management 103
Assessment 104
Acknowledgment 119
Attitude 126
Action 131
Analysis 141

5   Cross-Cultural Awareness in Conflict Management 147
Assessment 148
Acknowledgment 152
Attitude 154
Action 188
Analysis 195

6   How Writing Styles Can Create Conflict 203
Assessment: A Matter of Conceptualization 204
Acknowledgment: Reception 207
Attitude: Transmittal 208
Action 215
Analysis 217

7   Conclusion 223

References 225

Author index 240

Subject index 244

PREFACE

This book provides a communication skills approach to managing interpersonal conflict. The first three chapters focus on defining conflict and on identifying the communication skills required for effective conflict management. Chapter 1 explores the nature of conflict and provides a five-step model for conflict management. Chapters 2 and 3 delineate the principles and techniques of oral and nonverbal communication that facilitate conflict-handling behavior.

The second three chapters explore conflict in specific contexts—contexts not included in works that address other aspects of conflict. Chapter 4 addresses gender differences in communication and explains how the communicative behavior of both sexes may contribute to the ways in which women and men regard, express, and manage conflict. Chapter 5 considers the pseudoconflicts that often result from interacting with individuals from other cultures and explores how these cultural differences can be anticipated, assessed, and avoided. Chapter 6 addresses the act of writing as an often overlooked contributor to conflict and explores how to avoid the unnecessary misunderstandings that frequently result from written communication.

Each chapter concludes with several exercises. The suggested activities target the intervention strategies and communication skills essential for effective conflict management.

Our intention is to familiarize you with the many factors that can lead to interpersonal conflict and to provide you with appropriate communication skills to manage these differences effectively. We hope that those who read this book will no longer regard conflict negatively but will instead consider conflict as an opportunity for development, creativity, and change.

We wish to thank our colleagues for their helpful suggestions that have informed many of the revisions included in this edition. In addition, we would like to thank the reviewers of this edition: Lori Carrell, University of Wisconsin, Oshkosh; Alice Crume, the State University of New York at Brockport; and Mary Ellen Stepanich, Western International University. We are grateful, too, for the support of our families throughout the writing process.

INTRODUCTION

Conflicts are broadly defined as disagreements between and among individuals. Although this definition is obstensibly neutral, many societies—including that of the United States—have imbued the term *conflict* with a negative connotation.

Although disagreements occur routinely, many people regard conflict as a battle to win or a situation to avoid. People who engage in conflict are often considered aggressive, belligerent, and inflexible. Consequently many individuals experience anxiety when faced with a potential conflict. They want neither to enter into what they consider a negative encounter nor to be regarded in a negative light. They are therefore ill prepared to deal with conflicts, which inevitably arise.

Not every difference, however, need be so debilitating. Rather than accepting and perpetuating the negative stereotypes that surround conflict, it is important for individuals to recognize its positive aspects.

The prospect of change can be a compelling and highly motivating force. It is difficult, however, for people to achieve the changes required for managing differences without damaging relationships. The purpose of this book is to help people understand (1) the nature of conflict, (2) the appropriate communication skills for managing conflict, and (3) how gender differences, cross-cultural differences, and writing styles can be sources of conflict. Much of the literature on conflict and on the various contexts of interpersonal communication addressed in this book comes from diverse disciplines. Consequently the references cited reflect the works of noted anthropologists, linguists, psychologists, sociologists, and speech-communication specialists.

The first aim of the book, to enhance the reader's knowledge of the nature and dynamics of conflict, is presented in Chapter 1, which introduces the concept of conflict and conflict-managing behavior. Moreover the chapter provides a five-step model—assessment, acknowledgment, attitude, action, analysis—to enable individuals to handle disagreements effectively.

Chapters 2 and 3 address the second intention of this work: to provide the reader with an understanding of the appropriate communication skills for productive conflict management. These chapters address the action stage of conflict management and detail the communication strategies conducive to a supportive communication environment.

Chapter 2 explores oral communication: the words we choose to express ourselves and the syntactic structures we select to deliver these messages. These aspects of verbal communication influence our listeners' reactions to us. We must therefore develop an awareness of and sensitivity to the potential negative effect our oral assertions can convey.

Oral communication, however, is not the only source of conflict; nonverbal behavior is often a more potent indicator of how we truly feel. This topic forms the core of Chapter 3. Our tones of voice, the ways we use our eyes, facial expressions, and body movements reflect aspects of nonverbal communication. The unspoken messages we send can speak volumes in a business meeting, in a courtroom, in the classroom, and in the home. Thus the effect of nonverbal communication in preventing, initiating, and managing a conflict is enormous.

The third aim of this book is to address specific sources of conflict. Three major sources have been selected for exploration: (1) the effect of gender differences on communication, (2) the effect of cross-cultural differences on interaction, and (3) the effect of writing on creating interpersonal conflict.

Recent social changes exacerbate the potential for conflict. For example, women and men are working together in greater numbers than ever before. When men and women work as colleagues, their different styles of communication may lead to conflict because each sex's communicative behavior reflects distinct acculturation processes and behavioral expectations. Chapter 4 reviews the stereotypical and discernible communication behavior patterns of women and men in the United States and explores how this behavior can be channeled toward constructive conflict management.

International politics and global economics have brought nations closer together. But as we see in Chapter 5, proximity does not necessarily result in mutual understanding, especially when members of different cultures are required to negotiate with one another. To manage cultural differences—differences that often turn out to be pseudoconflicts—it is important for individuals to extend beyond their ethnocentric views of the world and to understand how people from other cultures feel and think.

Pseudoconflicts do not occur only in cross-cultural communication. In Chapter 6 we explore the potential and often avoidable differences that arise from written communication. Much of our daily interaction is handled through the written memo, letter, and report. Because the writer is not usually present to respond to the reader's interpretation of the message, however, careful writing strategies can be extremely useful in averting possible conflict.

Conflict will not vanish merely because individuals are reluctant to deal with disagreements. People who have grown up in an environment in which conflict was ostensibly absent are often ill prepared to deal with others under adverse circumstances. Such individuals lack experience handling disagreements productively. People who have been raised to regard conflict as a direct clash are often equally ill equipped to manage productively the give-and-take aspects of interpersonal relationships.

Individuals will be better prepared to deal with the problems that conflict can create if they are able to replace the notion of conflict as solely a hostile encounter with the more positive attitude of approaching disagreements as a normal part of developing and maintaining personal and professional relationships. When people embroiled in conflict are able to convey a cooperative attitude toward handling disagreements and to demonstrate the communication skills required for effective conflict management, they will embody the best qualities of the empathic, open-minded, and cooperative communicator.

1

THE NATURE OF CONFLICT

Points to Be Addressed

1. Traditional definitions of and views on conflict;
2. Altering assumptions about conflict: Viewing conflict as an integral part of our personal and professional lives;
3. The application of a five-step model to managing conflict productively: Moving from assessment to analysis;
4. Third-party intervention: Benefits and limitations of mediation and arbitration;
5. The rhetoric of apology as an effective tool to reduce or manage conflict.

> *"In my civilization, he who is different from me does not impoverish me—he enriches me."*
> —*Saint-Exupery, 1939*

There are several definitions for the term conflict. Coser (1956, p. 8) introduced the conflict perspective into American sociology with his definition of conflict as "a struggle over values and claims to scarce status, power, and resources in which the aims of the opponents are to neutralize, injure, or eliminate their rivals." Cross, Names, and Beck (1979, p. v) define conflict as "differences between and among individuals."

These differences are created by the nature of the conflict—for example, over goals, values, motives, ideas, and resources. Thomas (1976) provides a process definition of conflict—a process that originates when one individual perceives that another party has frustrated, or is about to frustrate, a goal or concern of his or hers. Deutsch (1971a) distinguishes five types of conflict: intrapersonal (within the self), interpersonal (between individuals), intragroup (within a group), intergroup (between groups), and international (between nations).

Deutsch (1971a, p. 51) further elaborates the term by stating that "conflict exists whenever incompatible activities occur. . . . An action which is incompatible with another action prevents, obstructs, interferes with, or injures, or in some way makes it less likely or less effective." Finally, Hocker and Wilmot (1985, p. 23) provide a communication perspective for the term conflict: "Conflict is an expressed struggle between at least two interdependent parties who perceive incompatible goals, scarce rewards, and interference from the other party in achieving their goals."

The common elements to these definitions include the terms *differences, expressed struggle, incompatible, frustration, interference, perception,* and *interdependence.* There are three distinct but interrelated reasons why members of the U.S. culture have heretofore experienced difficulty in dealing with conflict. Part of this difficulty stems from the pejorative connotation any type of discord conveys in a society that values harmony, compatibility, satisfaction, and independence. Therefore, there has been a tendency in the past to avoid conflict.

A second source of difficulty in dealing with conflict is rooted in how individuals learn to manage conflict. One of the authors, who has been teaching courses and conducting workshops on conflict management for nearly two decades, indicates that with rare exception, students and workshop participants have received little or no exposure to prior training in conflict management. The early experiences of these individuals at home, in school, and with forging friendships have informed their attitudes about conflict and their strategies for coping with differences. Their willingness and ability to deal with conflict, consequently, often reflects a wide range of behavior: Many regard conflict as a competition to be won at all cost; others find ways to continually avoid dealing with conflict.

And yet, in spite of the divergent ways students and workshop participants manage the conflicts in their lives, they share two things in common. First, they are surprisingly consistent in the terms they associate with conflict: "problem," "struggle," "threat," "difficulty" that creates "anxiety," "frustration," "stress," and "anger." By engaging in conflict, they believe that they will risk "rejection" or that they will lose "face," "pride," or "love." To the extent that these associations with the term conflict reflect the larger cultural values or their own personal experiences, we do not know, although we suspect that both are important factors that have shaped their negative orientation toward conflict.

The second commonality shared by those who enroll in courses in conflict management or who participate in conflict-training workshops is their awareness of the pervasiveness of conflict in their personal and professional lives and their desire to become more proficient in managing these conflicts. This leads us to the final difficulty we encounter in dealing with conflict: what we know about the subject and what skills we would presume to teach for managing differences.

The systematic study of conflict is, relatively speaking, in its nascency, having emerged as a field of scholarship in the early 1950s. Despite the impressive growth since the 1970s in workshops, training programs, and courses that address multiple approaches to conflict management and intervention within organizations, schools, and other institutions, Deutsch (1991) suggests that we approach such training with caution, for in his view, "there has been little systematic research on these efforts" (p. 52). According to Deutsch, those who study and teach conflict management and resolution need to address the following issues: (1) how we define conflict management in the first place and measure its effectiveness; (2) the extent to which an individual's ability to manage conflict effectively is influenced and/or varies across situations, contexts, and relationships and the extent to which these variations shape behavior; (3) the identification of age appropriateness for teaching conflict management skills (that is, when is too early or too late to learn such behavior); and (4) the determination of effective training techniques for diverse populations (that is, taking into consideration such factors as culture, ethnicity, gender, age, education, type of work, and so on). We hasten to point out that these issues apply not only to the field of conflict but also to all areas of communication. In Chapters 4 and 5 we explore more fully some of these issues as they apply to gender and culture in managing conflict.

Despite the need for ongoing scrutiny, Deustch acknowledges significant strides in the field. Perhaps one of the most significant achievements that research in conflict management has brought to bear on U.S. culture is the growing recognition of the influence conflict plays in our daily lives and our simultaneous need to view conflict as an opportunity to become more proficient communicators. In our personal relationships, for example, the literature suggests that the major factors in couples' dissatisfaction are the inability to listen and to resolve conflict productively. According to Howard Markman, "what keeps couples together or breaks them up is not how much they love each other or whether they have good sex, but how they handle conflict. . . ." (cited in Hoban, 1992, p. 33). In fact, "the early stages of a relationship can predispose or predict the later stages" (Duck, 1991, p. 98). Duck says that researchers report that "the style and amount of conflict that occur in premarital relationships are accurate predictors of conflict and distress in subsequent marriage" (1991, p. 98). To respond to the pressing need to help couples manage conflict, the American Association for Marriage and Family Therapy has grown significantly (from 9000 to 19,000 members between 1982 and 1992); varying approaches to resolving differences between couples has emerged as a primary focus of therapy (Hoban, 1992, p. 32).

The organizational setting is similarly rife with conflict. The American Management Association reported more than twenty years ago that CEOs, vice-presidents, and middle managers spent nearly 25 percent of their time at work dealing with interpersonal conflict deriving primarily from communication failure, personality clashes, and value differences (Thomas and Schmidt, 1976). For school and hospital administrators, the figure was nearly 50 percent (Lippitt, 1982). As women, minorities, and members from other cultures have increasingly entered the professional ranks, it would seem that the percentages would be even higher today because the more diversity introduced into an environment, the greater the likelihood that misunderstandings and miscommunications will occur (Deutsch, 1991). The growing number of workshops, seminars, and training programs on sexual harassment, diversity, and managerial skills attests to organizations' willingness to respond to the need to prevent and manage conflict productively.

Despite the variations in how conflict has been defined, viewed, studied, and taught, two attributes of conflict management remain constant. First, fundamental to understanding conflict is understanding communication. Because of our differences, we communicate, are challenged, and are driven to find creative solutions to problems. Barnlund cautions that were we all to agree with one another on every topic, conversation would come to a grinding halt, for "where men see and feel alike there is nothing to share. Talk is primarily a means of confronting and exploring differences" (1968, p. 9). Thus communication behavior is at the root of both creating and managing conflict. Second, conflict-handling behavior is not a static procedure. Rather, it is a process that requires flexibility and continual evaluation to be truly productive and effective.

Fisher and Ury (1981), Hocker and Wilmot (1985, 1991), Lulofs (1994), Stuart (1980), and Wehr (1979) are among those who present step-by-step procedures for effective conflict intervention and conflict management. We believe that examining steps for communication can also provide a productive vehicle for presenting and evaluating notable theorists as well as traits and skills required for effective conflict management. In contrast to providing conflict-management techniques as the culmination of understanding, we will use the process of conflict management itself to discuss the issues of conflict, for the process of management or resolution depends on the effective integration of theory and interpersonal communication skills.[1]

Our model for conflict management consists of five steps: assessment, acknowledgment, attitude, action, and analysis. A thorough understanding of each of these components will result in both heightened awareness of the dimensions of conflict and, ideally, in a greater ability for conflict-handling behavior.[2]

ASSESSMENT

Two department heads disagree about how their limited budget should be allocated. A worker is deeply offended, feeling unjustly passed over for an important promotion, and wants to confront the boss. A couple has two distinct views of each other's responsibilities for household tasks. Parents have divergent positions on the freedom they feel their teenage children should have. In each of these examples, the individuals are cognizant of their opposing viewpoints. How they choose to deal with these expressed differences will likely affect the quality of their relationship.

Assessment is an important initial step in managing differences, for it provides each party with an initial understanding about the nature of the relationship, the course of the conflict, and the appropriate communication strategies used in addressing the differences. Five aspects of the communication environment should be assessed during this first stage: (1) the individual traits of the participants and the nature of the relationship, (2) the nature and cause of the conflict, (3) the clarification of

---

[1]Arguably the result of conflict is not always resolution. In fact, there are occasions when individuals feel that it is appropriate to instigate a conflict, to escalate one that already exists, or to refuse to engage in conflict. Regardless of the intent of the disagreement, however, all conflict needs to be managed. An extreme example of violent conflict includes the country that feels that it must retaliate with a military strike for a perceived transgression. In direct contrast to this aggressive act is the use of interpersonal nonviolence to refuse to engage in conflict (as Hocker and Wilmot [1985], for example, assess Gandhi's pacifist stance). In this book we do not advocate one style of conflict-managing behavior. Rather, we advise individuals to become sufficiently familiar with the different types of conflict-handling behavior and with the appropriate interpersonal communication skills that will allow them to productively manage differences when they occur.

[2]Although the five steps for managing conflict are designed especially as strategies to be used before differences erupt into full-blown conflict, they also provide a vehicle for individuals already embroiled in a conflict to step back, evaluate, and, ideally, ameliorate the communication between themselves.

each party's goals, (4) an examination of the communication environ-ment climate, and (5) a preliminary determination of the appropriate conflict-handling behavior.

Individual Traits

Consider the individual traits of the participants and their relationship with one another. These two factors, according to Deutsch (1971a), affect both the development and the course of the dispute, for it is in the relationship, not within the individual, that the conflict resides. For example, a cordial relationship between the president and vice-presi-dent of a firm is qualified by the fact that the president controls their professional relationship. In the event of conflict, the power imbalance between the two is exacerbated by the discrepancy in their roles.

According to Watzlawick, Beavin, and Jackson (1967), the two ele-ments in any communicative act are the content of the communication and the relationship that mediates the content. Consequently in the conflict design described by Deutsch, we would include in our assess-ment consideration of the status of the parties involved, the nature of their prior relationship, how they communicate (style), the perceived threat of loss or change engendered by the relationship, and the com-munication environment in which the conflict occurs.

Nature and Cause of the Conflict

Different belief or value systems are likely to produce a conflict when individuals harboring these fundamental differences vie for goals in such a way that they perceive that only one goal can emerge. For exam-ple, such a difference in belief may emerge when two colleagues dis-agree over which type of computer will best service the needs of their division or when a couple dispute whether to save or to invest a sub-stantial amount of money.

A difference in values can be illustrated if we consider the example of two directors competing for how to spend their limited $60,000 bud-get: One wants to put money into student scholarships; the other believes that the department cannot function adequately without sorely needed equipment. The key in this example is in the term *limited*, for it is the perceived (as opposed to the actual) scarcity of resources that may produce a conflict. It is important to bear in mind that one's definition of the term *limited* is in itself a matter of individual interpretation.

Depending on whether the conflict is one of values, ideas, belief sys-tems, or resources will ultimately determine the approach in managing the conflict. The more a person feels that personal identity and basic values are compromised, the more likely a conflict will ensue and the more difficult it becomes to resolve such differences. Thus debates over religious issues, ethical dilemmas, and basic values—such as pro-life versus pro-choice, capital punishment, and capitalism versus socialism—are not easily resolved.

Individuals who find themselves embroiled in an argument over such issues are not likely to compromise or cede those beliefs they hold strongly. In contrast, when individuals hold certain goals in common but differ in how to achieve them, managing differences is far more likely. For example, two professors may share the same goal of increased student enrollment, but one faculty member might favor scholarships as a means to attract qualified students, and the other may believe that improving the quality of existing equipment will enhance the department's reputation. In the event that funds could be applied to either scholarships or equipment, even though one faculty member would be disappointed, at least that person's goal of hoping to recruit students would not be compromised.

Clarification of Goals

Related to determining the nature of the conflict is the need to clarify one's goals. This is often a difficult step because one's goals are frequently more than merely the ostensible issue at hand.

To continue the case of the directors, although the superficial problem may appear to be a matter of priority, that is, of whether funds should be spent on equipment or on scholarships, the root of the conflict may lie deeper. Perhaps the director who wants the equipment is adamant because the other director has received funds for scholarships over the past several years. The director in favor of scholarships may be similarly adamant because although granting agencies continue to provide for equipment, the number of available scholarships has been reduced drastically during the past decade, thereby preventing otherwise qualified students from pursuing an education. Thus the issues may be joined due to the practical matter of how to spend limited resources and, of equal importance, because of philosophical divergence and the perception by both directors that the other has or could receive the desired funds by means other than the money at hand.

As long as the underlying issues remain buried, it will be extremely difficult, if not impossible, for the participants in this conflict to reach a satisfactory agreement, for each will adhere strongly to her or his point of view without being clear why they are fighting so strenuously. Only when the unarticulated issues are acknowledged can the parties involved begin to resolve their conflict productively.

Examination of Climate

A fourth step in the assessment process is the examination of the communication environment. It is impossible to deal effectively with a
problem without knowing that one's efforts and approach will be appropriate within the structure.

In their book *Managing Job Stress*, Brief, Schuler, and Van Sell (1981)
observe that the type of institution, the stress factor, and the precedents
for dealing with conflict are important variables that determine how
problem solving can be handled effectively within an organization.
Consequently it is important to ask the following as part of the initial
assessment:

1. Does the environment facilitate or discourage open communication?
2. Are there established and fair procedures for addressing and resolving problems effectively (appeals and grievance procedures, for
   example)?
3. Are there designated channels and personnel who are empowered to
   deal with problems?
4. Is the problem typical of the kinds of difficulties that arise in the
   institution or organization?
5. Have similar problems been resolved satisfactorily in the past?

If we consider again the conflict between the two directors, it is obvious
that they will be unable to proceed in reconciling their differences until
they know they can do so openly in an environment that allows for
expressed divergence of opinions without reprisal.

Preliminary Determination
of Conflict-Handling Behavior

Once the nature of the conflict has been defined and clarified and the
climate of the communication environment has been examined, the
parties involved can begin to determine the proper approach for dealing
with the problem. Blake and Mouton (1964) are credited with identifying five conflict-solving strategies: smoothing, compromising, forcing,
withdrawal, and problem solving. Thomas and Kilmann (1974) later
developed a conflict-mode instrument designed to determine managerial conflict-handling behavior and labeled their approaches accommodating (smoothing), compromising, competing (forcing), avoidance
(withdrawal), and collaborating (problem solving).

Although labels for these strategies may have been altered, the
essential aspects of each of these approaches have remained consistent,
and the basic dimensions of each of these modes are important to con-

sider when dealing with conflict. According to Blake and Mouton (1964), the five conflict-handling modes represent a degree of cooperation, or willingness to satisfy another's needs, and assertiveness, or need to satisfy one's own needs (see Table 1.1).

Competing behavior reflects the extreme example of concern for one's needs at the expense of the other party. Identified with win–lose behavior, all-out competition may be appropriate in such contexts as a sporting event or a battle or when a company is trying to beat out the competition.

When dominance, or win–lose, strategies are employed in interpersonal relationships, however, the effect on the party who has lost can be frustration or dissatisfaction. Filley (1977), for example, reports that in corporate settings the least-effective managers rely on win–lose strategies when dealing with subordinates. Similarly, as evidenced by the extensive research on relationships between women and men in U.S. culture, personal settings are also an arena for dissatisfaction when one party dominates the other (Beck, 1988; Bernard, 1981; Henley, 1977; Jamieson, 1995; Kramarae, 1981; Rubin, 1983; Stockard and Johnson, 1980; and Tannen, 1994).

Although competing may not be suitable for bolstering interpersonal relationships, it may be the appropriate technique if the goal is to win at all costs. An actor trying out for a part, a dean determined to get the biggest budget for his or her school, or a major company fending off the competition will feel justified in employing any means necessary to accomplish their respective goals.

At the other extreme of competing behavior is avoidance. Identified with withdrawal from or denial of a problem or conflict, the inability or unwillingness to deal with a problem can be "a painful, disconfirming experience," according to Hocker and Wilmot (1985, p. 113), because avoiding a problem may convey that one person's needs or goals are unimportant.

TABLE 1.1   Conflict-Handling Modes

Mode	Level of Assertiveness	Level of Cooperation
Competing	High	Low
Compromising	Moderate	Moderate
Collaborating	High	High
Avoiding	Low	Low
Accommodating	Low	High

Summary of Thomas and Kilmann's (1974) communication styles of conflict-handling behavior based on Blake and Mouton's (1964) categories of conflict style.

It is essential during the assessment stage to determine whether the conflict should be acknowledged at all. For example, a coworker might decide not to confront a colleague about regularly coming in late, knowing that the coworker will be leaving the firm at the end of the month. The person does not wish to create a tense environment and will avoid the issue during this brief period. On the other hand, for an employee who resents being passed over for special assignments and promotion, avoiding the issue will only sustain, if not exacerbate, the employee's negative feelings toward the boss.

Compromise is considered the middle-ground position on the conflict grid, and certainly it is one of the easier tactics to employ. If we return to the example of the two directors pursuing the $60,000, an ostensibly simple method to resolve the issue would be to divide the money evenly. Although on the surface this would solve the problem, both parties may in fact lose; that is, half of the money may be insufficient either to purchase adequate equipment or to provide for meaningful scholarships.

In other circumstances, however, a compromise might be indicated. For example, a secretary might be induced to work late for several nights if allowed to come in later for work on these days. Or one director might be willing to forego the money this year if assured of receiving an equal amount the following year. Although compromising often leaves one or both parties dissatisfied (Filley, 1977), Jamieson and Thomas (1974) have found that compromise is often a highly viable approach when time and resources are limited.

Accommodation, the fourth mode of conflict-handling behavior, reflects the highest degree of cooperation on the part of one of the parties but the lowest amount of assertiveness. Associated with smoothing behavior, or ceding to the other party's wishes, accommodation, as with avoidance behavior, satisfies only one party's concerns and fails to consider the needs and feelings of the person who is seeking to establish harmony.

As with other modes, however, the situation and parties involved often require accommodation. One spouse may be especially accommodating to the other spouse's needs if the latter has recently been laid off from work. A manager might accommodate his colleague's wishes to select her office first, because having a window facing in a particular direction is not that important to him.

The willingness or ability of an individual to act in an accommodating way over a period of time is highly individual. Depending on whether one is concerned with relational or task-oriented goals, accommodating may or may not satisfy the needs of the accommodating party. If a group of people are concerned about the quality of a relationship, they may find accommodating others rewarding, whereas those who are less concerned with the nature and quality of interpersonal relationships may find this approach to problem solving unsatisfactory. (In Chapters 4 and 5, which deal with gender differences and cross-cultural issues and conflict management, this concept will be further explored.)

Collaboration is the conflict-handling behavior that requires a high level of both assertiveness and cooperation. Recognized as a "win–win" mode by Thomas and Kilmann (1974), it is the most integrative method of problem solving, for it acknowledges the concerns of the parties involved and identifies clearly their motives and goals. Although generally recognized as the most productive conflict-handling behavior, a collaborative approach requires a great deal of energy, creative thinking, empathy, and activity, and not all conflicts may warrant such intensity. For example, a collaborative approach may not be necessary when a couple given a gift of $100 disagree on how to spend the money. Such an issue may be resolved simply by dividing the gift in half.

If we return to the initial dilemma of the two directors, however, the most effective way to solve their problem might be a collaborative approach. One way to address the problem, for example, would be to analyze carefully the health of each program. The program seeking equipment may lease/purchase the equipment, thereby reducing an initial outlay of funds and allowing for scholarship support. Another way of approaching the problem might be an integration of programs. Perhaps scholarships could be awarded to students in one program, who in turn would contribute certain hours to working in the lab, thereby reducing personnel costs in the other program. This would allow the savings to be invested in equipment. Certainly an approach such as this is at best difficult and requires both commitment and cooperation from both parties. This approach may also, however, allow most fully that both programs get what they are seeking.

As we have seen, the effectiveness of each of the five conflict modes depends on the circumstances and conditions underlying the ostensible conflict. Only through an accurate assessment of the situation can we preliminarily select the most appropriate conflict-handling behavior for dealing with a problem.

ACKNOWLEDGMENT

Although all the steps designated in the assessment phase are important, they are essentially ineffective unless one acknowledges the other party involved. A key concept in Deutsch's (1971a; 1991) social psychological approach to conflict management is that one is dealing with an individual's perceptions, which may or may not correspond to an objective assessment of the situation. Yet unless one is able to demonstrate an awareness and to articulate fully the beliefs, goals, ideals, and personality traits of the other party involved, it will be unlikely that the conflict can be handled productively.

A useful process for understanding and acknowledging others is to follow the ideas proposed by cross-cultural experts Edward T. Hall (1961, 1966) and Harry C. Triandis (1976), for the works of both rely on the ability to understand and to acknowledge the similarities and differences between people.

A crucial issue in cultural evaluation stems from the fact that most people behave in ways Hall calls "out-of-awareness." That is, people make certain assumptions based on their own backgrounds, experiences, and culture about how they behave and about how others behave. When those expectations are violated or intruded on, a person experiences discomfort and anxiety.

Hall illustrates this concept with the example of how time communicates. For example, if a U.S. businessperson arrives for an appointment in certain Latin American countries approximately ten minutes ahead of the scheduled appointment, the individual will become extremely irritated if forced to wait for more than twenty minutes beyond the time scheduled. The reason for this response, according to Hall, is that U.S. businesspeople value time and view it as a commodity that should not be wasted. The other culture, in contrast, may not have such a restricted view of time, and being late for an appointment may not demonstrate rudeness or disregard for others. Therefore two individuals may regard the same objective fact from diametrically opposed positions.

To illustrate this concept from a monocultural perspective, consider the vice-president who always sets "rush" deadlines for her director. To meet the continually "urgent" deadlines, the director would have to submit incomplete materials. To avoid this, she consistently turns in complete and accurate documents—but they are inevitably late. The director is frustrated by her inability to function well under pressure, as demonstrated by the fact that she is always late with urgently needed materials.

A conflict will inevitably erupt if the vice-president and the director do not acknowledge the following information: When the vice-president demands urgent material, she does not expect a perfect document; for the director, "crucial," "urgent" materials also mean totally correct. Once the vice-president and the director are able to recognize and acknowledge each other's expectations, a frustrating situation for both can be turned into a productive relationship.

During the acknowledgment phase, therefore, it is incumbent upon each party to recognize that the other individual's perspectives may differ from his or her own. Without such awareness, the ability to deal with a problem is thwarted. Concepts related to language use, time, proxemics, kinesics, and haptics are particularly vulnerable to misperceptions and should be clearly and accurately defined and explained. (Chapters 2 and 3 address more fully the verbal and nonverbal communication required for effective conflict management to occur.)

ATTITUDE

To ensure productive conflict management, it is not sufficient to assess the situation and to acknowledge the other parties involved. Simply acknowledging another person's beliefs, goals, and values does not necessarily imply that one's attitude toward the other party will be conducive to dealing with the problem.

For conflict to be managed productively, the participants must demonstrate their willingness to engage in a mutually dependent exchange that includes rather than excludes the parties involved. In fact, research indicates that individuals who demonstrate conciliation, compassion, and concern are willing to take risks, take responsibility for their own actions, and are able to trust and are more effectively able to deal with conflict than are individuals who do not evidence these qualities (Cummings, Harnett, and Stevens, 1971). Thus one's attitude toward others becomes a crucial dimension in effective conflict management.

To create an atmosphere that generates trust and cooperation, individuals must address their attributions of behavior (or comparing their own behavior to the behavior of others) that can serve as barriers to conflict management. Consequently in addition to acknowledging the other individual's perspective, one's attitude toward that individual needs to be a willingness to engage in a productive communication exchange.

Individuals develop perceptions about themselves and form opinions about others. This, Hall (1961) observes, is the result of cultural experiences. But socialization also causes people to apply labels to their own and others' behavior (Knapp, 1980; Williams and Best, 1982).

To illustrate this concept, consider U.S. cultural expectations of ectomorphic, or thin, men to include mistrustfulness (Knapp, 1980). By link-ing appearance to expected behavior, we may therefore ascribe certain behavioral responses to a thin man and adjust our own behavior to that person in anticipation of his responses. In other words, if we anticipate the thin man's response to be unfriendly and/or suspicious, we are likely to act in a mistrustful and suspicious way toward him, thus eliciting a mistrustful or negative response, even if it is not in his nature to act unfriendly.

The implications of assumptions about others for conflict management are clear: To deal effectively and productively with others, it is essential to suspend stereotyped assumptions and to enter into a communication encounter with an open-minded attitude. Certainly we are aware of the debilitating effects of stereotyping behavior and the danger of attributing a trait to others based on our own assumptions even when the other party does not possess this characteristic. Labels about culture, ethnicity, gender, and religion attest eloquently to the damage that can result from attitudinal attributions.

In addition to examining our own stereotyping behavior, it is important to explore how we perceive our own behavior compared with the other party's behavior. This process will also influence directly our attitude toward the other individual in a conflict situation. Thomas and Kilmann (1977) postulate four reasons why individuals in a conflict situation are inclined to regard their own behavior as reasonable and appropriate while viewing the other party's behavior as just the opposite.

First, we often fail to understand fully why the other party is acting or feeling as she or he does. Our attitude thus becomes an assumption that the other individual is being unreasonable in contrast to our own reasonable actions. A manager who states, "I am always bending over backward to meet her deadlines," in response to a supervisor's criticisms may be unaware that his boss is equally pressured to meet her own unit's schedules. To prevent the escalation of a conflict or to manage an already evident problem, one's attitude should be willingness to suspend judgment of the other party's behavior until all sides of the issue have been articulated.

A second reason why an individual will regard his or her own behavior as reasonable or fair in contrast to how the other party behaves is that people are often unaware of how their own behavior is perceived and interpreted by others. Because we are often unable to monitor our own nonverbal behavior, a woman, for example, may be unaware that her frowning and lip biting are communicating unhappiness and nervousness, thereby contradicting her verbal assertions that everything is fine in a relationship. Because nonverbal behavior is regarded as a more accurate measure of how an individual actually feels than what is said (Birdwhistell, 1970), it is reasonable to assume that the individual in conflict with the woman in this example will respond to her gestures instead of to her words. Because constructive conflict management requires open and honest communication, one's attitude toward the other party should include monitoring one's own behavior so that verbal behavior is consistent with what is being communicated nonverbally.

Related to how we manifest our own nonverbal behavior is how we interpret others' behavior. The third reason that attitude affects a relationship in a conflict situation is due to the implicit threat of losing to the other party. This makes us particularly sensitive to another's communicative behavior. Such sensitivity may also result in misperception and in misinterpretation. A worker, for example, might be suspicious of her boss's affirmation of a need to resolve a problem if the worker's attitude toward management in general is negative. Two colleagues pursuing a promotion to the same position may regard each other's behavior with skepticism and as a means of furthering solely the other's own chances for getting ahead. Such negative positions belie an attitude that can prevent productive resolutions to problems and that make it difficult to maintain satisfactory relationships.

In these examples attitudes need to change to turn destructive conflicts into productive ones. The worker needs to suspend judgment of her boss and to react on the merits of the interaction rather than on the basis of their positions within the company. For the two colleagues in the second example to work productively, they need to acknowledge their individual aspirations, but they also need to place the demands and well-being of the organization above their personal pursuits.

A fourth barrier to creating a trusting environment is the pressure on both parties in a conflict to regard themselves positively and to view the other individual negatively. A couple experiencing marital difficulties may consider their own respective contribution to the problem as minimal, placing the blame for their difficulties on the other partner. The husband, feeling that his wife wants to talk everything to death, turns off (justifiably so, in his opinion) many of his wife's attempts to discuss their problems. The wife, seeing her husband turn her off, accuses him of not wanting to listen to her and of not caring sufficiently about the relationship. As long as both parties remain defensive about their own behavior and critical of their partner's actions, their negative attitudes will likely make untenable any satisfactory resolution.

Assessment of a conflict or potential conflict situation is a crucial first step, for it enables the individual to consider the nature of the conflict, to clarify individual goals, and to preliminarily plan how each will interact initially with the other party. Acknowledging the other party's concerns and outlook is a second stage that will undoubtedly affect how an individual will bring the other party's perspectives to bear on his or her own behavior. The third step, examining one's attitudes toward the other party, engenders an encounter with an open and, ideally, unbiased perspective. Having completed the assessment, acknowledgment, and attitude phases, one is ready to proceed to the fourth stage, action.

ACTION

The ultimate aim of conflict management is to take productive action toward achieving one's goals. Anyone who has ever been involved in emotionally fraught conflict situations recognizes how difficult it can be to control consciously one's actions and how potentially destructive such a lack of control may be. A crucial stage of the conflict-management process is to integrate the assessment, acknowledgment, and attitude dimensions into the most appropriate action for the particular situation.

The primary manifestations of action are in the participants' choice of verbal and nonverbal cues. As noted by Gibb (1961), communication strategies are the central factors in the creation of either defensive or supportive climates. Verbal choices can create defensiveness when statements sound evaluative rather than descriptive, controlling rather than problem oriented, strategic rather than spontaneous, neutral rather than empathic, or superior rather than equal. Nonverbally, body position and orientation, distance between participants, and facial expressions such as frowning or looking away from the other party may put the other party on the defensive, thereby either exacerbating the conflict or even creating conflict.

Clearly the parties in conflict must be conscious of their actions and should work to become skilled at using various and appropriate communication techniques. On the verbal level a conflict participant must make active choices regarding a variety of issues. Language style must be appropriate to the situation. A conflict participant may sound condescending in certain instances by use of language style, which may in turn escalate a conflict. Slang, jargon, or obfuscation may also cause unnecessary problems, whereas thoughtful word selection may enable individuals to resolve their differences more efficiently.

Besides language style, decisions must be made regarding asking questions. Too many and poorly-timed questions may be detrimental, whereas judiciously-asked questions may indicate attentive listening and caring and may enhance effective communication when in conflict. Incorporating techniques such as dating (noting clearly when something occurred or how long ago observations were made), indexing (pinpointing the uniqueness of specific individuals or situations—avoiding stereotyping), and "to-me-ness" (a means by which a speaker indicates that his or her perceptions are not etched in stone, by making such statements as "it seems to me. . .") in one's language may also be productive in managing differences.

On the nonverbal level there is an equally broad range of choices. Participants must carefully select the setting of the confrontation. Would it be best to interact on home territory, on a neutral front, or on one's opponent's home court? What kind of object language should participants choose for their encounter? It may be more appropriate to dress down for some conflicts and to dress up for others. Whether it is appropriate to touch fellow interactants is an important question about nonverbal behavior in conflict. A touch from a subordinate may indicate insubordination when in conflict and may contribute to punitive measures in the workplace, whereas touch between a battling couple may be the right choice to move communication in a productive direction. Appropriate facial expressions, decisions regarding eye contact, and tone of voice are also crucial to productive conflict management. Smiling may indicate that one does not take the conflict seriously, staring may appear to be a challenge, and sounding hesitant may bring sincerity into question.

Much work provides insight into the action dimension of communication strategies that are crucial for effective conflict management: researchers Barnlund (1968), Condon (1965), and Gibb (1961) exploring semantics and verbal coding; Birdwhistell (1970), Knapp (1980), and Mehrabian (1981) investigating nonverbal cues; psychologists Watzlawick, Beavin, and Jackson (1967) studying human interaction; and sociologist Goffman (1959) discussing the nature of the situation. Although the work of most of these scholars focuses primarily on interpersonal theory in general terms, specific applications to the field of conflict studies can be made. Conflict management is, after all, effected through communication. To take productive action in conflict situations, one must therefore develop both an understanding of communication techniques and the ability to apply these techniques.

Using verbal and nonverbal communication strategies in an environment that facilitates rather than inhibits interaction, participants in a conflict should attend to the following transactional stages:

1. Establish credibility with the other party. According to Gahagan and Tedeschi (1968), compliance depends on the credibility of one's opponent.
2. Early on in the encounter, establish a level of trust so that the

transaction can proceed toward a resolution of differences. Zand (1972, p. 178) defines trust as "the conscious regulation of one's dependence on another that will vary with the task, the situation, and the other person."

3. Articulate the problem from both points of view so that all parties have a clear understanding of the other person's position and motivation.

4. Use accurate and appropriate verbal and nonverbal communication. (See Chapters 2 and 3.)

5. Ascribe equal status to the participants during the exchange. Watson and Johnson (1972) observe that only when both parties are empowered to articulate their goals and feelings can productive conflict management occur.

6. Early on during the exchange, establish common goals. For example, to thwart an actual work stoppage in a pending strike, both labor and management will have to agree that preventing or ending the strike is a mutual goal.

7. Try to anticipate the concerns of others so that communication is not one-sided.

8. Seek continual feedback. The only way to ascertain that one's statements and concerns are clearly understood is to elicit questions and information from others. Fisher and Ury observe that whereas statements often generate resistance, questions can be a powerful tool to encourage answers (1981, p. 117).

9. Demonstrate willingness to modify one's communication behavior. Because conflict management reflects a process and not a static procedure, it is important to reevaluate one's conflict-handling behavior and to adapt one's behavior according to the needs of the interaction.

10. Generate as many potential options or solutions as possible that integrate both sides of the issue. In their study on effective leadership, Maier and Sashkin (1971) propose that a combination of integrating needs and suggesting creative solutions is a highly desirable and successful conflict-management strategy.

11. Keep the channels of communication open in an atmosphere that supports interaction. It will be extremely difficult to achieve satisfactory solutions to a problem if one's needs, ideas, and feelings are continually misinterpreted or denied a voice. Barnlund (1968) contends that those who are impervious to the words of others, while staunchly defending their right to assert their concerns, serve only to deny individuals any meaningful role in the transaction.

12. Review and summarize the expectations and decisions of all parties.

ANALYSIS

The final step in our conflict-management model is analysis. It should be clear that analysis is employed throughout the conflict-management process as part of the assessment, acknowledgment, attitudinal, and action stages. It is important, however, to designate analysis also as a separate, culminating step.

Once the decisions have been reviewed and summarized, it is important to consider whether

1. the concerns of all parties have been met as adequately as possible;
2. the decisions can be implemented swiftly and/or effectively;
3. the short- or long-term effects of the solution are viable; and
4. the relationship between the conflicting parties has been modified productively.

Hocker and Wilmot (1991, p. 39) observe that conflict brings both danger and opportunity. Although certainly the notions of frustration, loss, and threat represent undeniable dimensions of conflict, as Deutsch (1971a; 1971b) notes, the potential value of conflict should be neither ignored nor denied. We can propose that the value in conflict emerges from the fact that through conflict, stagnation can be ended. Also, conflict can provide a vehicle for presenting and solving problems. Equally important, social and personal change, and, ideally, growth can result from addressing differences. Finally, we can generate creative approaches to problem solving through how effectively we manage conflict.

If indeed we are living in an era that supports and requires communication, conflict can, as Hocker and Wilmot (1991) observe, bring about a great deal of opportunity. No longer subjected to subjugating our needs and concerns, ours is now an environment that encourages open and honest, albeit at times painful, exchange. Yet it is through such exchange that we can truly avail ourselves of the opportunity to grow. Conflict assuredly is a part of our culture. How we choose to deal with it, however, belies the changes and strides emerging today.

THIRD-PARTY INTERVENTION

A summary of the five steps to managing integrative conflict is presented in the box. In some situations, however, individuals are unable to manage conflict on their own. In such instances it may be appropriate to seek an outsider, someone skilled in bargaining or problem solving.

Steps to Integrative Conflict Management

Assessment:	Allow yourself time to calm down and to evaluate the situation.
	Determine the true source of the conflict.
	Gather appropriate information or documentation.
	Assess the points you are willing or unwilling to compromise on.
	Assess what the other party wants.
	Make a preliminary determination of the appropriate conflict-handling behavior for the situation, for the relationship, and for the environment.
Acknowledgment:	Listen to the other party's concerns.
	Try to understand his or her viewpoint.
Attitude:	Avoid stereotyping and making predeterminations.
	Try to remain objective.
	Remain as flexible and open as possible.
Action:	Watch your own use of language.
	Watch your nonverbal communication.
	Observe how the other party communicates verbally and nonverbally.
	Stick to the issues; don't go off on tangents.
	Don't make promises you can't keep.
	Don't present issues in a win–lose context.
	Don't sidestep the issues.
	Be sincere and trustworthy.
	Try to remain open-minded and flexible.
	Use the conflict-handling behavior appropriate for the situation, and be able to

	revise your behavior according to how the interaction progresses.
	Listen, repeat, and clarify information.
Analysis:	Make sure all parties' concerns have been articulated and considered.
	Summarize and clarify decisions. Review procedures for implementing any changes.

Mediation

Mediation is a form of alternative dispute resolution that is often sought when disputing parties are unable to resolve their differences on their own. As a process, mediation is defined by the following characteristics:

1. An impartial, mutually acceptable, and neutral third party (or parties) is called on to assist disputants reach an agreement (Coulson, 1983; Kressel and Pruitt, 1985; Moore, 1986).
2. This third party facilitates isolating the disputed issues, developing viable options and alternatives, and attaining an acceptable settlement that accommodates the needs of the disputing parties (Folberg and Taylor, 1984).
3. This third party has no authoritative decision-making power in the process but rather must rely on the disputants' responsibility and willingness to reach a mutually acceptable settlement (Folberg and Taylor, 1984; Moore, 1986).

These three traits define and underscore the importance of the mediator's role, deemphasize status and power differences between disputing parties, and stress the empowerment of both sides of the dispute in order to explore and to articulate fully all goals, needs, and concerns.

As a process, mediation appears to be a viable and cost-effective vehicle for resolving differences. Its use in the United States began formally in the late nineteenth century as a means to resolve disputes between management and labor, although its use as a way of resolving differences has been traced back to the teachings of Confucius (551–497 B.C.) (Wall and Blum, 1991) and to the inception of religious institutions in Western culture (Folberg and Taylor, 1984). Since the mid-1960s, the use of mediation in dispute resolution has expanded in the United States to help resolve community disputes, minor criminal issues, divorce and child-custody settlements, student-versus-student and student-versus-teacher disputes in educational settings, international differences, and environmental disputes (Araki, 1990; Duffy, Grosch, and Olczak, 1991; Fisher, 1988; Fisher and Ury, 1981; Gourley, 1994; Hauser, 1995, 1996; Keltner, 1994).

Regardless of the types of disputes in which mediation is employed, those who practice and study mediation agree that this process requires a fairly prescribed format, that mediators require special competencies, and that as an area of practice, mediation faces certain challenges. We turn to a brief examination of each of these areas.

Stages in the Mediation Process

Although practitioners may vary in the number of steps they indicate in the mediation process, we can summarize the goals of each phase of mediation in the following five general categories:

Initiation/Orientation. During this initial phase, the mediator explains his or her role in the mediation process, establishes credentials as a mediator, indicates his or her role as an impartial facilitator, and explains the format of the mediation process. Building a foundation of trust and establishing a productive rapport with the clients are the desired outcomes of this initial stage, a foundation required for all subsequent phases if the mediation process is to be productive.

Information Gathering. During the second stage of the mediation process, the mediator encourages clients to identify and to articulate in their own words the issues to be negotiated. Haynes (1981) refers to this phase as the fact-finding stage, for at this point, both sides exchange considerable information.

Problem Identification. This phase differs from the second phase in that during this stage, the mediator helps the clients to recognize the full extent, intensity, and range of differences, as well as potential points of agreement. According to Keltner (1994, p. 125), at this point in the mediation process, the mediator helps the clients to prioritize the issues to be negotiated, to establish a framework or an "issue agenda" of what will be negotiated, and, most important, to set the criteria that all solutions or alternatives must meet in order to be acceptable.

Generation and Evaluation of Options. Once the agenda and the criteria have been established, clients begin the process of proposing potential solutions, assessing the value of those solutions, and identifying possible areas for compromise. The mediator plays a critical role in helping clients not only generate viable options but also evaluate those options. That is: How closely will each of the options complement the basic needs, goals, and concerns of the parties? What potential trade-offs have been generated to allow the parties to both compromise and reach a settlement? (Keltner, 1994, p. 126)

Finalization of the Agreement. When clients have reached an agreement, the mediator executes the settlement in writing, using, whenever possible, "the disputants' own words" (Hauser, 1996, p. 69), and has all parties sign the agreement. Keltner notes that the most valuable agreements "clarify what is to be done or exchanged, cover all the issues, and hold firm, thereby terminating the dispute" (1994, p. 127).

Competencies and Challenges for Mediators
Beyond possessing and demonstrating the communication competencies outlined earlier in the box, the skilled mediator must understand the role of advocacy (Keltner, 1994, p. 108). In addition, the mediator ought to have "considerable substantive knowledge about the issues around which the conflict centers" (Deutsch, 1991, p. 49).

Despite the potential for mediation to be one of "the most promising sectors" of the conflict-regulation field (Wehr, 1979, p. 34), three fundamental challenges confront those who serve as mediators. First, the range, duration, and competencies provided by programs designed to train mediators vary among agencies and fields. Because of a lack of coherent standards and certification requirements, the potential for a wide variation of quality has led to a call for a substantial assessment of the type of training needed to produce competent and effective mediators (Davis, 1993; Deutsch, 1991; Folberg and Taylor, 1984; Hauser, 1996; Keltner, 1994; Zack, 1985).

The second challenge relates to factors that help identify and assess what communication competencies contribute to effective mediation. Deutsch (1991), for example, calls for the need to investigate what conditions allow for the resolution of difficult disputes.

Hauser (1996) and Keltner (1994) acknowledge the need for effective mediators to be sensitive to and aware of cross-cultural and intercultural issues. We would underscore the importance of cultural awareness. The effective mediator must be cognizant of such cultural conditions as value differences, how communication is displayed and interpreted, and what constitutes appropriate behavior, promotes trust, or reflects neutrality. These are just a few of the diverse cultural factors that affect the quality of a communication exchange and are elaborated more fully in Chapter 5.

The effect of gender on communication is an additional factor that needs to be recognized. Borisoff and Hahn (1995) and Wood and Inman (1993) are among those who argue for the need to consider how we interpret, value, and/or devalue modes of communication that are linked to sex-role or to sex-trait stereotypes. The effective mediator needs to be aware of potential variation in communication that is informed by gender and to make sure that all parties articulate fully their own needs and goals and that all parties are understood by others.

The third challenge confronting the process of mediation is related to the extent to which this proces is voluntary. In her chapter on mediation in cases of abuse, Charity Gourley (1994) indicates that many agencies and courts have increasingly come to rely on mediation to resolve disputes. Often mediation is mandated. In such instances the voluntary dimension of the mediation process, which, as indicated earlier, contributes to the successful resolution of differences, is undermined. Gourley cites several cases that indicate that outcomes are often compromised and qualified when mediation is imposed on disputants.

Arbitration

When individuals or groups are unable to resolve their differences through negotiation, they may resort to arbitration. There are two fundamental aspects to the process of arbitration:

1. An impartial, mutually acceptable, neutral third party is called on to hear all aspects of a case and to make a decision that is usually final and binding (Coulson, 1973; Elkouri and Elkouri, 1960; Keltner, 1994).
2. This third party is responsible for obtaining as much evidence from the disputants as possible in order to determine the truth about a case. (Venues for obtaining evidence may include the submission of written records, the presentation of relevant exhibits, conducting hearings, interviews, and so on.)

There are two fundamental differences between the mediation and arbitration processes. First, whereas the mediator serves more as a facilitator and advocate to help the parties contribute to their own resolution of a dispute, an arbitrator serves more in a quasijudicial role. That is, the arbitrator determines which side is right and which side is wrong in a case. Thus making judgments is an integral role of the arbitrator. The mediator, by contrast, enables the disputants to formulate their own mutually acceptable judgments about the conflict.

The second distinction between these two processes is related to the first; that is, individuals involved in mediation are highly vested in identifying issues and generating viable options that both sides can adhere to and live with. Because the articulated goal of arbitration is to determine the veracity of a case and to make a determination for one side in the dispute, this process is more reflective of a win–lose orientation and relies, therefore, on the strength of the evidence presented by both sides. Those who resort to mediation to resolve a dispute retain their power in the negotiation process. Those who turn to arbitration give up this power.

Despite these differences, there are three basic similarities between these two processes. First, like mediation, arbitration has a long legacy. According to Keltner, arbitration has been practiced informally and formally from the time of King Solomon up through the Middle Ages (1994, p. 152). Moreover, although arbitration also may be applied to the resolution of a wide range of disputes, its use in U.S. culture has been primarily to resolve labor–management and collective-bargaining issues.

The second similarity between these two practices has to do with practitioner training and competencies. The arbitrator, like the mediator, does not require special certification or training in order to practice. This presents a potential problem. However, because the arbitration process is usually more formal in nature and depends on the presentation of evidence, effective practitioners, according to Keltner (1994, p. 155), usually possess significant "real-world" experience, have acquired an appropriate education (e.g., in law, labor relations, or conflict training), and have developed a reputation for being effective.

The third similarity between mediators and arbitrators is their reliance on communication. As we indicated in the section on mediation, the effective practitioner must be sensitive to variations in communication informed by such factors as culture, gender, and ethnicity. Similarly, the effective and ethical arbitrator must be aware of how communication is shaped and influenced, including his or her own attitudes toward others and toward the communication process.

EXPLAINING: THE RHETORIC OF APOLOGY

The dimensions of conflict management presented so far have dealt with advocating and defending one's case. Frequently, however, problems arise because events have gone awry or mistakes have been made. How these events or mistakes are explained can have an enormous impact on the situation. Failure to acknowledge or to address a situation adequately can exacerbate difficulties between individuals.

An often-heard excuse for not submitting a paper or report on time is that "the computer was down." Although many faculty members or administrators have accepted such explanations in the past, in many instances further elaboration would be warranted, such as "I have taken my material to an outside company. The report will be to you within thirty-six hours." or "My computer is being repaired today. I'll have the data ready this evening."

Although the communication skills required for effective conflict management are addressed in the next chapter, some basic steps for explaining or apologizing for a situation include, according to Goodman (1983):

1. *Acknowledging and explaining your role in the situation.* ("I realize that we will not be able to meet the order because of equipment break-down, and I am aware that this is my responsibility." "I know I am in charge of this unit, and the high absenteeism of personnel has seriously hampered our ability to function.")

2. *Explain the problem in general terms.* ("Our department has been experiencing many problems with these machines. They have been breaking down on the average of twice a month." "Apparently there has been an outbreak of the flu in our community—our department, unfortunately, has not been spared.")

3. *Offer a solution to the immediate problem.* ("I have already contacted a manufacturer that makes the same equipment we have, only its machines have a superior performance record. We have arranged to lease its equipment on a short-term basis with an option to purchase." "I have contacted several local placement firms. They are sending over temps to cover our office until our employees are able to return to work.")

4. *Explain controls and make assurances.* ("I have begun to take steps to ensure that this type of situation will not happen again. I am negotiating a contract with the other manufacturer to include regular equipment inspections that will prevent breakdowns." "I have set up a system with our personnel department to inform me when three cases of the same illness are reported, so that I can either make arrangements to borrow personnel from other units or contact temporary agencies before absenteeism reaches crisis proportions.")

5. *Explain the impact of the situation.* ("I realize that this breakdown cost the company several thousands of dollars, but I have assessed the productivity we will be able to handle with the new equipment. My estimation is that we will be able to increase sales by 10 percent next year, an increase that will far surpass this loss." "We were fortunate that

because this is a relatively slow period for us, frayed nerves and inconvenience seemed to be the greatest impact.")

These steps for explaining or apologizing for a situation are especially applicable to situations that arise in professional settings. When it comes to apologizing in personal relationships, students indicate that they are more ambivalent. They acknowledge that apologizing to a friend, a family member, or a romantic partner may be positive, because such actions "make us feel better," "assuage guilt," "clarify our intentions," "repair relationships," and "open the channels to communication."

In light of the positive aspects of apologizing, why, then, do people experience such ambivalence? Over the years, students have generated the following factors that affect their willingness to apologize to or to accept an apology from those closest to them:

1. The fear of rejection, that is, that the other party will not accept the apology;
2. The fear of loss of power, that is, by acknowledging one's own contribution to a problem, the other party will have the upper hand in the relationship;
3. The fear of loss of pride, that is, one's own self-esteem may be lowered if one admits that one may have been wrong; and
4. The fear that too much time has passed to repair the relationship.

By contrast, factors that influence willingness to apologize to another include the following:

1. The extent to which one is vested in the relationship (e.g., a best friend for ten years; parents or close family member; a long-standing romantic partner);
2. The type of "wrongdoing," that is, hurting another's feelings, betraying one's trust, a pattern of inconsiderateness, and so on; and
3. The extent to which the hurtful behavior was intentional or unintentional.

If we consider that most of us were raised to associate apologizing with being wrong (e.g., "Apologize to your brother for taking his toy.") and that apologies were often demanded rather than given freely (e.g., ("Apologize to your mother right now!"), it is understandable that as adults, we view personal apologies primarily as admissions of wrongdoing; that we are not always sincere when we apologize to others.

Therefore the aforementioned barriers become understandable. None-theless, however, students acknowledge the importance of learning how to repair relationships, to change their relationships with others, and to put closure on past conflicts.

Using four of the five steps (Goodman, 1983) provided at the beginning of this section, consider the differences in tone and language use when we attempt to rectify conflicts in our personal relationships:

1. *Acknowledge and explain your role in a situation.* ("I realize that between school and work, I have a million things on my mind, which is why I often forget to let you know that I'll be late." "As your best friend for so many years, I was concerned that you changed so much after you began dating Shelly. That is why I responded the way I did when you asked me what I thought of her."

2. *Explain the problem in general terms.* ("I'm aware that you are concerned about my safety and that when I'm consistently late, this affects your plans as well." "I now realize that as a friend, I should not try to impose my own feelings on another person. What is important is that you are happy."

3. *Offer a solution to the immediate problem.* ("I've begun entering our plans in my date book. From now on, being late will be the exception, not the rule." "I'm aware that any new relationship will have an impact on us and on our friendship. Perhaps if I get to know Shelly better, I won't be so concerned about changes in our own relationship."

4. *Explain the impact of the solution.* ("I'm now more sensitive to the fact that we have different views about lateness. I also realize that being considerate will strengthen our relationship." "I realize that we can't easily replace friends. I know we won't always agree, but more important, I want you to know that I will always support you and be there to listen to you."

Whatever mode of communication we use to apologize—face-to-face, e-mail, telephone, or letter—a sincere and appropriately-timed apology can have a powerful influence on the quality of our personal relationships. The act itself forces us to empathize with others and, ideally, to view our own actions from a different perspective.

SUMMARY

The term conflict has many definitions. Common elements among these definitions include conflict as an expressed struggle between individuals over perceived incompatible goals, resources, or rewards.

Effective conflict management requires a positive attitude toward appropriate interpersonal communication and toward conflict itself. Rather than regard all conflict as a threat or a negative condition, individuals need to consider expressed differences as the potential for creativity and growth.

We propose a five-step model for conflict management that encourages a flexible attitude toward managing differences. This model integrates both conflict theory and interpersonal communication skills.

During the initial, or assessment, stage, individuals are encouraged to examine the context of the communication environment. They must first consider the participants engaged in conflict and their relationship to each other. Second, they need to identify the ostensible areas of contention, along with the communication climate in which these issues are expressed. Only after these initial assessments can people make a preliminary determination of the appropriate conflict-handling behavior, choosing from the five styles—competition, avoidance, accommodation, compromise, and collaboration—initially identified by Blake and Mouton (1964).

The second step, acknowledgment, involves the ability to understand and to articulate both sides' views. The ability to manage differences productively is greatly impeded if individuals lack fundamental information about each side's perspectives regarding issues of contention.

The third step in the conflict-management process is for individuals to develop and display an attitude conducive to productive interaction. An appropriate attitude includes the ability to trust in the other party, or at least in the process of communication, and to enter a communication exchange unencumbered by negative stereotypes, pejorative attributions of intent, or erroneous assumptions about the other party.

Action comprises the fourth step in our conflict-management model. This step encompasses interpersonal communication skills, for it is through communication that we are able to effect conflict management. Accurate communication, appropriate verbal and nonverbal behavior, flexibility of communication style, and the ability to keep the channels of communication open reflect in part aspects of productive action.

The fifth and final stage of our model is analysis. Although analysis is in fact an ongoing process of transactional communication, conflict participants need to consider the feasibility and effectiveness of implementing mutually agreed-on decisions.

In many instances individuals engaged in conflict are unable or unwilling to manage their disputes on their own. When an impasse occurs, conflict participants often resort to third-party intervention.

Through mediation, individuals are encouraged to work out their disagreements. If negotiation fails, conflict parties may resort to arbitration as a means to resolve differences.

Elaborate procedures are not always required for disagreements. In some cases differences can be appropriately handled through an apology. By acknowledging their role in and responsibility for a situation or event, communicators demonstrate their willingness to address and manage conflict constructively.

SUGGESTED ACTIVITIES

The following activities focus on various aspects of conflict management.

A. FOCUS ON PERCEPTIONS ABOUT CONFLICT

At the start of the course or workshop, participants are asked to generate a list of the words they associate with the term conflict. Participants may then be divided into small groups and asked to consider the following, based on their list:

1. What types of nouns, adjectives, and/or verbs were generated?
2. Do these terms reflect positive or negative associations with the term conflict?
3. Were there any commonalities or differences among these associations that might reflect cultural, ethnic, and/or gender differences?

An open discussion considering items 1–3 would follow. Additionally, the group members would address why the term conflict creates negative and/or positive associations for them.

B. FOCUS ON CONFLICT STYLE: SELF-ASSESSMENT

Most individuals do not demonstrate one way of dealing with conflict across situations and relationships. As a way of getting at their own patterns of behavior in conflict situations, individuals are asked to consider the following in both their personal and professional relationships:

1. Consider the individuals with whom you have either had a conflict or feel you would want to confront about a certain issue or problem (e.g.,

a conflict with a roommate about sharing chores, with a girlfriend or boyfriend about amount of time spent together, with a parent about future goals, with a colleague at work about assuming one's share of the work, with a superior who has passed you over for a bonus or promotion).

2. Make a list of those conflicts you react to and those you avoid, and consider what it is about the nature of the conflict and the other party involved that causes you to respond to some issues and to avoid others.

3. Make a list of goals and/or potential behavioral changes that you would like to develop for the way you manage conflict. Some of the general conflict issues, rationales for behavior, and goals may be used as a basis for open discussion: Are there commonalities we share in conflict types, in certain relationships, in specific contexts?

C. FOCUS ON APOLOGY

1. Consider a recent conflict between you and a friend, family member, or colleague at work. Write a letter of apology to this individual. As part of the discussion, consider the intention of the apology and the extent to which the letter may accomplish the goals (e.g., to repair a relationship, to defend one's position, to put closure on the situation or on the relationship.)

2. Using the same or a different situation, write a letter of apology that you would like to receive from another individual.

D. FOCUS ON CONFLICT MANAGEMENT: SELF-EVALUATION

At the beginning of the course or workshop, each participant is asked to begin a journal to follow his or her conflict-handling behavior over a period of time. Each entry should include the date and the following information:

1. Assessment

    a. Describe briefly the conflict in an objective manner.
    b. Who were the participants in the conflict?
    c. What is their relationship to one another?

2. Acknowledgment

    a. Describe the conflict from your perspective.
    b. Describe the conflict as well as possible from the other individual's viewpoint.

3. Attitude

    a. In your opinion, were you being reasonable?

    b. In your opinion, was the other individual acting reasonably?

    c. Specify why or why not for (a) and (b).

4. Action

    a. What conflict-handling behavior(s) did you employ?

    b. Describe your verbal and nonverbal communication strategies.

5. Analysis

    a. Was the conflict successfully resolved?

    b. What was the outcome?

    c. If you were not satisfied with the outcome, what steps might have been taken that would have led to a different solution?

At the end of a designated period, individuals should review their overall development in their ability to assess and manage conflict and set goals for continued improvement. Individual cases may be used as a basis for open discussion.

E. FOCUS ON CONFLICT: MEDIATION AND ARBITRATION

1. Students should be assigned and asked to role play the following situation:

   - *Employee's Side*: The employee contends that the employer "dumps" work on him. Frequently the employer gives the employee work and says it is urgent. The employee believes he is trying to get the work done: He likes the office and his coworkers, but he cannot cope with the overbearing and demanding employer. After working for eight months in this position, the employee has been cautioned by the employer that he may be let go if his job performance does not improve.

   - *Employer's Side*: The employer contends that after eight months, the employee should know the job and not have to be told what is important. In fact, there are a lot of important materials and many items that are urgent. Somehow the employee always manages to find time to take a coffee break in the morning and in the afternoon. If that time were spent working, perhaps the job would get done.

As the mediator called in, what questions would you ask? What recommendations would you make?

The remainder of the group should address the following issues:

    a. What were the attitudes of the employee and the employer toward the situation and toward each other?

     b.   What traits of an effective negotiator were demonstrated by the mediator?

     c.   What conflict-handling behavior(s) were employed?

     d.   Assess the outcome of the interaction.

2.   Consider the following situation: A new manager has been hired to oversee a unit of seven employees. After a few months, it becomes evident that the manager's organizational style conflicts sharply with the communication environment to which the employees were accustomed. The employees were used to an informally run office in which interaction among colleagues and feedback to and from the former director were encouraged. They are therefore resentful of the more formal attitude and expectations of their new supervisor. The employees have communicated their frustrations to the vice-president. The new director has also related concern about the employees' poor attitude and lack of cooperation to the vice-president. The vice-president has determined the need to mediate the conflict between the two sides before productivity is negatively affected.

The class or seminar group should be divided so that there are approximately three groups, each composed of two directors, two employees, two vice-presidents, and one observer. Each group works independently to address the issues from the perspectives of both the employer and the employee. The vice-president will listen to each side and endeavor to mediate the conflict. One member of each group will act as "observer" and will record what transpires within each group.

The entire group reassembles, and each "observer" presents what occurred in his or her group. A discussion and assessment of the effectiveness of each mediator's actions/decisions should follow.

F. FOCUS ON FLEXIBLE CONFLICT-HANDLING BEHAVIOR

Consider the following situations:

1.   A wife wants to develop a career after spending eight years raising two young children who are now in school. The husband believes that he should provide their income and that she is needed to attend to the family's needs.

2.   A young man has been invited back for a second interview at a major accounting firm. The partners he has met seem impressed with his credentials. He is equally impressed with their reputation and with what they can offer him in terms of experience and remuneration. Toward the end of the interview, the partner casually states to the candidate, "Our policy is that no mustaches or beards are allowed. You will, of course, need to shave your mustache when you start to work here." The candidate has had a mustache for several years; it is part of his identity.

3. Two directors who have worked in the same corporation for one year are having lunch. One director mentions his ideas to help increase productivity at no additional cost to the company. The other director asks questions about this idea. Two weeks later at their monthly divisional meeting, the vice-president proudly announces that the company will be adopting the plan presented by one of the directors and asks the director to present her ideas. She proceeds to describe in detail the plan that her colleague presented to her over lunch. The director who conceived of the initial plan is outraged by the fact that the colleague whom he trusted "stole" and claimed full credit for his ideas.

4. Two coworkers have been with a company for three years and have developed a positive and productive professional relationship. A new supervisor has recently been hired. After a few months, it becomes evident to one of the workers that the supervisor favors another worker, who receives what she considers "plum" assignments, is praised more often, and is granted preferential treatment in general. When the first worker raises her concerns with her coworker, he tells her that she is imagining differences in the way they are treated. The worker, however, is convinced that she is being treated neither equally nor fairly.

5. For the past twelve years, a husband has run his family's business and provided the primary monetary support; his wife has taken care of the children and now works part time as a nurse. The husband admits that he has been unhappy with his work. He wants to change careers and become an attorney. The wife believes that he has too many responsibilities and commitments to start making a costly career change at this time in their lives.

Different members of the class or seminar group should be assigned a role in one of these five situations. Participants should determine which conflict-handling behavior they feel will best serve dealing with the situation (accommodating, avoiding, competing, compromising, or collaborating). Each situation should then be role played. The rest of the group should assess the effectiveness of the conflict-handling behavior selected. If the group feels that a different approach would be either more effective or appropriate, the individuals enacting the roles will redo the encounter, using a different conflict-handling mode.

G. FOCUS ON APOLOGY

Consider the following situations:

1. You are in charge of a foreign-exchange program for a university, bringing foreign students to your university for six weeks. Thirty students are scheduled to arrive on Friday. Apparently the dormitory space was never confirmed by your office, and now space is available for only

half the group. This means that your office will have to pick up the tab for hotel accommodations for fifteen students for six weeks. This terribly overextends the approved budget for the program. What do you tell the dean in charge?

2. You are in charge of publicity for a major manufacturing firm. Brochures showing your fall line were supposed to be mailed out by June 1 to stores on the coast. It is now one month later, and the brochures have not yet gone out. The president of the firm anticipates an enormous loss in orders because of this delay and calls you in for an explanation. What do you say?

3. You are cochairing a local fund-raising event for a charitable cause. For several months many volunteers have been soliciting donations and selling raffles. A great deal of money has been collected, and you are scheduled to make a financial report at a meeting with all the volunteers. A few days before you are to make your report, you discover that $60,000 (of the $80,000 collected) is missing. An executive committee of five had access to the safe. What report do you make to the volunteers?

Divide the class or seminar group into six small groups. Each group will be assigned one of these three situations. Half the members of each group will prepare a statement that they will deliver orally. The other half of each group will prepare a written explanation. In addition to discussing how effectively each situation was handled, note what differences appear in the oral and written statements.

2

THE LANGUAGES OF CONFLICT MANAGEMENT

Oral Strategies for a Supportive Communication Climate

Points to Be Addressed

1. The integration of Gibb's traits for a supportive communication climate with the language of conflict management;
2. Descriptive speech: The impact of the words we choose;
3. Problem orientation: Focusing on issues;
4. Spontaneity: Promoting a climate receptive to ideas and solutions;
5. Empathy: Strategies that facilitate "feeling with" others;
6. Equality: Making our voices heard—strategies to overcome barriers to managing differences;
7. Provisionalism: Keeping the channels of communication open.

In the preceding chapter we addressed the nature of conflict and presented a five-step model for effective conflict management. Although understanding each stage is important to the overall effectiveness of dealing with conflict, it is during the action phase that transactional communication occurs and when it is important to demonstrate the requisite communication skills for productive conflict-handling behavior.

Individuals embroiled in a conflict are likely to focus on their own concerns and interests (Blake and Mouton, 1962). This tendency toward self-absorption often results in the inability to attend fully to those individuals who hold differing ideas, concerns, and views. For example, in a dispute over wages, employees are likely to consider the impact of insufficient wages on their lifestyles. If their attention is focused primarily on what they regard as the dire consequences an insufficient wage hike will produce, it is unlikely that they will be prepared to acknowledge sufficiently the problems that a wage increase will create from management's perspective.

Because of this tendency to focus intrapersonally rather than interpersonally, the participants are likely to ignore any similarities among the opposing parties. Thus the workers might overlook the fact that they stand to benefit by the company's increasing expenditures to raise profits—profits that would ultimately translate into earnings for them. Instead, their focus on the employer's decision to step up production as a direct barrier to their own need for more money makes the management of their differences untenable.

To manage conflict productively, the participants need to be able to communicate. In their work on intergroup conflict, Watson and Johnson (1972) elaborate the four kinds of communication required for effective conflict management. First, it is important for the conflict participants to have a clear perception of the other's underlying motivations and position. This, we acknowledged earlier, is a difficult process because individuals tend to focus on their own concerns. Second, accurate communication is essential for true understanding between individuals. Third, an attitude of trust must be conveyed for productive interaction. Fourth, a shared assessment of the conflict as a mutual problem is needed to motivate participants to attempt to ameliorate their differences.

The kind of communication posited by Watson and Johnson (1972) represents the need to engage both parties in managing the conflict. Furthermore, the prescribed attempts to achieve mutual understanding and to acknowledge the concerns of all parties also reflect efforts to integrate the needs of both sides into the process of handling the conflict. Considering both parties' concerns and viewing the conflict-management process as a "win–win" situation enables individuals to establish a collaborative style.

Blake and Mouton (1964) initially identified five types of conflict-handling behavior: competing, withdrawing, smoothing, compromising, and collaborating. Of these five types of behavior, conflict theorists maintain that collaboration may be highly effective in managing differences (Blake and Mouton, 1964; Filley, 1975, 1977; Folger and Poole,

1984; Thomas and Kilmann, 1977). Because collaboration requires the effort, effective communication, and open-minded attitude needed to ensure that the concerns of both sides are fully articulated and addressed, the likelihood of arriving at solutions acceptable to both sides is greatly enhanced.

It was observed in Chapter 1 that not all differences merit the effort and energy that characterize collaboration. Because collaboration can be achieved only by employing the basic oral and nonverbal communication skills that reflect effective interpersonal communication, however, we will focus on the types of environments that enhance the productive communication strategies required of collaborating behavior.

Barnlund (1968) has observed that misunderstanding, alienation, and frustration often result when people do not listen to one another and are quick to interrupt or disregard what has been said. He portrays in this instance interpersonal communication at its worst. The inadequacies, misunderstanding, and alienation to which he points can be avoided if one can interact in an environment characterized by trust. Jack Gibb's (1961) seminal work on communication defines the nature of such a supportive communication environment.

Gibb posits two opposing climates and describes the effects of each climate on communication. One type of climate he describes is defensive and threatening. A defensive climate is characterized by communication that is evaluative, controlling, strategic, neutral, superior, and certain. The other climate Gibb presents is supportive and provides an atmosphere conducive to mutual trust, openness, and cooperation. In contrast to the defensive climate, the supportive climate is characterized by communication that is descriptive, problem oriented, spontaneous, empathic, equal, and provisional. (See Table 2.1.)

TABLE 2.1 Traits of Contrasting Communication Climates

Defensive	Supportive
Evaluation	Description
Control	Problem orientation
Strategy	Spontaneity
Neutrality	Empathy
Superiority	Equality
Certainty	Provisionalism

Summary of Gibb's (1961) behavioral traits for supportive and defensive communication environments.

Although Gibb's work addresses communication climates in general, his observations apply to the communication evidenced in conflict-managing behavior. The defensive climate reflects the type of atmosphere characteristic of competition—an atmosphere that Deutsch (1973a, b) notes inhibits the mutual trust required for effective conflict management. The supportive climate presented by Gibb characterizes the type of environment reflective of collaboration—an environment that Filley (1975) observes leads to mutual trust and to an atmosphere conducive to managing differences. Therefore if we consider the interpersonal communication skills reflective of the supportive communication climate described by Gibb, we are also providing skills that facilitate a willingness to engage in a cooperative and integrative approach to conflict management.

DESCRIPTIVE SPEECH

Gibb (1961, p. 144) defines descriptive speech as that which "tends to arouse a minimum of uncertainty. Speech acts which the listener perceives as genuine requests for information or for materials with neutral loadings is descriptive." In an environment characterized by dissension, it is not so easy to decrease uncertainty and to gather information. According to Rogers (1961), individuals tend naturally to be judgmental and evaluative of others. They therefore create barriers to productive interpersonal communication. If Rogers' claim belies a natural tendency, individuals who want to communicate in nonjudgmental, nonevaluative, and nonthreatening ways need quite consciously to employ verbal strategies that will result in disclosure, comprehension, and information sharing free from negative connotations. The following five verbal strategies are intended to enable parties embroiled in a conflict to participate in the supportive descriptive environment that Gibb proposes.

Admitting One's Assertions

In conflict situations it is often difficult to remove barriers to effective interaction between participants. Barriers are especially resistant to change when individuals are reluctant to acknowledge their own feelings and ideas about a problem.

According to Mehrabian (1981), it is far easier to ascribe blame to a third party, and therefore to distance oneself from the other party, than it is to admit one's position about a situation. For example, a manager lashes out at his colleague with a statement such as, "Everyone thinks you're not pulling your weight in this company." By claiming that *everyone* shares this perception, he is likely to provoke defensiveness, for his colleague will become concerned with who has made these statements.

If participants in a conflict want to open rather than impede a dialogue, they will find it more productive to admit and to acknowledge their own ideas. The manager might open the conversation with a statement such as, "It seems to me" or "I believe that you are not pulling your weight in the company." By owning his own assertions, the manager has enabled his colleague to respond directly to the individual who holds these views rather than to some anonymous other.

Stating Issues Clearly and Specifically

How clearly and specifically individuals articulate their ideas and concerns will have an enormous impact on the way individuals respond in a conflict. Deutsch (1991) cautions against employing generalities. Generalities occur when individuals resort to abstract, ambiguous, or exaggerated rather than concrete terms when describing feelings, events, and situations.

The attorney who tells her associate, "Jim, I'd like to talk to you about your performance," creates, according to Mehrabian (1981) a negative effect. This occurs because she has excluded substantive information about Jim's performance. Until she clarifies her statement (e.g., "You have not been bringing in sufficient clients to merit your salary," or "We are delighted with the number of clients you have brought to the firm"), Jim will be unable to respond appropriately to the term *performance*.

Similarly, exaggerations are often employed to substantiate claims. The administrator who accuses her employee of "always" making personal telephone calls on company time or of "never" being on time opens herself up to criticism unless, of course, literally every telephone conversation is of a personal nature and the employee has never been punctual.

If individuals are concerned with how others respond to them, it is incumbent on them to articulate their concerns as clearly and as accurately as possible. Thus the administrator who states, "I have observed that you made twelve calls in the past two days" has provided specific information to which the employee can respond. By avoiding the accusatory sweeping claim ("You are always making personal calls!"), the administrator does not put the employee totally on the defensive. Perhaps making personal calls is habitual and is therefore a problem. But it is also possible that extenuating circumstances, such as an illness in the family, have necessitated these actions. By being specific and concrete rather than general and unclear, the administrator has opened the channels to a productive exchange.

Semantic Selection: Word Choice

A dual-career couple has spent considerable time and energy negotiating an equitable plan for executing household tasks but soon becomes critical of the arrangement. Each individual claims that he or she has more to do than the other partner. The couple's ability to manage the disagreement will be unlikely if the two are unable to agree on their perceptions of the facts. For example, they may disagree over how much time constitutes too much time spent weekly on tasks. Agreement may also be untenable if they have divergent perspectives: For instance, one task is considered either easier or harder, more menial or meaningful, depending on one's orientation.

Many writers suggest that individuals' experiences, identities, roles, and cultures serve to shape their *Zeitgeist*, or world view (Barnlund, 1968; Barry, 1970; Goffman, 1959; Hall, 1961, 1966; Rogers, 1961; Simmons and McCall, 1966). Yet when individuals, in Barnlund's terms, "project private significance into the world" (1968, p. 7), the potential for managing conflicts productively diminishes because these individuals hold values significant only unto themselves.

Perspectives are highly personal. This notion conflicts directly with the idea that definitions of problems and information conveyed must be understood by all the participants in a conflict (Blake and Mouton, 1962; Deutsch, 1973a, b). The semantic, or word, choices each individual makes consequently will affect the quality of a communicative exchange.

Denotative Meanings of Words

The denotative, or dictionary, definitions of words are normally clear and readily understood. The vice-president tells her director, for example, "I need the report next Monday." If this statement is made on Wednesday, the director knows that he has five days before he must submit the report to his boss. Ostensibly there is no difficulty understanding both the intent and the content of the message: The report is needed by the vice-president on Monday. Indeed, if this type of request is routinely made, a minimal chance exists for a misunderstanding.

Connotative Meanings of Words

In contrast to the clearly defined denotative meanings of words, the connotative meanings reflect individual interpretation and are highly personal. As indicated earlier, our experiences shape how we react to certain words. For example, two men reading the statement "The boy was hungry" may have quite different responses. One may accept the statement at face value, assuming that the boy will satisfy his hunger shortly. The other man, however, may react quite strongly to the same sentence, recalling with trepidation his own hunger as a child growing up during the Depression.

In a conflict situation the intention of individuals may be to select carefully words that both parties understand clearly. As the example indicates, however, the potential to use words that produce divergent reactions among individuals may create a real barrier to managing a conflict. (The possibility for misunderstanding created by connotative interpretations of words is exacerbated further if one introduces gender and culture as variables. These ideas are further elaborated in Chapters 4 and 5.)

It is impossible for individuals to be fully acquainted with every person with whom they interact. Thus individuals cannot be expected to avoid using all the words that may unintentionally provoke adverse reactions. Additionally words may become highly charged when they reflect current problems or especially debatable issues. The words *conscientious objector*, for example, had a highly subjective meaning in the mid- to late-1960s. More recently the terms *surrogate mother* or gun control may be highly provocative terms.

To the extent that individuals embroiled in a conflict need to be sensitive to the other party's concerns, it is important to try to anticipate what words are likely to increase the difficulties between individuals and to avoid these words if possible. Thus in a labor dispute, if the goals of management and labor are truly to ameliorate differences, it would behoove the labor representative to avoid using the term *strike*, just as the management representative might judiciously avoid the words *lay off*.

Semantic Obstacles to Communication: The Use of Slang, Stereotypes, and Automatic Phrasing

If supportive communication climates employ descriptive rather than evaluative communication, individuals engaged in a conflict should avoid using verbal conventions that aim to hurt others or that exacerbate differences between people. Slang and stereotypes reflect overt examples of language intended to damage interaction. The use of what Mehrabian (1981) terms *automatic phrasing* reflects subtler forms of avoiding open communication.

Slang

In contrast to the accidental use of words that may create differences between people, conflicting parties often resort to slang expressions to make their point. In other instances individuals intentionally employ words to provoke others, such as expletives, purposefully incorrect grammatical statements, or mispronunciation. This differs from the unintentional language misusage discussed in Chapter 6, as the communicator is aware of the effect he or she creates. By breaking from societal norms, or what Goffman terms *situational propriety* (1959), individuals distance themselves from the other party.

Thus the ordinarily articulate supervisor who, in response to his colleague's request for a report, responds, "There ain't no way in hell that you'll have the report by Friday!" is challenging his coworker through the language he chooses. He intentionally conveys a negative message that would not have occurred had he instead responded, "I'm sorry, but I won't be able to have the report ready by Friday."

Stereotyping

Stereotypes used to substantiate one's beliefs all too often convey misinformation. Rather than conveying descriptive communication, asserting opinions that belie stereotypical assumptions creates a defensive atmosphere. Although it is a normal and even helpful (Casmir, 1985) part of a person's information-coding process to attempt to categorize information and people, Knapp (1980) and Simmons and McCall (1966) caution that in the process of ascribing or excluding certain traits to groups of people, one is likely to make errors of commission or of omission.

It is not necessary to look too far to observe the damaging effects stereotypes can have on certain groups. Opposing sides in a conflict are not likely to move closer to each other if one or both parties resort to stereotyping behavior. For example, a personnel director proposes new hiring policies to reflect ethnic diversity and gender equality in the organization. Her plan may be met with such stereotyping comments as "Those people can't be trusted" or "Women are too emotional to hold positions of responsibility." These derisive responses are likely to produce anger and to increase the distance between her and her supervisor.

Automatic Phrasing

In contrast to the use of slang or stereotyping remarks as intentional strategies to distance people from one another, often individuals unintentionally employ verbal forms that can convey suspicion or doubt. Mehrabian (1981) identifies three types of automatic phrasing that may serve as barriers to descriptive communication: fillers, tags, and pauses.

Fillers.   Fillers, words that are linguistically unnecessary to the content of the message (such as "um," "you know," and "just") minimize the speaker's association with the message, thereby diminishing its impact. Examples of statements that reflect the inclusion of fillers are: "I, um, want you to listen to me" or "It's just a few dollars we're talking about." If the speaker wants to own his or her words, the more assertive "I want you to listen to me" or "It's a matter of a few dollars" would be more appropriate.

Tags. The addition of tags to statements is the second type of automatic phrasing Mehrabian (1981) identifies. Although there are examples of appropriate use of tags (see Chapter 4), when individuals employ tags in order to assert their opinions, the use of the tag may be construed as seeking approval or verification of their assertions from the listener. For example, "I believe that the director has made the correct decision" becomes less assertive when "don't you?" is tagged onto the end.

Pauses. The third example of automatic phrasing is the overuse of pauses when speaking. Certainly the thoughtful pause as conveyed by the example "Uh . . . let me think about your suggestion for a few minutes" is appropriate. When individuals employ pauses to convey that they don't wish to discuss a topic further, however, this strategy conveys uncertainty and ambivalence.

When two parties are in conflict, the likelihood of managing differences is impeded when pauses are employed. For example, a person may say, "Let's discuss the areas where we are at odds with each other." If the other party responds, "I, er . . . don't, uh . . . want to discuss this now," this statement may be interpreted as attempting to avoid the issue.

Mehrabian's (1981) description of automatic phrasing reveals that the three examples he describes—fillers, tags, and pauses—all serve to distance individuals. Such distance often creates barriers to open, honest, and disclosing communication, which is the type of communication characteristic of Gibb's (1961) supportive communication climate. If conflict participants are truly concerned with managing the differences between them, such management will be facilitated by their choosing their words with care and by paying attention to the little slips, or automatic phrasing, that may contradict productive efforts.

Syntactic Selection: The Impact of Threats, Hostile Joking and Sarcasm, and Hostile Questioning on Managing Conflict

Selecting words carefully and appropriately is essential for achieving the supportive communication climate characteristic of collaboration. Semantic tactics form only part of the communication, however.

Syntax, or how these words are formulated into phrases and sentences, also affects the ability to manage conflict productively.

Threatening Statements

Several types of statements inhibit the flow of ideas between individuals (Barnlund, 1968; Deutsch, 1973; Hocker and Wilmot, 1985). The use of threats is but one example. Threats may be direct, as reflected by the example "If you don't meet this deadline, you will be fired." In other situations threats may be veiled. The following example is, for instance, not so overtly obvious: "The organization does not look kindly on individuals who are unwilling to travel."

Gibb (1961) observes that threatening behavior presents the most obvious barrier to creating a supportive environment. The reason is that threatening behavior creates defensiveness in those who are the object of the threat.

That threats can serve as effective deterrents has been documented (Watson and Johnson, 1972). For example, in international politics the implied threat of nuclear retaliation keeps many countries' aspirations in check. Yet scant empirical support appears to substantiate that the results of threatening postures are as productive a strategy as collaborative attempts to manage differences (Watson and Johnson, 1972).

Rather than resorting to the coercion that results from threatening tactics, a far more effective compliance-gaining strategy is to explain clearly the rationale for certain behaviors and the implications a lack of cooperation or defiance engenders. These strategies form a part of the intent model for impression management described by Thomas and Kilmann (1977) and are particularly effective for productive conflict management. For example, a manager who explains, "This position requires that individuals must be willing to work under tremendous pressure and time constraints" or who expresses her reservations about a subordinate by saying, "I am concerned that you will not be able to meet the established deadlines" is asserting the organization's and her own expectations while allowing the other party to participate in the communication exchange.

Hostile Joking and Sarcasm

Although threatening behavior creates discomfort, at least individuals are clear about the intention of the message. If a person does not perform a certain task, some type of punitive action will be taken.

In contrast to the direct use of threats, the use of hostile joking and sarcasm represents insidious tactics for opposing or criticizing others. A manager, for example, says to her department head, "I'm upset that you went ahead and implemented these policies without consulting us." The department head responds with the statement, "Oh, come on, now, Carole. Don't get so nervous about a couple of tiny, little procedural changes. You've already got enough important matters to worry about." By teasing Carole about the relative importance of the procedural changes, the department head attempts to defend her actions by trivializing the manager's concerns.

Using the same example, the department head might also react sarcastically: "If I could ever get this department together at the same time, perhaps we could meet." The explicit message is that it is difficult to convene the group. The implicit communication, however, may be interpreted as follows: The department members are not where they are supposed to be. Otherwise it would not be so difficult to bring them together.

Both of these responses serve to silence the manager. Both serve to diminish the ability of the two parties to participate in an honest communication exchange. Both responses, in sum, increase the distance between these two individuals who presumably need to work together.

To turn a defensive exchange into a productive encounter, the recipient of defensive communication tactics must avoid escalating further the destructive communication cycle that has been initiated. Thus the manager needs to articulate clearly her feelings about the procedural changes. For example, she might say, "I feel that the changes you implemented will have a major impact on how the organization functions." Further she might suggest ways to rectify the department head's perception about the members of the department: "I will be happy to convene the group so that we will all have an opportunity to consider the changes you have implemented."

Hostile Questioning

When individuals employ questions to accuse or to find fault with the other party's behavior, such actions are also likely to create defensiveness. For example, when management fails to approve what the workers regard as an equitable cost-of-living wage increase, a union representative might feel justified in asking the management representative, "Don't you care at all about the quality of life of your employees?" Because the union representative has attempted to link care about employees solely to a wage increase, the employer must guard his or her response. To admit that the company cares about its employees is likely to invite further criticism about the way it deals with those about whom the organization presumably cares. Thus a countering statement, such as, "Of course we care about our employees," may be met with further accusations. A likely union response to this might be, "If you admit that you care about your workers, how can you deny them the basic necessities of survival?"

By using hostile and therefore accusatory questions, the labor representative has put management on the defensive. In such a situation apparently any answer offered will provoke additional accusatory lines of questioning.

For management to prevent this conflict from escalating further, the representative might enumerate specifically the ways it has demonstrated the company's positive attitude toward its employees. For example, the management representative could say something like "Our company has initiated the following plans that reflect our concern and commitment to our employees. . . ."

PROBLEM ORIENTATION

A primary aim of communication is to persuade or to enable another individual to share our perceptions and view of reality. We either consciously or unconsciously initiate communication to change the other party. As Barnlund observes, "If difference is the raw material of conversation, influence is its intent" (1968, p. 10). This inclination toward control, however, is likely to create a defensive environment, especially if the attempts to regulate others are indirect or hidden. When this occurs, managing conflict can be thwarted because the ability to trust others is in part dependent on openness (Zand, 1972).

In contrast, a cooperative conflict-management process is characterized by openly acknowledging the views of both parties. Gibb (1961) observes that listeners are more likely to cooperate when they perceive that speakers are similarly cooperative. Speakers may demonstrate their willingness to work jointly by communicating their desire to work together to define the problem, to generate viable solutions, and to refrain from purporting preconceived agendas or solutions. Consequently it is essential for participants engaged in conflict to assure each other of their intentions and efforts to work together toward managing the differences that exist between them. Further, they must endeavor to separate the people from the problem (Fisher and Ury, 1981.)

If we consider again the example of the couple dissatisfied with the allocation of household responsibilities, we can compare how effective the different processes of problem versus solution orientation will be in managing the disagreement. It is rather simple to seemingly resolve the problem of sharing chores by merely dividing up the tasks. For example, the wife may assume responsibility for taking and picking up clothes from the cleaners; the husband may agree to do the wash. This solution will not be satisfactory, however, if either party believes that the other has manipulated him or her into agreeing to the solution. Nor will the couple be satisfied if problems related to the solutions have not been addressed. Maybe the wife resents having to alter her work schedule in order to get to the cleaners before it closes.

Maier and Solem (1962) and Maier (1963) propose a three-step plan that not only considers solutions to problems but also emphasizes the process of uncovering the basic problems from which conflict has originated. They propose that first, individuals need to identify the problem. Second, persons engaged in a conflict must attempt to generate as many viable and appropriate solutions as possible. The third and final step in the process is assessing the quality of the solutions generated.

Identifying the Problem

An important first step is to acknowledge the problems. In the example of the couple, several areas of disagreement may lie below the surface relationship. The wife, for example, may believe that she works harder than her husband and therefore feels strongly that an equal amount of household duties should not be required of her. The husband may feel that his position is more important than his wife's and that therefore he should not be asked to perform what he considers menial tasks.

Rogers' (1961) contention about the tendency of individuals to make judgmental assertions would create, in this instance, a highly defensive and destructive communication environment. One party might assert, for example, "Your job isn't nearly as important as mine. I don't see why I should have to be bothered with housework." These comments connote an evaluation about the other party's work and about the other party's relative importance within the relationship.

Without acknowledging the fundamental issues of each party's status within the relationship, managing differences will be greatly impeded. Employing the descriptive language characterized by Gibb (1961), however, will enable both parties to express their differences without offending each other. Thus the husband may assert, "I have worked very hard to achieve my position. I don't want to perform the same task I was doing when I first started out." Similarly the wife may state, "I work extremely long hours. I am too tired to perform many of the household duties as well." These statements reflect attempts to bring out into the open feelings both parties have about certain tasks. Equally important, neither side has made judgments about the other partner.

Proposing Solutions

Once problems have been acknowledged, individuals can attempt to propose solutions. Important to the process of managing conflict cooperatively is that these solutions reflect the concerns of both parties. Furthermore these tentative solutions should be articulated in an open yet nonevaluative manner.

For example, the husband who is adamant about not doing the laundry may feel less negative about preparing meals or cleaning dishes. Similarly the wife may be willing to stop at the cleaners if on those days, she brings home dinner. If, as Barnlund (1968) has observed, there are neither perceived hidden attempts to control each other nor overt power struggles over whose time, job, or role is more valuable, reaching solutions that have addressed the couple's attitude toward doing housework is possible. If, as Maier and Sashkin (1971) have posited, both parties have generated as many solutions as possible that integrate the needs of both sides (the husband's need for recognition, the wife's need for a lighter work load), reaching solutions acceptable to both sides is also more likely.

Assessing Solutions

Conflict management does not end merely because an agreement has been reached. Of equal importance is how individuals choose to deal with solutions to problems that have failed to meet their expectations or needs.

Dissatisfied parties who resort to defensive communication tactics as, for example, accusations ("You did this on purpose!"), negative judgments ("Your idea was stupid!"), threats ("If you ever force me to do this again, I'll leave!"), or stereotypes ("It's typical of people like you to act this way") are likely to find their verbal assaults met with equal resistance and defiance. In contrast, individuals who include descriptive communication strategies when asserting their feelings are likely to find their concerns responded to. Thus a wife might say, "When I agreed to bring home dinner, I didn't anticipate the impact it would have on our budget. Let's talk about what we can do." By acknowledging the source of the problem (the cost of dinner) and a willingness to work jointly toward a new solution, she is far more likely to initiate a more productive interaction than would be possible in an atmosphere charged by accusations and defensiveness.

Pruitt has defined negotiation as "a process by which a joint decision is made by two or more parties" (1981, p. 1). We contend that assessing the quality and viability of decisions is also a process, for effective interaction with others and integration of the needs of both parties does not cease once a decision has been reached. Assessment is merely a continuation of the conflict-management process. Consequently it is subject to the same variables that allow for productive or destructive communication.

SPONTANEITY

Gibb (1961) explains the difference between strategy and spontaneity as the difference between deliberate manipulation (through feigned guile-lessness and other forms of pretense or deception) and genuine responsiveness and openness to a communication exchange. Strategic behavior often results in defensive behavior in the other party. In contrast, spontaneous communication encourages mutuality and cooperation.

Zand (1972) contends that an essential factor in effective conflict management is the extent to which individuals have confidence in or trust each other's assertions. The ability to trust is possible in a communication environment that is unfettered by deception and that is characterized by co-orientation.

Although manipulative individuals do not typically verbalize their intention to control or to deceive, such strategies are all too familiar. For example, people are able to sense when the other party withholds relevant or important information by use of automatic phrases, especially fillers and inappropriate pauses. Individuals are often able to detect another person's lack of genuine interest, as when he or she changes the topic or does not provide appropriate feedback. (The topic of feedback is addressed in the next section.) Individuals become aware of hidden agendas by the way in which ideas or propositions initially not evident in the negotiation are brought to the forefront. And people are loathe to confide in others if they fear that their comments will be either divulged or used against them at a future time.

In contrast to the defensive environment that can result from manipulation or deception, a supportive environment is possible when communication is open and spontaneous. Conflict theorists Maier and Sashkin (1971) encourage an exhaustive search for ideas and solutions to problems. Filley (1975) adds to this process when he proposes using choices between solutions to generate new problem statements.

The technique of brainstorming—defined as "literally bombarding a problem and generating as many ideas as possible" (De Vito, 1986, p. 48)—allows for the spontaneous exchange of views in a nonevaluative atmosphere. Although brainstorming as a problem-solving technique is generally employed within cohesive groups, the process also includes those aspects of cooperation that facilitate conflict management. Citing

Osborn's (1957) work on the process of brainstorming, De Vito (1986, p. 48) briefly summarizes the following general procedures for this process, aspects of which have been introduced earlier in the sections on descriptive communication and problem orientation.

Avoid Negative Criticism

Individuals involved in negotiation should treat equally and without prejudgment all the ideas each party generates. It is tempting to assume a position of "we" versus "they," which reflects a competitive win–lose orientation. An attitude of "we" versus "the problem," however, is likely to encourage the generation of ideas that may eventually be incorporated into the adopted solution.

The department head, for example, who strongly believes that achieving financial equilibrium can be accomplished only by personnel cuts must initially refrain from criticizing another department head's proposal to achieve a balanced budget by reducing space. To judge negatively another's ideas without allowing for the full expression of thought is likely to discourage communication. If individuals perceive that others do not judge them or their ideas fairly, they are likely to maintain staunchly their original positions.

Generate Viable Solutions

Participants in a conflict may initially regard solutions to a problem as an either/or situation. For example, one party may propose either reducing personnel or cutting back on space. Yet negotiation that encourages creative rather than inflexible approaches to managing differences is less likely to obstruct cooperative efforts to diminish or to resolve disagreements.

For example, if the two department heads do not feel that they will be criticized for proposing divergent ideas, they are likely to feel encouraged to seek additional ways to solve their financial problems. One department head may suggest restructuring the units to make the most efficient use of extant personnel and space. The other department head may recommend leasing rather than purchasing equipment. It is important to reiterate that the verbal communication employed to express these ideas needs to be as descriptive and nonevaluative as possible. Thus one department head may meet resistance if she states, "As far as I'm concerned, there is only one way to solve our fiscal crisis, and that is by cutting our staff." She would be far more likely to have her ideas considered if she were to propose, "One approach to solving our financial difficulties is to reduce staff."

Combine and Integrate Proposals

Although entire proposals may not be acceptable to all parties, aspects of different ideas can often be incorporated into developing viable plans acceptable to both sides. In fact, Maier and Sashkin (1971) contend that integrating and combining the ideas of both sides to formulate creative solutions is a highly effective approach for managing conflict.

As with the other steps in the brainstorming process, assertions need to be descriptive and should reflect co-orientation among the participants. Moreover, Barnlund (1968) cautions that individuals who resist being open to new ideas and experiences are likely to remain prisoners of their own constructs and will be unlikely to maximize the potential for reaching sound decisions.

Extending the example of the department heads, one might state, "Although I am opposed to the concept of staff reduction, if we explore your suggestion to reorganize some of the units, we might find that several individuals are performing the same functions. Perhaps we could reallocate some of these individuals to areas where we are currently understaffed, thereby saving on new office positions." This individual has asserted his beliefs (to not reduce staff), acknowledged the idea of the other party (to reorganize), and built on this proposal (to reallocate staff) to achieve their mutual goals (financial stability).

Appraise Proposals

Once ideas have been articulated and expanded upon, a realistic appraisal (not a personal attack) is warranted. For example, one department head states: "Although I am open to your suggestion to merge several units, we need to consider the costs involved with relocating staff. I don't believe we are in a position to support a major reorganization at this time." Here he specifies the area of disagreement (the cost of moving personnel) without attacking the other party directly.

Thus individuals engaged in conflict need to match the ability to generate solutions with the ability to assess them. Both steps, however, are best achieved in a communication environment characterized by cooperation, mutuality, and trust.

EMPATHY

The term *empathy* derives from the German *einfülung*, which means, literally, "to feel with" another person's ideas, emotions, and desires. In Gibb's analysis of supportive communication environments, he describes the ability to empathize as "particularly supportive and defense reductive" (1961, p. 146). To achieve empathy with another, individuals must willingly attempt first to understand the other party. Second, individuals must judiciously suspend their tendency to judge others.

Understand the Other Party's Perspective

An important first step in achieving empathic bonds with another is to make an effort to understand the other individual. A mutual framework is essential to facilitate understanding, especially in a conflict situation.

For example, one party demands parity within an organizational hierarchy. The other individual will experience difficulty understanding fully his colleague's demand if he does not share a framework for the concept "parity within an organizational hierarchy." This illustration reflects a barrier to understanding that is typical of cross-cultural communication and international conflict (see Chapter 5).

The causes for misunderstanding, however, need not be so obvious. Gender, ethnicity, religion, geographical location, educational background, professional status—in sum, who we are and what we have experienced—affect our personal constructs and inform our ability and willingness to respond to others. Therefore regardless of the numerous differences that exist between people, the ability to manage differences between conflicting parties depends in large measure on the willingness and efforts of both parties to understand each other.

Avoid Evaluating the Other Party

Fred and Johanna have taken their vacation at the same time for the past ten years. When Johanna is promoted within her company, she learns that although she has not lost the amount of vacation time available to her, one of the two weeks' vacation coincides with the company's deadline for completing its budgetary projections. Johanna believes that she cannot be away from the office during this week. She therefore proposes to her husband that they try to reschedule their vacation. If this is impossible, she would meet him for one of the weeks. When she expresses her ideas to Fred, he feels hurt that his wife would willingly forego their time together. He believes that she values her position more than their relationship.

Ed and John are close friends who get together for dinner at least once a month. John confides that on two separate occasions during the past year, he has been passed over for a promotion. Nonetheless he continues to assume additional assignments with the hope of gaining the recognition and reward he feels he deserves. As Ed listens to John's account, he secretly believes that John is acting too passively. He feels that his friend should fight for his promotion. That is what he would do if he were in John's position.

Both of these examples illustrate the tendency for individuals to evaluate others and reflect a response typical of individuals engaged in conflict. That is, we tend to project on the other party our own motivations, understanding, and interpretation of events. According to Triandis (1976), such responses serve as major obstacles to understanding fully the other party's position. Certainly such responses impede our ability to feel with the other person.

Given the barriers to empathizing with those with whom we disagree, what steps can individuals take to ensure that their ideas and feelings are listened to and understood? How can they ensure that they will understand others? The process of providing and soliciting feedback is perhaps the most effective means for achieving empathy.

Exchanging information, viewpoints, and responses in the communication process is called *feedback*. Many individuals are threatened by the implicit change implied by feedback. For example, they fear that others will reject, criticize, evaluate, or misunderstand their messages. When managed properly in a supportive communication environment, however, feedback is a powerful mechanism for demonstrating empathic communication. Three basic oral strategies to elicit or to provide feedback include questioning, paraphrasing, and role reversal.

Oral Constructs for Feedback

Questioning
The use of questions can lead to divergent reactions. For example, a hostile leading question that is accusatory in tone and content may exacerbate rather than ameliorate differences. To illustrate this kind of question, consider the director who feels that his colleague is being unreasonable. He asks, "Do you really expect that your obvious attempts to avoid me are going to make me forget our differences?" An emotionally charged question such as this is intentionally provoking. In turn, the recipient of a hostile question will likely feel defensive and may respond unfavorably.

Not all questions in a conflict need be hostile. Questions judiciously used, and the tone in which they are communicated, can also facilitate communication and enable individuals with differences to gather important information and obtain feedback from each other. The three basic classifications of questions—(1) open or closed, (2) primary or secondary, and (3) neutral or leading—can be used appropriately during a communication exchange (Stewart and Cash, 1988). Moreover, the language employed, the tone in which the questions are articulated, the point at which they are employed during the interaction, and the ability of the recipient of the questions to respond adequately will affect the quality of the encounter. Used appropriately, the questioning process will convey that each party's concerns and ideas are being fully listened to and understood (Wolvin and Coakley, 1985).

If establishing credibility, developing an environment of trust, and facilitating rather than impeding a shared understanding of the problem are the goals, obtaining feedback by asking, "Do you feel that there is only one way to resolve this dispute?" or "What is your reaction?" or "Are you avoiding me?" or "If I understand you correctly, you're upset with my tone of voice" will be far more productive than the hostile question presented at the beginning of this section.

Paraphrasing

DeVito defines the term *paraphrase* as "a sentence or phrase that conveys the same meaning but is presented in a different form from another sentence or phrase" (1986, p. 221). More than merely repeating another person's message, restating the sentence or phrase assures the other party that the content or intent of the message has been understood.

An employee may lash out at her colleague: "You never let me finish what I'm saying!" The colleague may reflect that she understands the message by responding, "If I understand you correctly, you are upset because you feel I interrupt you too much" or by asking, "Do you feel that I interrupt you too often?"

Regardless of whether paraphrasing takes the form of a statement or a question, the ability to paraphrase is an essential aspect of providing and receiving feedback to the other party. Moreover, this technique demonstrates a willingness to attend to and to acknowledge the concerns of others.

Role Reversal

It is important for individuals in a conflict to be able to express their own perceptions and ideas regarding the nature of their differences. Yet the inability to articulate the viewpoints of others impedes the ability to understand differences.

One verbal strategy that enables individuals to state what Rogers (1951) calls the inner world of another individual is role reversal. In role reversal an individual assumes the role of the other party and attempts to articulate the other individual's viewpoint, using that person's communication style.

For example, a couple experiencing marital difficulty may be asked to assume each other's role and to express in the role of the spouse why they feel they cannot communicate. Similarly two members of a management team who staunchly disagree on how to reorganize their unit may be requested to enact their differences in the role of the other.

When individuals are willing to cooperate, role reversal is particularly effective because both parties are mutually responsible for ensuring that accurate and constructive communication occurs. Furthermore, because role reversal enables individuals to see clearly each other's ideas, views, and feelings, it provides a powerful process for clarifying differences when misunderstandings or false expectations are the source of disagreements.

Regardless of the verbal techniques used to provide or receive feedback, clearly the ability to understand fully or to feel with the other party is possible only when individuals are willing to ensure that they understand, and are understood by, each other.

EQUALITY

The previous section explored how feedback can enable individuals engaged in conflict to empathize with the other party. Communication is likely to remain both unbalanced and unproductive, however, if individuals do not have equal access to the communication exchange and if they endeavor to manipulate the interaction through either avoidance or control.

Most conflicts reflect efforts to equalize the power between parties. Moreover, without a relative power balance, it becomes increasingly difficult to manage conflicts productively. Therefore, if one participant in a conflict is denied a voice in the conflict-management process, the belief that his or her own concerns have been ignored will negatively affect that person's willingness to accept the other side's position.

For example, a manager is likely to discourage feedback about a problem if she states: "I've been with this company for five years. I know that this is the only way to settle the matter." Similarly a husband may silence his partner momentarily by asserting: "Listen, I'm the one who brings home the money. I'll decide how we're going to spend it." It is highly improbable, however, that his wife's silence means that she is satisfied with his self-aggrandizing tactics.

Both examples reflect attempts to maintain superiority or control in the relationship and contradict a basic assumption about effective conflict management, that is, that all members should be encouraged to interact freely (Blake and Mouton, 1962).

Barnlund has observed that "human understanding is facilitated where there is a willingness to become involved with the other person" (1968, p. 20). Several strategies exist to accomplish such involvement. Each strategy aims to empower conflict participants with the ability to articulate their concerns in the supportive communication environment described by Gibb (1961).

Encourage Participation in the Communication Process

One way to ensure equal participation in a communication exchange is to request it, even when participants represent different positions of status within the organization or within the relationship. A director, for example, may say to her assistant: "I realize that we have different views about how best to accomplish this project. However, I would like to hear your viewpoint as well as your objections to my proposal." Despite the status differential, the assistant will be more likely to present her views if she feels that they will be attended to.

Status differences, however, need not be the only barrier to equal participation in the conflict-management process. Parties who share equal status in a relationship may feel reluctant to articulate their ideas if they believe that the other party really does not want their input. Thus if two professors knowingly oppose each other about which courses in the program should become requirements, one colleague may initiate a dialogue about their differences by stating: "I realize that we disagree about which courses should form part of the core. I'd like to hear your rationale for including courses other than the ones I have proposed." In so doing, this individual has made clear his intentions and willingness to listen openly to his colleague's ideas.

Respect the Other Party's Ideas and Experiences

If experiences shape perspectives, it is important to remember that each individual's experiences are unique. Therefore two individuals' points of view will not always coincide.

A woman who is accustomed to spending every Christmas with her family may become defensive when her husband suggests that this year they go away for the holidays. If she remains unwilling to respect his desire to take a vacation, he in turn might be reluctant to respect her desire to adhere to familial traditions.

To defuse the conflict that is likely to erupt if both the wife and the husband fail to understand each other, a cooperative attitude and willingness to attend fully to the other person's concerns becomes essential. Only by engaging in an open and equal exchange will the couple be able to generate potential solutions to their disagreement.

In this example several solutions are possible. The husband may be willing to go away during another time period. The wife may be willing to celebrate the Christmas holiday with her family a week or two ahead of time. The couple may determine to alternate years: to spend Christmas with her family one year and to travel the next year. Or they may decide to spend Christmas day with the wife's family and to leave the following day for vacation. As the possible solutions suggest, the ability to manage and resolve differences is limited only by the willingness of both parties to acknowledge and respect each other's perspective.

Confirm the Other Party's Assertions

A supervisor disagrees with his manager over the allocation of staff to his unit. He feels severely understaffed to meet the company's production deadlines. The manager staunchly disagrees. He feels that he has already assigned an adequate number of personnel. Further, he believes that they are not performing to their fullest potential.

The manager, in an effort to placate his complaining supervisor, calls regular meetings, ostensibly so that the supervisor may air his differences openly. Rather than leaving these meetings with the feeling that he has been heard, because nothing ever happens in these sessions, the supervisor feels that these meetings are a waste of time. Instead of feeling encouraged, respected, and positive, he becomes increasingly discouraged, frustrated, and negative. Basically, the supervisor has had a disconfirming experience. He believes that the manager has been unresponsive to his concerns.

Several writers address disconfirming responses (Borisoff and Merrill, 1992; Cahn, 1987; DeVito, 1986; Hocker and Wilmot, 1985; Sieburg and Larson, 1971). Following are seven examples of disconfirming responses. Included in these examples are brief exchanges that illustrate verbal strategies for turning disconfirming experiences into productive exchanges.

Denial or Excuse Making

As a basic tactic to avoid dealing with a conflict, individuals often deny or offer excuses for a problem.

Personnel Director: It's not my fault that so many staff members have been sick.

Vice-President: Admittedly you cannot prevent illness. However, you can take steps to ensure that offices are covered. For example, you can establish an internal procedure for sharing staff in emergency situations.

By acknowledging the director's assertion that she is unable to control attendance and by providing concrete examples about how to deal with staff problems, the vice-president forces the director to address and to manage the problem.

Underresponsiveness
The failure to address adequately another's concern represents a frequent criticism by those who feel ignored or dismissed. When individuals believe that others do not give adequate or appropriate attention to their ideas or problems, they need to enlighten the other party to the seriousness of the problem, as the following example illustrates:

Director of Staff Development: Many of the employees feel that they are not being considered for the promotions they believe they deserve. Some are considering leaving the firm.

Director of Budget: This kind of griping is common around evaluation time. Don't worry about it.

Director of Staff Development: I am convinced that the staff is serious. I would like us to review our promotion policy.

By not allowing her colleague to dismiss her concerns, the director of staff development will be able to explore further her ideas for retaining and promoting qualified staff.

Trivialization of the Problem through Joking or Sarcasm
Superficially jokes or sarcastic remarks can be defended (e.g., by the statement "I was only kidding"). Their use, however, may create or exacerbate problems, as demonstrated by the following exchange:

Husband: Ever since you've gone back to work, the house hasn't been as clean as I'd like it to be.

Wife: You've got two hands and two legs. If you want a clean house, why don't you use them to push a broom or carry out the garbage!

In this example we can see how little it would take to escalate this exchange into a full-blown conflict.

Admittedly a great deal of control and a willingness to cooperate are essential for individuals to respond cutting remarks. If individuals can view sarcastic or joking remarks as attempts by others to get their own way or to defend themselves, however, this attitude makes it easier to avoid retaliating with similarly hostile comments.

If a clean house, and not the derision of his wife, is the husband's ultimate aim, he can avoid exacerbating differences further by responding with a comment such as, "I'm sorry I criticized your work. Let's discuss what we can do to get the house cleaned."

Silencing

An effective way to avoid dealing with another individual's concerns is to silence her or him, thereby also avoiding possible conflict. Four basic strategies to silence another individual include interrupting behavior, changing the topic, avoiding the topic, and blaming external procedures. Here are examples of these four strategies, as well as ways to prevent being silenced.

- Interrupting behavior

Maria: I want to discuss our monetary situation . . .

Kurt (interrupting): I am so overwhelmed with cases right now, I can't even think about money. All I want is a nice, quiet evening at home.

Maria: I realize that you have been extremely busy. However, I am concerned that we stop postponing making decisions regarding the house and starting a family because you are always busy with work. When would be a good time to talk about this?

- Changing the topic

Chairperson: We've already spent enough time on this issue. Let's move on to the next agenda item.

Committee Member: I realize that we have an agenda to follow. However, I feel that this issue is so important that we should include it on our agenda and address it now.

- Avoiding the topic before it can become an issue

Personnel Manager: We've all had a long day. Let's not get into raises right now.

Supervisor: I realize we've had a difficult day. However, if we don't address salaries, I'm afraid we're going to have a strike on our hands.

- Ascribing blame to external procedures

Director: Look, we have a week to complete this report. We can't consider equipment now.

Assistant: I am convinced that including equipment needs will only strengthen our report because . . . .

These examples reveal many ways to avoid dealing with issues. The four illustrations demonstrate, however, that individuals do not have to remain silenced because the other party wants to avoid certain issues or topics. In each instance the individuals who want to discuss the topic that the other party is avoiding may not in fact finish addressing the issue at this particular moment. Still, each has acknowledged why the other individual may not want to discuss the issue at present. Each has also articulated why it is important not to ignore the issue. In effect, each individual has asserted his or her equality in the conversation.

Generalizations and Stereotypes
This type of response aims to refocus the issue or problem. It is often employed to justify not having to deal with an area of concern. The following exchange illustrates the use of ascription to justify avoiding a problem:

Case Worker: We desperately need these funds to institute a viable program to prevent drug abuse in our community.

Supervisor: Drug abuse is just one of many problems these people have. No one program can begin to meet their needs.

In such an example it is important for the individual wishing to discuss an area of disagreement to address specifically his or her concerns. Thus the case worker might follow up with a statement such as, "Studies have shown that the program we are proposing has been highly successful. If you will agree to consider . . . ."

Definitional Side Tracking

Definitional side tracking occurs when parties engaged in conflict attempt to focus on a specific word or example, thereby avoiding the larger (or real) area of contention. The following exchange between boyfriend and girlfriend illustrates such side-tracking strategies:

Dan: You never have time for me anymore.

Joyce: That's not true. Last night we had dinner together.

By responding with an example of a time when they were together, the woman avoids addressing the real issue: her boyfriend's perception that they do not spend enough time together. To make her respond to his feelings, the boyfriend may react with a statement such as, "I want to spend more time with you" and specify ways to accomplish this.

Incongruity

Frequently individuals try to avoid a conflict by asserting that there is no problem. Their nonverbal communication, however, contradicts their verbal assertions. Typical of this kind of reaction is the manager who says, "It's good to see you" but whose lack of eye contact and rapid tone of voice indicate that she is extremely busy and does not wish to be disturbed. The recipient of contradictory messages needs to determine whether to acknowledge the verbal assertions or the more accurate nonverbal message. For example, he could say, "I realize you are busy now. However, we do need to discuss the project."

Individuals who feel that others dismiss or ignore their concerns by using any of the aforementioned tactics are likely to experience frustration and annoyance at having to suppress their ideas, feelings, or beliefs. Managing differences is an important function of communication. For individuals to feel that they can voice their concerns, they must be able to participate equally in the communication exchange. They must not allow others to disconfirm their concerns, ideas, and opinions.

Communicate Fairly

In addition, disconfirming strategies, controlling tactics, characteristic of competitive behavior also inhibit equality (Argyle and Furnham, 1983; Ting-Toomey, 1983). If individuals are able to identify the basic controlling strategies that are conflict productive, they can counter these types of confrontative behaviors with responses that are conflict reductive.

The following seven examples of competitive behavior reflect in part the work of Filley (1975, 1977), Hocker and Wilmot (1985), Thomas and Kilmann (1977), and Triandis (1976). Incorporated in the examples are brief situations that demonstrate how participants in a conflict can counter destructive communication and thereby reestablish a more equitable balance in the relationship.

Ascribing Blame

Accusing the other party of certain actions or beliefs is a common strategy that deflects attention from the speaker and forces the listener into a defensive posture. A manager, for example, makes the following accusatory statement to his assistant: "I told you the forms had to be processed by today! Now it's your fault we've lost the account!" Such an accusation is likely to provoke a defensive reaction. If the accusation is true, the assistant may respond with what Thomas and Pondy (1977) call a repairing statement. For example, the assistant may say, "I'm very sorry for this error. . . ." She might go on to indicate how she will avoid future errors. On the other hand, if she feels falsely accused, she may counter her boss's accusation by asserting: "I admit I was late with the forms. However, because you were out of the office for the past three days, I was unable to finalize the proposal."

Although accusations generally flow vertically in a hierarchical structure (Brief, Schuler, and Van Sell, 1981), individuals in positions of less power need to assert themselves when confronted with what they regard as an unfair or unjustified accusation.

Denial of Responsibility

Individuals who adamantly refuse to admit any responsibility for a problem may engage in defensive rather than participatory tactics. This is evidenced in the following exchange:

Director: Did the shipment come in?

Assistant: It won't be in until tomorrow.

Director: I told you we needed the materials by today at the latest!

Assistant (raising his voice): You never mentioned any shipment to me!

At this point, it is likely that, unless the director or the assistant attempts to focus on the issue rather than on the other party, a conflict about responsibility is starting and will escalate into an issue about who knew what. For example, the director might defuse the situation by responding, "That may be. However, I need your help now to track down the items."

Judging Others by Asserting One's Own Values

It is normal in a conflict situation to believe in and to want to defend one's position. Differences between individuals may be exacerbated, however, when one party asserts that his or her claims are correct and thereby diminishes or devalues the other party's views. The following exchange illustrates the debilitating effect of making such judgments:

Wife: I've been thinking about taking a leave when the baby is born.

Husband: Being a full-time parent is just an excuse for not wanting to work. There's no reason you can't maintain your job and be a good mother.

The husband's response indicates his own assumptions about parenting (that it does not require a great deal of effort) and his belief that his wife should be able to handle both parenthood and her career.

Individuals faced with evaluative remarks from those about whose opinion they care need to determine the basis for the remark. For example, the wife may wish to determine whether the husband's mother resented giving up a career to be a full-time parent. In addition, the wife should consider the context in which the husband issued the remark (financial difficulties, perhaps) and the consistency of the assertion (the degree to which the husband usually supports his wife's decisions and actions). Finally, the wife must consider the appropriateness of the husband's comments; although the husband may have legitimate concerns about his wife's career, how he chooses to articulate them is provocative and inappropriate. Only by assessing the nature of the remark in the context of the relationship can an individual determine how to respond.

Personal Attacks

One dictionary definition of the word attack is "to set upon forcefully" (*Webster's*, 1981, p. 71). If all-out competition and winning are the goal, this meaning of attack would not be regarded negatively. The dictionary provides other definitions of this word, however, which include "to assail with unfriendly or bitter words" and "to begin to affect or to act on injuriously." All too often, in an attempt to change the behavior or to gain compliance of another, individuals resort to strategies designed to injure the other party.

Two examples of personal attacks include beltlining and gunnysacking. DeVito (1986) defines beltlining as using privileged information inappropriately or unfairly (from the cliché "hitting below the belt"). The employer who uses his employee's confidences against her or the wife who uses her husband's weaknesses to influence his actions are examples of using personal attacks to influence behavior.

Gunnysacking, or storing up and unleashing grievances on the other party, is another divisive strategy (DeVito, 1986). To illustrate this tactic, consider the teenager who arrives home one hour beyond curfew. Instead of addressing the issue of breaking curfew, his irate parents instead assail him with a barrage of complaints about his behavior in general. They complain about how he dresses, his grades, his messy room—issues they have been harboring against him but have left previously unarticulated.

All their concerns may stem from their belief that their son's behavior reflects irresponsibility and inconsideration for others. Yet by raising criticisms without addressing the fundamental issue of responsibility, the parents are likely to provoke defensiveness and to escalate rather than resolve differences with their child.

Deutsch (1971a) has observed that a competitive orientation often results in communication that is destructive rather than productive. To the extent that personal attacks are likely to provoke suspicion and to foster an environment of mistrust, those who employ beltlining and gunnysacking are not likely to obtain long-term behavioral compliance from the other party. In fact, such destructive strategies are likely to distance others and to increase alienation and hurt feelings.

Sarcastic Remarks

As with personal attacks, sarcasm and hostile jokes are likely to exacerbate differences and to contribute to a defensive climate (Gibb, 1961; Kramarae, 1981; Pearson, 1985). Consider the following remarks: "*I* don't have to worry about making the meeting. You're never on time, anyway"; "How can *you* claim to want nice furniture? This place is like a pigsty"; and "You want a window office? Why? You're *never* here to look out the window." The initiators of such statements can claim that they were only teasing. The recipients, however, are not likely to misinterpret the intentions of the comments.

When individuals are the objects of sarcastic remarks, they must determine the most effective and appropriate way to address the implicit criticisms. If the relationship is a valued or necessary one, it will further be required to correct the other party's perceptions without engaging in similarly offensive tactics. For example, a roommate may counter the statement regarding the cleanliness of the apartment with a suggestion such as: "I realize the apartment isn't as clean as we would like. Perhaps we should consider using a professional cleaning service." This statement focuses on the problem, not on the other roommate. Consequently it is a far more productive response than resorting to a similarly sarcastic retort as, for example, "This place is a pigsty because you refuse to lift a finger to help clean up!"

Reprisals

The threat of sanctions to control or to manipulate the behavior of others belies a struggle for power in the relationship and conveys a win–lose orientation. Many familial differences and professional differences, for example, are often conveyed in statements meant to assert authority, control, and power over the other party. Examples of such attempts to control another include the parent's warning to his child ("If you don't finish your homework, you won't be allowed to watch television") or the supervisor's admonition to her staff member ("If you are not at the meeting on Friday, don't bother showing up for work on Monday!").

Individuals may feel that threats are justified when initial attempts to gain cooperation or compliance have failed. Indeed the staff member may be motivated to show up for the Friday meeting, and the child may work harder to complete her assignment. That the quality of the relationship will be improved or strengthened, however, is, according to Watson and Johnson (1972), doubtful when negative sanctions are employed to change or to motivate behavioral compliance.

Attribution of Belief

In an attempt to justify their own anger or discomfort with another person, individuals often will accuse others of holding certain views, even when these accusations are not necessarily justified. For example, an employee is passed over for a promotion by her boss. Rather than determine whether she was qualified for the position, she is quick to accuse her boss of being sexist and of not wanting to promote women to management positions in the organization. Such action may provoke defensive communication because the recipients of accusations will endeavor to defend themselves if they believe that they have been falsely accused.

Certainly examples of sex stratification in the workplace abound (Bernard, 1981; DeWine, 1987; Powell, 1993; Stockard and Johnson, 1980). When individuals generalize behavior and apply pejorative labels or intentions to others, however, alienation and anger are likely to result. Rather than attempt to ameliorate differences, the parties focus on how best to defend themselves.

Barnlund (1968), Deutsch (1973a, b), and Gibb (1961) have found that it is relatively easy to create a defensive communication climate. Furthermore, they maintain that productive communication and conflict management become increasingly difficult when either or both parties perceive in the other an unwillingness to cooperate.

The ability to ensure equal communication between conflicting parties seems at first glance to be a logical and easily achieved condition. The ability to empower the participants and to ensure equal communication is, however, impeded when perceived differences exist and emotions are fraught. To ensure that participants in a conflict are able to voice their concerns and ideas, individuals need to encourage, respect, and confirm the other party as well as to communicate fairly.

PROVISIONALISM

The final verbal strategy for ensuring the supportive communication climate proposed by Gibb (1961) is to adopt a provisional attitude toward reviewing decisions that have emerged from the conflict-management process. If individuals are willing to expend the effort required to integrate and to reflect the concerns of all parties, they will likely want to maintain this same sense of openness in reviewing the effectiveness of these decisions after they have been implemented.

Maier (1963) encourages conflict participants to consider solutions from both objective and subjective standpoints. The following statements reflect a willingness to remain open to the concerns of both sides:

> "We'll try out this new procedure and review its effectiveness in six months."

> "Let's see how the new plan will affect morale."

> "Let's meet periodically so that we can adjust the plan if needed."

These examples of provisional statements reflect what Putnam (1987) terms *problem-solving communication*. All three examples allow for further assessment interaction and communication.

SUMMARY

Effective communication, even under normal conditions, is difficult because individuals tend to view events from their own perspectives and want to articulate their feelings. They often therefore fail to attend fully to the concerns and ideas of others. Differences that result from conflict further exacerbate barriers to productive interaction.

These tendencies toward self-absorption belie traits that characterize what Gibb (1961) calls a defensive communication climate. He singles out aspects of communication that are impervious to productive communication. However, if individuals are willing to engage in communication strategies characteristic of Gibb's supportive climate—that is, communication that is descriptive, problem oriented, spontaneous, empathic, equal, and provisional—the ability to manage differences and to achieve productive communication is enhanced considerably.

If participants in a communication exchange are able to achieve the co-orientation and mutuality that reflect a willingness to engage, they have the opportunity to share in a process of productive communication.

SUGGESTED ACTIVITIES

The following exercises focus on strategies for using verbal communication to assess, understand, and manage conflict.

A. FOCUS ON CONNOTATIVE MEANING OF WORDS

Students should write down approximately ten words that for them provoke strong negative responses. The group should share the words they have chosen. Discussion may address the following issues:

1. What types of words were selected?
2. Are there similarities with the words chosen?
3. What events or experiences led to the pejorative meaning of the words?
4. Assuming that several of the group's words coincide, what assumptions can be made about the word choices made when people communicate with others?

B. FOCUS ON THE EXPRESSION OF DIVERGENT VIEWPOINTS

Consider the following statements:

1. "Marijuana is not as harmful as other drugs. Therefore it should be legalized."
2. "All people arrested for drunk driving should be treated like criminals."
3. "Instead of putting so much money into defense, we should be pouring these funds into education."
4. "In spite of what the Women's Movement has done for women, in fact men are still expected to provide for the family. Thus higher-paid positions should be given first to men."

The group should be encouraged to contribute additional statements that are likely to produce diverse reactions. Each statement should then be read to the group. On a scale of 1 to 5 (1 being "strongly disagree" and 5 "strongly agree"), each participant should record his or her responses to the statements.

Individuals read aloud the numbers they have ascribed to each statement. The class should then be paired off, with each pair representing opposing sides to one of the statements.

In turn, each pair should be asked to begin a dialogue about the reasons why they agree or disagree with the statement.

The rest of the group should observe each pair's discussion, keeping in mind the following:

- The areas of agreement and of disagreement;
- The extent to which both participants shared equally in the exchange;
- Assessment of the verbal tactics used (that is, direct statements, generalizations, sarcasm, and stereotyping, among others);
- Assessment of communication style (that is, tone of voice, volume, rate of speaking, and so on);
- Assessment of word choice and grammatical structures employed; and
- Assessment of the overall effectiveness of the interaction.

C. FOCUS ON SUPPORTIVE COMMUNICATIVE ENVIRONMENTS

Students describe a recent conflict they have experienced (as either a participant or a witness). Using the following criteria from Gibb's (1961) supportive communication climate, indicate how effectively each participant in the conflict engaged in the following:

1. Descriptive communication;
2. Problem orientation;
3. Spontaneity;
4. Empathy;
5. Equality; and
6. Provisionalism

What was the outcome of the conflict? If the participants engaged in defensive communication, how, specifically, would you alter their communication to achieve a supportive climate?

D. FOCUS ON FEEDBACK

Students or group members should be divided into pairs. One partner chooses to be the speaker; the other becomes the listener. Each listener is instructed to look at the speaker but to refrain from providing any discernible verbal or nonverbal feedback. The speaker selects a topic—preferably one about his or her own experiences—and begins to speak. After a few minutes, the pair switch roles: The speaker becomes the listener; the listener becomes the speaker.

Following the exchange, discussion should focus on the role of feedback in interaction:

1. How did the speaker feel when her or his statements were not responded to?
2. Was it difficult for the listener to refrain from responding? Why?
3. Can the group think of relationships they have with others in which they feel they are not listened to? Specifically, what kinds of behaviors do these individuals demonstrate?
4. What are the functions of feedback in a communication exchange?

E. FOCUS ON PARAPHRASING

The class should be divided into small groups of approximately five members each. Each group selects an issue that is likely to generate debate (that is, a political, moral, or ethical topic). The group is instructed to discuss the topic. After each speaker makes a statement, however, another member of the group must paraphrase it. The initial speaker either confirms or clarifies the paraphrased statement before discussion continues.

After five to ten minutes of discussion time, the entire group should consider the following:

1. How accurately were group members able to paraphrase the statement?
2. Did the individuals experience difficulty paraphrasing others' statements? Why or why not?
3. Did the act of paraphrasing help clarify others' ideas?
4. Do you feel that paraphrasing can facilitate interaction? Why or why not?

F. FOCUS ON ADAPTATION OF CONFLICT-HANDLING BEHAVIOR

Consider the following situations.

1. Colleagues Judy, Alec, and Curtis have agreed to undertake a consulting project that represents a significant amount of money. They are scheduled to make a presentation on the fifteenth of the month and have agreed to review their portions of the presentation on the first.

    At the meeting on the first, Curtis indicates that although he has done preliminary work for the presentation, due to family problems, he will not be ready by the fifteenth. Aware that their deadline cannot be extended, Judy and Alec conclude that they will now have to do Curtis's work under extreme pressure.

The presentation goes well. Judy and Alec, however, feel that Curtis should turn over his portion of the fee for services to them because they have, in fact, done his work. Curtis does not agree. He feels that without his contribution to the project, Judy and Alec would not have been able to complete his work. He should not be penalized for circumstances beyond his control.

2. Charlotte and Anne have lived together amicably for 1 1/2 years. They have agreed on most issues. Anne, however, meets Randy and starts to date him regularly. At first Randy visits on occasion. After a while, Charlotte feels as if a third roommate is living in their apartment.

Charlotte's attempt to voice concern about Randy's presence is met by resistance, especially because Anne feels that the apartment is half hers. She can do what she wants with her half. Charlotte feels strongly that she wanted one, not two, roommates.

3. Kathy and Jim have been married for four years. Kathy is an account executive for a large firm. Jim is an actor. Kathy earns about 2 1/2 times what Jim makes. When they were first married, they earned approximately the same and routinely shared costs.

Recently Jim has observed that Kathy has begun to make significant purchases without discussing them with him. This is a departure from past practice. One day she appears with a $250 pair of gold earrings. Another time she shows up with a $600 ring. On another occasion she brings Jim a leather jacket that cost $400.

Jim is upset by the fact that Kathy is making all of these purchases and is not discussing priorities with him. Kathy responds: "Look, I work hard for this money. And I buy nice things for you too. I don't think you should have an equal say in how I spend my money unless you contribute an equal amount." How does Jim respond?

The group should be divided into pairs or groups representing the three situations. Turns should be taken enacting these situations, using the following conflict-managing styles:

- The situation with the three colleagues (Curtis, Alec, and Judy):
  - Curtis, Judy, and Alec are competing.
  - Curtis and Judy are competing; Alec wants to compromise.
  - Curtis is competitive; Alec and Judy are accommodating.
  - Curtis is competitive; Judy and Alec assume a collaborative approach.
- The situation with the two roommates (Anne and Charlotte):
  - Charlotte is competing; Anne is avoiding.
  - Charlotte and Anne are competing. After a few minutes of enacting the situation, Anne and Charlotte should reverse roles.
  - Charlotte and Anne are willing to collaborate.

- The situation between the couple (Kathy and Jim):
  - Jim and Kathy are competing.
  - Kathy is avoiding; Jim is compromising.
  - Jim tries to collaborate; Kathy is competitive. After several minutes, Jim and Kathy should reverse roles.
  - Jim and Kathy are willing to collaborate.

G. FOCUS ON DESCRIPTIVE VERSUS EVALUATIVE LANGUAGE

The class should collect magazine or newspaper articles or advertisements that represent opposing viewpoints about the same issue. Discussion may focus on the following:

1. What words in particular evoke the article's or picture's tone?
2. What do the words actually mean? What are they supposed to connote?
3. Is the intended message conveyed effectively? Why or why not?
4. Distinguish between the explicit and implicit messages of the material. Which words reflect these messages?

3

THE LANGUAGES OF CONFLICT MANAGEMENT

Nonverbal Strategies for a Supportive Communication Environment

··

Points to Be Addressed

1. The definition and influence of nonverbal communication;
2. Direct nonverbal communication: Appearance, body language (kinesics), eye contact (oculesics), touch (haptics), and spatial distance (proxemics) as potential sources of conflict;
3. Paralanguage: Effects of vocal aspects of communication as potential sources of conflict;
4. Monitoring and interpreting nonverbal communication to facilitate a supportive communication environment.

··

To this point we have discussed communication only as it regards verbal, or spoken, messages. Much of what we communicate, however, is conveyed without words. Indeed, according to Ray Birdwhistell (1970), the receiver of a message derives as much as 65 percent of the meaning of that message from the sender's nonverbal communication.

Additionally culture and gender issues may markedly affect the degree to which an individual relies on nonverbal communication. One of the clearest examples of the effect of gender and culture on nonverbal communication comes in Gallimore, Boggs, and Jordan's study (1974) of Native Hawaiian ("Aina Pumehana") and white Hawaiian school-children. The study showed that Native Hawaiian schoolchildren sought help verbally from the teacher 19 percent of the time, whereas white schoolchildren sought help verbally 93 percent of the time. The study showed that Native Hawaiian children sought help but did so through nonverbal means, such as increased eye contact or standing near the teacher. This chasm was made even more dramatic when the factor of gender is considered. Among the schoolchildren studied, none of the verbal communication used among the "Aina Pumehana" children came from the girls. Native Hawaiian boys sought help verbally. By contrast, among the white schoolchildren in the study, white boys relied on verbal communication to seek help much less often than white girls. White boys sought help verbally 86 percent of the time, whereas white girls sought help verbally in every recorded instance, that is, 100 percent of the time (pp. 215–216; 221).

Although not all contrasts in the use of nonverbal communication across sex and culture are likely to be so dramatic, the Hawaiian example brings to the fore the complexity of the situation. Were the teachers in the classroom involved in this study to have ignored all nonverbal signals from their female "Aina Pumechana" students, they would in effect have received no communication from them at all. Such a situation is not out of the question, moreover, since (as detailed in Chapter 5), the way in which nonverbal communication is expressed remains subject to marked cross-cultural differences of interpretation.

In any given exchange, even in the same culture or among the same sex, a message receiver who is unaware of the nonverbal elements in that message risks missing more than half of what is conveyed. This, in turn, leaves a great potential for misunderstanding that leads to conflict. For instance, a favorite ploy in spy films is to have the spy point to a hidden microphone and with a significant wink tell a visitor a piece of information both know is incorrect. Pointing out the microphone and the knowing wink nonverbally communicate to the visitor that the spy is deliberately telling a falsehood to mislead the counterspies listening to their conversation. Were the visitor to contradict the falsehood and provide the correct information, the spy would justifiably believe that the visitor belonged to the opposing espionage group. It is unlikely that the spy would consider that the visitor merely did not understand the significance of the pointing and the wink.

The nonverbal signals used by the spies in the movies, however, are more consciously sent and often considerably more blatant than the average nonverbal communication sent between communicators. A bitten thumbnail can—in the proper context—express a wide range of things from nothing more than a bothersome hangnail to extreme nervousness. The nailbiter can in turn be very aware that he or she bites the nail or almost unconscious of having done so at all. Yet how the person observing the bitten nail interprets this act can seriously affect whatever else the two communicate. To reduce the likelihood of such conflict, the sender must take steps consciously to control his or her nonverbal signals to convey the intended message.

In turn, the sender of a message may be unaware that the person to whom he or she communicates is interpreting not only the words used but also the nonverbal elements in the message. For example, a manager who is exasperated with the long-winded explanation of a subordinate may verbally tell him, if asked, to continue. Nonetheless she may give what are to her very clear nonverbal signals to him to end his speech. She may roll her eyes, drum her fingers on the desk, and sigh audibly. The enthusiastic subordinate, however, if he is caught up in his idea, may be totally oblivious to these nonverbal messages. The result may be an abrupt verbal message from the superior telling the subordinate to stop talking and leave. The subordinate, unaware of the signals his boss had expected him to understand, would likely feel greatly surprised and probably hurt. A conflict situation resulting from these differences in perception would likely follow. In such cases the disparity between the words the sender uses and the way in which the receiver interprets the nonverbal messages accompanying that message may convey an entirely different meaning to the message's receiver than that which the sender intended. If the receiver interprets the nonverbal message in a way that contradicts or undermines the message of the words, a defensive climate and a sense of anger or distrust are likely to occur, leading to a very real conflict.

Conflict may result simply from misunderstanding the nonverbal messages one party sends to another. Even when the source of conflict is real rather than perceived, nonverbal signals can influence markedly the degree of conflict by adding elements of bias into the information being sent and received. Nonverbal messages can distort information by appearing to emphasize, understate, or contradict the intended meanings.

Thus to minimize the likelihood of unwanted conflict situations, it is useful for communicators to be aware of the role nonverbal messages play in communication. To do so communicators must remain cognizant of both the nonverbal signals they send and of the way in which others understand their nonverbal messages.

WHAT IS NONVERBAL COMMUNICATION?

The importance of communication sent and received through media other than words is increasingly beyond debate. Much disagreement exists, however, over what precisely is meant by nonverbal communication. Since this debate, although important, does not necessarily concern us here, we may agree to accept nonverbal communication expert Randall Harrison's definition for our purposes in this book.

Harrison (1974) defines nonverbal communication as "the exchange of information through nonlinguistic signs" (p. 25). In this definition Harrison defines *signs* as "a stimulus which, for some communicators, stands for something else"; *nonlinguistic* as "nonword signs"; and *exchange* as "more than one communicator linked in some way so that at least one of them can respond to the signs produced by the other" (1974, p. 25).

Part of the debate alluded to earlier stems from the fact that in many instances the verbal messages simultaneously communicated with the nonverbal messages are meshed together so that the verbal element is for all intents inseparable from the nonverbal one. Such elements as voice production, vocal expressiveness, and the various nonword noises (such as grunts, giggles, and ums) that accompany verbal messages fall into this category. Although some question exists as to whether these are *truly* nonverbal signs, they still fit within Harrison's definition of "the exchange of information through nonlinguistic signs." To distinguish these from the more direct nonverbal signs, however, we will call these elements *paralanguage*.

Nonverbal communication, however, is by no means limited to paralanguage. The way we move, our use of eye contact, touching behavior, how we position ourselves relative to others, and our outward appearance and dress all communicate nonverbally but without the use of sound. Perhaps the most important discussion of these elements is Albert Mehrabian's *Silent Messages* (1981). Yet the title of even this classic description of the importance and pervasiveness of these aspects of nonverbal communication is misleading. Not all nonparalinguistic, nonverbal communication is silent. Snapping fingers, hand clapping, table pounding, burping, and expelling gas are all forms of auditory nonverbal communication that belong in this category. Moreover, not all nonauditory communication is nonverbal, most notably sign language for the deaf. We shall refer to these types of nonverbal behavior as *direct nonverbal communication*.

TYPES OF DIRECT NONVERBAL COMMUNICATION

As discussed, direct nonverbal communication takes many forms. The five most important of these are appearance; body movement, or kinesics; eye contact, or oculesics; touching, or haptics; and the use of personal space, or proxemics. All five of these direct nonverbal communication forms can significantly influence the way in which a message's receivers interpret information. Consequently all five types of direct nonverbal communication can affect the nature and level of conflict.

Appearance

People judge others by appearance, particularly in establishing first impressions. Moreover, some experts assert that these first impressions are often quite accurate (Burgoon and Saine, 1976). Appearance helps us determine key impressions regarding gender, age, profession, relative economic position, and race or culture about those with whom we speak.

Appearance falls into two categories: artifacts and physical traits. Artifacts are those items of personal appearance over which one has control. The clothing and jewelry one wears are artifacts. Other artifacts include items associated with one's status or trade. An expensive automobile is often an artifact of a wealthy person. A collection of lenses and cameras dangling around one's neck and shoulders are artifacts of a photographer.

Artifacts themselves are affected by social expectations. At the most obvious level, nude beaches are a social norm in much of Europe, whereas most public nudity is illegal in the United States. Yet the messages conveyed by clothing and other artifacts are often much more subtle than this. For example, considerable disagreement exists over what is appropriate and inappropriate dress in the workplace. In a survey of 200 U.S. corporations, McConville (1994) found that 78 percent had no formal dress codes and that more than half (55 percent) allowed casual dress on weekdays (p. 12). Nonetheless even in companies with casual-dress codes, what clothing is appropriate is subject to debate. "As in many companies," McConville writes, "casual dress has limits at Ford Motor Co., where slacks and sweaters are fine for men and women, but blue jeans, spandex, sneakers and tank tops are not" (p. 12). A similar casual-dress policy at General Motors carries a warning that the relaxed dress code "does not interfere with important meetings" (p. 14), a clear indication of the communicative value of dress artifacts.

Physical traits, by contrast, are characteristics that on the whole cannot be easily changed but by which people are nonetheless judged. Indeed, in his seminal works on the subject of physical appearance and behavior, William Sheldon (1940, 1942) categorized people into three physical types (endo, or heavy; meso, or muscular; and ecto, or thin) that to some extent affected how people could be predicted to behave. Finally, certain physical traits can be altered or added to—such as false fingernails or dyed hair—combining both the artifact and physical-trait categories.

The categorization of individuals into body types arguably may not be problematic in and of itself. Potentially conflict-causing judgments, however, often occur from the ensuing valuations and character associations that have become linked with physical traits in general. The tension between expectation and reality can cause conflict when these valuations and associations do not necessarily correlate to the actual behavior. Examples of such ungrounded associations with physical appearance are well documented. In their study of facial stereotypes, for example, Berry and McArthur (1986) found that weakness, intellectual naivete, and submissiveness were attributed to adults who were described as "baby faced." Similarly Roberts and Herman (1986) have found height to correspond positively to perceptions of competence, status, and attractiveness.

More serious sources of conflict may arise when appearance-linked associations draw on gender, racial, or ethnic stereotypes. For example, regardless of gender, physical attractiveness has been shown to be a potential advantage in initial hiring decisions (Cash, Gillen, and Burns, 1977; Dipboye, Arvey, and Terpstra, 1977). Yet several observers have indicated that when women are viewed as very attractive (an asset in social relationships), the chance increases that others will judge them as unqualified for certain high-level positions in the workplace—especially in positions that men have traditionally dominated (Hatfield and Sprecher, 1986; Heilman and Saruwatari, 1979; Tarvis, 1992; Wolf, 1991).

Race and ethnicity may compound these observations. Racial and ethnic groups in the United States may be subject to a host of unfounded negative racial stereotypes by those belonging to other races and ethnic groups. Even when stereotyping is minimal or absent, the labeling of race may be typically the most prevalent attribute of an individual belonging to a racial minority. As Conrad Harper, a partner at a prominent law firm and formerly the head of the Association of the Bar of the City of New York, describes in an interview with Ellis Cose, many attorneys are often "bitterly scarred by not being seen first as lawyers . . . but always first as African Americans" (Cose, 1995, p. 60).

Additionally, racial and ethnic stereotypes may result in pigeonholing individuals based on race. Several authors have observed prejudices in which Asian Americans may be "tagged as technical people, not as people who can be trained as managers" (Thomas, 1991, p. 102) or "when they are being selected for employment, they are sought in science and technical areas but not in sales, human resources, or executive-training positions" (Blank and Slipp, 1994, p. 38). Similarly Ellis Cose notes that *black executives have landed, out of all proportion to their numbers, in community relations and public affairs, or in slots where their only relevant expertise concerns blacks and other minorities. The selfsame racial assumptions that make minorities seem perfect for certain initially desirable jobs can ultimately be responsible for trapping them there as others move on. (1995, p. 65)*

Many of these stereotypes combine with gender-linked differences. For example, Blank and Slipp (1994) observe that, based on appearance, Asian American women are stereotyped as "highly pliable and sexually available" and that

although sexual harassment—and complaining about it—is a problem facing all women in the workplace, it is a special problem for Asian-American women because they may be conditioned by their culture not to complain when they are mistreated. They are vulnerable because they are seen as pliable. (p. 43)

Conversely, Blank and Slipp observe, Asian American women who do act assertive are more likely than other women to be viewed as "manipulative, powerful and sexually lethal." For instance, Blank and Slipp (1994) describe an example of a Japanese American attorney who indicates that if "she acts too assertively in her firm, she is called The Dragon Lady" (p. 44).

Nor are such judgments limited to racial or ethnic minorities or women. Corporations have begun offering training workshops for employees to deal with prejudice against white males. AT&T spokesperson Burke Stinson explains, "White men don't want to be categorized or reduced to a cliche any more than anyone else does" (Caudron, 1995, p. 56).

To the extent that appearance influences perceived credibility and competence, physical traits exert a powerful influence in daily social and professional interaction. This in turn affects self-esteem (Graham and Jouhar, 1982; Mathes and Kahn, 1975). How people internalize cultural prescriptions for appearance may be a source of interpersonal conflict. How others respond to a given individual on the basis of his or her appearance may also be a source of interpersonal conflict.

The key thing to keep in mind is that mere physical appearance communicates a message. For example, a client walks into a U.S. law firm office and sees a middle-age graying man dressed in a three-piece dark suit and a young man with jet black hair wearing a cardigan, an open-neck shirt, and contrasting slacks. The client, on the basis of her impressions of how attorneys should look, may begin to address the older man in the suit as the partner in charge, based on nothing more than the clothing he wears (U.S. corporate attorneys traditionally wear dark three-piece suits) and his physical traits (partners in major law firms are more likely than not to be older and thus graying). Although the client and the attorneys have not exchanged a single word, communication has taken place indicating which of the two men the client faces is likely to be the person in charge.

Conflict occurs when what the person observes communicates a different message than actually exists. For instance, it is possible that the younger, more casually dressed man could have been the partner and the older, more formally dressed man his assistant or even a paralegal or other lower-ranked position. The younger man may feel sensitive about having been mistaken for the lower-ranked position. The client, in turn, may feel uncomfortable working with an attorney who does not fit her impression of how an attorney ought to look. This alone lays the foundation for a possible conflict.

The chances of this increase when misjudgments based on appearance play into external elements to which one or the other party is particularly sensitive. For example, as discussed in Chapter 4, conflicts based on gender differences are at times linked to appearance. To illustrate this, let us imagine that the client had entered the law office and seen—instead of an older man and a younger man—a man and a woman of equal age. Based on appearances and (based on a history of strong sex discrimination) the relative lack of female law partners in major U.S. law firms, the client would be justified in assuming solely on the basis of appearance that the person in charge was the man. If in fact the partner in charge were the woman and the man were merely a paralegal or other lower-ranked assistant, the client might play into the partner's sensitivity at being so mistaken, particularly considering that the reason for the client's assumption reflects a sexist bias in the profession to which the partner is arguably an exception. The irritation that the partner feels is likely, at least initially, to produce a counterproductive environment in which conflict is relatively likely.

Kinesics

How we move—or "body language," to use Julius Fast's popularized term (1970)—is called *kinesics* by social scientists. Great differences in kinesics occur from one culture to another and—at least within most of these cultures—between the sexes. These are discussed at greater length in Chapters 4 and 5. Regardless of culture or gender, however, the purposes motivating nonverbal communication fall into identifiably discrete categories. When the body movements are misinterpreted or uncontrolled, conflict may follow. These purposes and possible conflict situations associated with kinesics are discussed here.

In a series of seminal works (1969, 1972, 1974) Paul Ekman and Wallace Friesen have established five basic purposes served by nonverbal communication and particularly applicable to kinesics: emblems, illustrators, affects, regulators, and adaptors. Each of these five purposes, in turn, risks misinterpretation by those who observe them. Indeed, because nonverbal communication is often indirect, the possibility for misunderstanding and subsequent unintended conflict is greater than that of written or spoken communication. Examples of such conflict are described in this section with each of the five Ekman-Friesen types of nonverbal communication.

Emblems

Emblems are nonverbal messages that a receiver can translate directly into words. For example, a common emblem is one in which the sender's hand is raised with the palm facing away from the sender, the forefinger and the thumb touching to form a circle, and the other three fingers extended. Often the emblem is accompanied by a short jerk of the hand followed by a momentary holding in place before the sender releases.

This gesture, known to researchers as the ring, is universally held within the United States to mean OK, or good. When people from the United States see this OK emblem, they understand that the person showing the ring sign means OK. The receiver can translate the emblem into the word *OK* directly, and the sign is understood unambiguously.

Emblems like the OK sign are the least likely of nonverbal communication forms to cause unintended disagreement or unexpected conflict. This is precisely because emblems are so unambiguous. They act like words and—in the case of sign language for the deaf—may be viewed as being verbal rather than nonverbal communication.

Despite their seeming commonality, however, a very serious flaw occurs in the use of emblems. For the most part emblems are directly linked to the culture of the message sender. Later in this book, we will discuss how nonverbal behavior of all types is culture bound. This is nowhere more evident than in the use of emblems, since identical emblems very frequently have diametrically opposed meanings in different cultures.

For example, the ring emblem, which means good, or OK in the United States, has in Europe and North Africa alone four distinct meanings (Morris et al., 1979). In much of Britain, Ireland, Scandinavia, and the former Yugoslavia, the ring means the same as in the United States. In Tunisia, by contrast, the OK meaning of the identical emblem is entirely absent. Tunisians interpret the emblem, depending on the context in which it is used, to mean either "zero" or as a threat (deriving from the implication that the person to whom it is shown is nothing but a "big zero"). Similarly, although the OK meaning of the emblem is not absent in France and Belgium, it is more commonly interpreted to mean zero. Even though they share with the Tunisians the zero interpretation of the emblem, however, neither the French nor the Belgians share with the Tunisians the threat interpretation. In Greece, Sardinia, Turkey, and Malta, both the threat and the zero interpretations of the emblem are almost entirely absent, and the OK meaning is relatively rare. The ring emblem is very frequent in those countries, however, as an insulting obscene gesture representing an orifice, a symbol dating back to ancient times, with the gesture appearing on ancient Greek vases with this meaning. Even those who use the emblem as an insult differ, according to their culture, as to which orifice and which gender they refer to when using the emblem.

The impact of such cross-cultural differences is strong, since the users of emblems often feel that such emblems are at once universal and unambiguous direct translation of words into nonverbal symbols. Thus a U.S. tourist in Greece might indicate to the waiter pouring his wine that the exact amount was in the glass. Limited in the Greek he spoke, the tourist might not even think twice before using what he would take to be a universal sign for OK. In turn the Greek waiter—particularly if he were from a region not often frequented by foreigners—might likewise not think twice before deciding to pour the remainder of the bottle in the tourist's lap.

Illustrators

Illustrators, the next category that Ekman and Friesen describe, are movements that complement verbal communication by describing, accenting, or reinforcing what the speaker says. Among other things, illustrators can describe what size an object is, emphasize the key word in a phrase, or sketch a picture in the air of the object a speaker describes. Illustrators tend to be cross-culturally more universal than emblems, although, as discussed in Chapter 5, the frequency with which people use illustrators varies greatly.

Within a single culture one might expect the frequency of illustrators to increase when the speaker either is excited or senses a lack of understanding. Illustrators therefore both clarify what is said and act as indicators that the speaker is enthusiastic or trying hard to communicate. The presence or absence of illustrators is in itself unlikely to create conflict; however, the listener's perceived sense of the speaker's committed effort to communicate that accompanies the use of illustrators may establish a more collaborative atmosphere when difficult subjects or conflict situations are discussed.

Affect Displays

Affect displays are nonverbal messages of the body and face that carry an emotional meaning or display affective states. Emotional or inner states—hate, disdain, fear, love, and anger—may all be communicated nonverbally in a variety of ways.

For example, in the United States a bouncing gait generally implies a happy state of mind, whereas a slumped posture and a shuffling, slack walking style usually indicate depression. Similarly bursting into a big smile is an affect display of pleasure; frowning suddenly is an affect display of displeasure.

Because such affect displays are often done spontaneously in response to a strong emotion, they may lead to conflict, particularly in sensitive situations. For instance, a physician may wish to appear sympathetic and compassionate to patients. On first seeing a dramatically disfigured patient, however, the physician may be unable to prevent an affective display of revulsion. Even though the physician may have said nothing to give the impression of being disturbed or disgusted by the patient's disfigurement, the patient is aware of the doctor's reaction, due to the affect display. The patient consequently may distrust the physician's subsequent assurances that the disfigurement is not so severe. Indeed, the patient may no longer wish to deal with the physician, based solely on the one displayed affect, resulting in a complete rupture of their relationship.

Regulators

Regulators are nonverbal messages that accompany speech to control— or regulate—what the speaker says. Regulators are directly within awareness, but the communicators sending and receiving them are less directly aware of their use than they would be of emblems, illustrators, or affect displays.

Thus when two people hold a conversation, the person listening may nod his head periodically. He does so to show that he is listening, although he remains less aware of the nod than he would be, for example, of a ring emblem to communicate that what was said was OK with him. Conversely the speaker also is aware of the nodding but again at a lower level than a signaled emblem or illustrator.

Significantly, regulators appear to have more universality across cultures than do emblems. Even here, however, culture may play a part. For example, nodding is relatively common in most cultures as a way to communicate that one is listening in face-to-face discussions. Nevertheless in some cultures it is common to face the speaker directly while nodding and making eye contact. In other cultures it is common to lower one's eyes (at least within certain relationships based on rank or gender) but still to nod. Still elsewhere it is proper to nod while turning one's ear toward the speaker, since the ear is the listening organ.

The use of regulators increases when communication becomes more difficult. Thus in conflict situations we would expect participants to use more regulators than in nonconflict situations. Indeed, it is here that the less conscious perception of regulators (as compared to emblems, for example) becomes more evident. Neither party in a conflict situation (at least in most cases) would consciously indicate that the other party is being more or less cooperative or collaborative in resolving a difficult matter on the basis of the number of regulators being employed. No rough count of the number of head nods, for example, is tallied by either party to indicate that the other party is listening carefully to a given proposal.

Nonetheless, the absence of positive regulators or the use of negative regulators (such as drooping eyes) on the part of one party is very likely to give the other party the feeling that his or her position is not being well received. The lack of regulators therefore communicates a lack of interest and may impede delicate negotiations. The use of such neutral negative regulators as an impassive face or drooping eyes in itself causes significant misunderstanding. Thus if party A suggests a way to resolve a conflict with party B but party B sits motionless throughout the period in which party A makes the suggestion, party A may feel in an intangible way that party B does not favor the idea or has failed to hear out party A's suggestion in an unbiased manner. This may not be the case. Party B may have listened to party A's position very openly, but the fact that party A perceives that party B did not do so on the basis of party B's absence of regulators may lead to a hardening of party A's position. This in turn contributes to making conflict management more difficult.

Adaptors
The final category of nonverbal behavior that Ekman and Friesen have isolated is adaptors. These occur on a very low level of awareness and represent perhaps the most difficult of the categories to define. Adaptors are in general terms those movements used to fulfill a personal need. These can take several forms. Scratching or holding oneself are examples of adaptors that one performs on oneself. Other adaptors are more outward, affecting objects within the person's reach, such as chewing on a pencil or twisting paper clips while concentrating. Finally, some adap-

tors affect neither objects nor the body directly but represent movement without a direct outcome, as shaking or swinging one's legs.

Since people performing adaptors are fairly unaware of the adaptors they use, those with whom the adaptor user interacts are often more aware of the adaptors than the people using the adaptors. Adaptors may therefore act unintentionally as clues to how a person feels. In particular, adaptors stem back to behavior learned early in life. As Mark Knapp (1980, p. 9), observes, "Adaptors are not intended for use in communication, but they may be triggered by verbal behavior in a given situation associated with conditions occurring when the adaptive habit was first learned."

Significantly adaptors increase with an increased level of anxiety. Thus a person who feels uncomfortable may scratch more than a person who feels at ease. Therefore, attentive listeners can assess to some extent how much anxiety the person speaking to them feels, based on the adaptors that person uses.

Since the use of adaptors is associated frequently with an increased state of anxiety or nervousness, verbal assurances of calmness or control may be undermined by the adaptors that accompany them. This in turn can lead to a conflict.

For example, an advertising executive may nervously shift in her seat and scratch the back of her neck in an initial meeting with a new and very large potential client. Because she wants the huge account very much, she may unintentionally demonstrate her concerns through her use of these adaptors. The potential client may not trust the advertising executive fully but may not be sure why, as he, too, is likely to be only partially aware of the adaptors he observes. To satisfy his lack of trust, the potential client may ask the advertising executive how much experience she has had with accounts of his size. She may assure him verbally in a calm voice that she has much experience along these lines, even reciting past successes. As she knows that the potential client's cross-examination is a bad sign, however, her level of anxiety—high already—will increase even more. Now she may perform even more adaptors as a release for her uneasiness. She may bite at her cuticle and shake her leg under the desk. The potential client, now firmly aware that the advertising executive is for some reason nervous, may say that he has decided to look around a bit more before committing. The reason he gives is a nebulous lack of trust. The advertising executive, unaware to a large extent of the adaptor she has sent, may argue that the lack of trust is unfounded. The potential client is likely to agree with her that everything she has said to him should only build his trust. Since the potential client is unlikely to say that he has decided to look elsewhere on the basis of a bitten nail or a shaking leg, both parties focus on their verbal communication. In this case the client has little to support his lack of trust. The result is a conflict that remains at the unspoken level precisely because it is never fully realized. Often categorized as a personality conflict, the source of such conflict may never fully surface, as it is possible that neither party ever becomes totally aware of the adaptors that signaled it.

Oculesics

Oculesics, or eye contact, has long been recognized as a means of communicating without speaking. For centuries poets and novelists have been fascinated with the power of eyes to communicate. "Drink to me only with thine eyes, / And I will pledge with mine" (lines 1–2), wrote the poet Ben Jonson in his poem "To Celia," and Miguel de Cervantes in *Don Quixote* defined "the eyes those silent tongues of Love" (pt. I, bk. II, ch. 3). Yet communication experts have examined the field of oculesics only comparatively recently.

How one uses his or her eyes can convey a number of meanings. As with other nonverbal communication, oculesics vary markedly from one culture to the other (as discussed in Chapter 5). When all parties are from the same culture, however, the eyes can communicate in a number of recognizable ways.

Oculesics have been identified, at least within English-speaking North American culture, to serve four main functions: (1) cognitive, (2) monitoring, (3) regulatory, and (4) expressive (Argyle et al., 1973; Kendon, 1967).

Cognitive Oculesics

Cognitive oculesics are those eye movements associated with thinking. In general, people communicate that they are thinking by looking away from those to whom they speak. To look away indicates that the communicator is not open to receiving further information. Conversely people tend to make eye contact when they are open to receiving more information. A person who looks away from another indicates to some extent that the speaker should slow down the flow of information while the listener processes it. In turn, those who do make eye contact indicate that the communication they have just received has been understood.

Conflict may result from inappropriate cognitive oculesics. For example, in a labor-negotiation session a union representative may find that her management counterparts are not looking at her when she makes her demands. When this occurs, she is likely to interpret the management representatives' lack of eye contact as indicating that they have not listened to her position attentively or that they do not take her demands seriously. The labor representative's conclusion, however, may be erroneous. The management representatives—although appearing inattentive due to inappropriate cognitive oculesics—may well have closely listened to the labor representative's demands. No verbal message was ever given to indicate otherwise. Conflict, therefore, could easily be introduced when the labor representative verbally reacts in a hostile way to the negative messages she wrongly believes she has received. In response the management representatives would quite naturally respond verbally to the labor representative's hostile position, and the conflict would escalate.

Monitoring Oculesics

Monitoring oculesics are those eye movements associated with the receiving of responses to what the speaker has just said. For example, one would expect a listener who understands a speaker to look more steadily at the speaker than a listener who has trouble understanding the speaker (based on the nature of cognitive oculesics just described). To assess the extent to which a listener understands what has been said, the speaker would monitor the degree of eye contact provided by the listener. Monitoring oculesics are not only tied to observing the listener's eye movements, however, but also involve the entire range of the direct nonverbal communication behavior discussed in this chapter.

Conflict deriving from monitoring oculesics might occur when speakers misread the eye movements of their audience. For example, college professors often interpret the fixed gaze of their students as indicating that the students understand the course lectures. Conflict takes place when a large portion of the class later indicates through assignments or class discussion that it has not understood the lectures. Only then do these professors find that they have misinterpreted the class members' monitoring oculesics.

Similarly conflict may occur when speakers mistakenly interpret the gaze of a listener who does not look steadily at them as lack of understanding. For example, a salesperson may oversimplify her sales pitch or unnecessarily rephrase points she has already made if she interprets a knowledgeable potential buyer's eye contact as indicating a lack of knowledge. The buyer, in turn, may feel affronted by this *verbal* response to his unintended nonverbal cues.

Finally, conflict based on even an *accurate* reading of a listener's monitoring oculesics is possible. The listener may, for example, be unaware that he or she so clearly shows a lack of understanding. Believing the lack of understanding to be hidden, the listener may resent even the speaker's *correct* interpretation of the listener's *nonverbal* cues if the speaker treats these cues as if they had been *admitted* verbally rather than *detected* nonverbally.

Regulatory Oculesics

Regulatory oculesics are those eye movements associated with the willingness or unwillingness of a communicator to respond to what has been said. Relatedly the speaker may regulate the flow of communication by making eye contact to indicate that the listener should respond or by failing to make eye contact to indicate the desire to keep speaking. As with cognitive oculesics, the major indicator of regulatory eye movement is the absence or presence of direct eye contact. Thus listeners who do not wish to respond to what they have heard avert their gaze. Listeners who meet the gaze of the speaker indicate either that they are willing to respond at that point or that they have understood what has been said and that the speaker can continue.

Conflict based on regulatory oculesics also derives from misread cues. If, for example, a subordinate looks away from his boss when the boss asks him a question, the boss is likely to understand this eye movement to be a sign that the subordinate does not wish to respond. If in fact the reason the subordinate looked away was unrelated to the boss's question, the boss and the subordinate will base their commuunication on two different assumptions. The boss will respond to the subordinate's averted gaze in a manner that would suggest that the subordinate could not or would not answer the question. The subordinate, if unaware of this, will feel that the boss's behavior is unjustified and will respond accordingly. This exchange of responses will in turn escalate the misunderstanding and may well lead to actual conflict.

Expressive Oculesics

Expressive oculesics are eye movements associated with the emotional response of the communicator. Paul Ekman and Wallace Friesen (1975) have identified oculesic disgust, anger, happiness, and sadness and have based these indicators on the positions of eyebrows and eyelids, the tautness of skin around the eyes, and the amount of white shown in the eyes. By reading the emotions expressed through the eyes, communicators gain an insight into how their messages are received and the extent to which they have interested, excited, or in some other way emotionally involved the person with whom they are communicating.

Conflict based on expressive oculesics may arise when communicators misread the messages written in the eyes of those with whom they communicate. In particular, as discussed in Chapter 4, marked differences exist between the expressive oculesics of men and women.

Similarly, as discussed in Chapter 5, cultures vary greatly in how their members interpret standard oculesic expressions. As a result, conflicts due to distorted readings of expressive oculesics are very possible in communication between women and men or across cultures.

Haptics

Making or failing to make body contact is another form of nonverbal communication. Such communication through touching behavior is called haptics.

Perhaps no other area of nonverbal communication is fraught with more ambivalence than touching or being touched by another. Our need for touch—what Ashley Montagu (1971) has termed "skin hunger"—is abiding. Yet how we gratify our "hunger" for touch has emerged recently as a controversial area.

According to Julia Wood (1993), behavior, including touching, that was once regarded as flirtatious, natural, and complimentary has undergone considerable scrutiny. The same behavior, in certain instances, is often now viewed as "unwanted, unwelcome, unprofessional, and unacceptable" (p. 23). Stanley Jones (1995) devotes an entire book to understanding the power and need for physical contact and for developing the right touch in our daily lives.

How we construe "right" is influenced by several factors: the intention of the person who touches another; the context of the interaction; the interpretation of the person who is being touched; and the nature of the relationship (or the extent to which touch may be reciprocal). For example, when a father hugs his crying daughter, he reassures her and communicates that things will be better or that he loves her. No word has to pass between the two for this message to be exchanged.

Similarly haptics often communicates intimacy. The more affectionate people are, the more freely they will touch each other. Haptics are not limited to love or intimacy, however. Haptics—excluding openly hostile touching behavior (such as slapping)—can be categorized into five major types: (1) functional/professional, (2) social/polite, (3) friendship/warmth, (4) love/intimacy, and (5) sexual/arousal (Heslin, 1974). Each of these categories represents progressive stages, each leading to the next, so that one moves from professionally acceptable touching behavior to socially acceptable haptics, and so on. Each of these categories is duly proscribed by the social norms of the culture in which an individual lives, although the differences between cultures is marked (see Chapter 5).

In most cases, when the boundaries of what is permissible within a haptic category are exceeded, the person doing the touching does so to communicate a message regarding the interpersonal relationship between the person touching and the person being touched. What is communicated to the person being touched is that the person doing the touching either believes that the relationship is closer or more intimate than the previously appropriate category would imply or *wishes* it to be so. Conflict can occur when the one touching and the one being touched do not agree on the appropriate haptic category. When one person touches another in a way that is too intimate, the resulting tension caused by the touch can cause conflict.

Nancy Henley (1977) has indicated that a relationship exists between haptics and dominance. She asserts that those in power are more likely to touch their subordinates than they are to be touched by their subordinates. Thus it is more likely than vice versa for doctors to touch their patients, police their detainees, teachers their students, and advisors those they advise.

Consequently when a person touches another, it may not be a message of increasing intimacy but instead of dominance. If the two parties do not agree on the relative dominance such touching implies, conflict is possible. It should be noted that Henley pointed out in particular that in status situations, men tended to touch women more often than vice versa. The gender-linked status differences in this touching behavior are discussed in Chapter 4.

Proxemics

The way in which people use space communicates a message. How people use space in this way is called proxemics.

The use of space has a powerful effect on communication. As Edward Hall has observed, "Spatial changes give a tone to communication, accent it, and at times even override the spoken word" (1959, p. 160). If a person moves to a point that we believe is too close, we back up. Conversely we tend to move closer to a person we believe to be too distant. How close is too close and how far is too far, however, are carefully proscribed. Although the actual distance involved varies from culture to culture, the categorization of personal space according to appropriate and inappropriate distances when speaking is universal. Hall, in a later work on the subject (1966), observes four categories of personal space: intimate, casual-personal, social-consultative, and public.

Intimate personal space is, as its name implies, that space nearest the body, reserved for those with whom one is intimate. In the United States this area is a bubble extending approximately 1 1/2 feet around the body.

The casual personal area is acceptable only for the interaction of friends. In the United States this usually covers an area from 1 1/2 feet to 4 feet.

Social-consultative personal space is the space employed in conducting most day-to-day affairs. It is the space in which business is conducted and is impersonal enough for use with strangers. In the United States the acceptable area for social-constructive personal space is between 4 and 12 feet.

Finally, public space is the zone outside social-consultative space. Reserved for public-speaking situations, it is too distant for most other activities.

Many factors influence the distance between communicators, especially in intimate, casual, and social interactions. Several researchers have studied spatial distance (Eagly, 1987; Hall, 1959; Hall, 1984; Henley, 1977; Knapp and Hall, 1992). The following eight factors, summarized from their findings, may influence our proximity to others:

1. Culture and ethnicity—especially the extent to which individuals come from high- or low-context backgrounds;
2. Personal and physical traits—age, height, weight, and certain physical attributes (e.g., physical disabilities and disfigurations);
3. Interaction setting—the context of the encounter—which affects both our willingness and expectations for distance (e.g., an expectation to be seated more closely to strangers in a crowded airplane or restaurant than in a library);
4. Perceived power or status—greater distance given to those to whom we attribute, or who are vested with, power or status (e.g., a police officer, certain political figures, a company's CEO);
5. The nature of the relationship—whether we are interacting with friends, casual acquaintances, total strangers, coworkers, family members, or romantic partners;
6. The nature of the topic—the extent to which a topic being discussed is confidential, highly personal and/or sensitive, or neutral;
7. Sex roles—although there are many contradictory findings regarding sex and interaction distance, to the extent that affiliative and prosocial roles are often connected to women's behavior—the extent to which women approach and are approached more closely by others may reflect the assumption of these roles;
8. Personality traits—the willingness to approach and to be approached more closely by others is reflective of one's self-concept (e.g., high versus low self-esteem, extroversion versus introversion, high versus low affiliative needs).

It is important to keep in mind that although all eight of these factors influence distance, they are culturally determined. Moreover, even within the same culture, there are variations in how "comfortable" we feel with our proxemic distance in our interaction with others. When others exceed our "comfort zone," this behavior may be viewed as a "violation" of our space. Such intrusions, regardless of the intention, may be a potential source of conflict. Conversely when individuals alter their patterns of behavior with us (e.g., they now "keep their distance"), such a change may be confusing or provocative.

For example, since how close or far we choose to stand to someone communicates a strong message, a possibility for conflict deriving from miscommunication or disagreement exists. If a husband makes a sincerely intimate statement to his wife, she would expect him to do so from the intimate zone. If instead he does so from the social-consultative zone, his proxemics undermine his spoken message.

In response, the wife may feel affronted by this nonverbal incongruity. She may therefore return the husband's intimate statement more coolly than he expects, based on his verbal statement alone. The husband, in turn, is likely to feel affronted by his wife's response. These exchanges can rapidly build on one another, resulting in conflict.

PARALANGUAGE

As defined earlier in this chapter, paralanguage is the group of vocal elements accompaniing verbal messages. These elements include the qualities of voice production and expressiveness, as well as the various nonword noises that people use in speech.

The various qualities of a speaker's voice provide information about the speaker. Studies show that people make assumptions about intelligence, friendliness, rank, general attitudes, and honesty based on paralanguage, or *how* a speaker sounds (Addington, 1968; Davitz, 1964; Kramer, 1963; Williams, 1970).

Unskilled listeners are readily able to interpret accurately paralinguistic cues regarding the speaker. The average listener, however, is unaware of exactly from what he or she has obtained this information when it is conveyed paralinguistically. In short, the listener processes paralinguistic messages as unnamed feelings or intuitive hunches about the speaker without being fully cognizant of their source. As J. A. Starkweather explains: "Voice alone can carry information about the speaker. . . . Judgments appear to depend on significant changes in pitch, rate, volume and other physical characteristics of the voice, but untrained judges cannot describe these qualities accurately" (1961, p. 69).

The paralinguistic messages that Starkweather's untrained judges accurately assess but cannot describe *can* be identified. What is important for our discussion is that when communicators unintentionally convey messages through the paralanguage they employ or when the message they attempt to convey is not the same as the message the audience receives, misunderstanding and attendant conflict may follow.

Pauses

A subset of paralanguage meriting individual attention as a source of communication-based conflict is the pause. Pauses are powerful tools in speech, often conveying strong messages. These messages, though, are frequently imprecise, and in their imprecision rests the possibility of misinterpretation leading to unintended conflict.

Two types of pauses occur in speech: unfilled and filled. Unfilled, or silent, pauses and the use of silence, although nonvocalized nonverbal communication, are included here because their use depends on placement within speech, and they are used as a form of vocalized nonverbal message, that is, as the absence of vocalized messages. Unfilled pauses in speech are differentiated from silence as a matter of degree. A short silence is an unfilled pause; a long pause, an intended silence.

Unfilled pauses, depending on their frequency, act as a verbal cue to listeners. Hesitations and pauses—both filled or vocalized and unfilled or silent—are expected in spontaneous speech at spots other than those determined by grammatical closure. Indeed one way to differentiate a read speech and a spontaneously delivered speech rests in the relatively high consistency of grammatical pauses and the absence of nongrammatical pauses in the read speech. Knapp (1980, p. 222) indicates that in spontaneous speeches, "only 55 percent of the pauses occur at grammatical junctures, whereas oral readers of prepared texts are highly consistent in pausing at clause and sentence junctures." Thus one vocal cue listeners determine from the use of unfilled pauses is the degree to which the speaker's words seem to be spontaneous. Misevaluating these pauses, therefore, can skew the listener's perception of a speaker and his or her message, which in turn may lead to conflict based on misunderstanding.

Other studies have shown unfilled pauses to act as vocal cues in other ways. Unfilled pauses have been linked to listeners' perceptions of the speaker's conciseness and a decrease in predictability (Goldman-Eisler, 1961). Excessive use of unfilled pauses, however, appears to lead listeners to perceive the speaker as contemptuous, angry, or anxious (Lalljee, 1971). Conflict may result when the listener's emotions are colored in this way by the speaker's pauses, unbeknownst to the speaker.

Silences are intentionally used unfilled pauses of long duration.

Silence can be a very powerful nonverbal communication tool. One amusing example, although probably apocryphal, of the use of silence to communicate a message forcefully involves the address of Nikita Khrushchev to the Politburo soon after he succeeded Josef Stalin as head of the Soviet Union. Khrushchev was attacking Stalin for various atrocities and abuses in a vitriolic speech when an anonymous voice shouted from the back of the large room. "If Stalin was such a monster, Comrade Khrushchev, then why did no one—including you—stand up to him? Why did no one speak out?" The members of the Politburo gasped almost as one, and a hush fell over the room as Khrushchev set down his speech and looked over the faces of the men and women in the room. "Who said that?" he demanded and glared at his audience. Khrushchev allowed a long silence to follow his question. No one spoke. The huge room was so quiet that each Politburo member could hear the breathing of the member next to him. After more than a minute of this nearly palpable silence, Khrushchev smiled. "That, Comrade," Khrushchev said, referring to the sense of dread the silence just passed had communicated, "that is the reason why no one spoke out."

J. Vernon Jensen (1973) suggests that a wide range of meanings are attributable to silence. He suggests that silence indicates

1. mental activity, such as reflection or thoughtfulness;
2. evaluation and passing judgment;
3. revelation, for example, hiding or making known a fact by answering an inquiry with silence;
4. emotional expression, generally of strong emotions, such as love or disgust; and
5. an accent or underscoring of a point, as in the Khruschev example.

Due to this variety of possible interpretation, listeners may relatively easily misinterpret a speaker's use of silence. Although misinterpretation in itself may not necessarily create conflict, the perceptual gap between the received and sent messages can strongly affect reactions to information exchanged in a conflict situation by contributing an element of bias that may be unfounded.

The other type of pause, the filled pause, is much more akin to other paralanguage. Filled pauses are hesitations and pauses that the speaker fills with various nonword vocalizations. In English these commonly include such sounds as "um," "eh," "er," and "ah." Filled pauses also include word repetition or false starts, stuttering, and verbal expressions acting as fillers (such as "OK" or "you know" when used out of context). On the whole, filled pauses are less well received than unfilled pauses.

Filled pauses have been associated with long-windedness and the predictability of what the speaker is attempting to express (Goldman-Eisler, 1961).

As discussed in Chapter 2, filled pauses have been shown to lead listeners to perceive the speaker as bored or anxious (Lalljee, 1971; Mehrabian, 1981). When these perceptions do not reflect the reality of a situation, each party may behave in what seems to the other party to be an incongruous manner. For example, if an attorney uses numerous filled pauses, her client may grow irritated with the attorney after a very short period, since he anticipates a long-winded speech. He therefore feels justified in interrupting the attorney after only a few minutes. He may even tell her to get to the point. However, she is likely to be surprised at her client's abruptness, since she has spoken for only a few minutes. It would be unlikely that she would be aware that her client is reacting to her filled pauses. Consequently she would respond to her client's interruption as an unmotivated rudeness. The client would, in turn, react to her reaction and so forth until the initially harmless misinterpretation of a nonverbal cue escalates into a very real basis for conflict.

NONVERBAL COMMUNICATION STRATEGIES FOR CONFLICT MANAGEMENT

In this chapter we have discussed the ways in which nonverbal communication can affect the environment in which the whole communication process takes place. Messages conveyed nonverbally, both while speaking and while listening, help to establish what we have termed in Chapter 2 a *collaborative climate for interpersonal communication.*

Nonverbal behavior, as we have noted, is often overlooked by those who send the message. Thus a speaker may be unaware of what her body motions or facial expressions convey while she speaks. Those who watch the speaker, however, are unlikely to remain equally unaware of these nonverbal signals. Thus the first step in maintaining a supportive climate likely to avoid interpersonal conflict is self-awareness of our own nonverbal behavior.

The insights that an observer may draw from watching another's nonverbal behavior are varied and rich, although often imprecise. Consequently the second step for maintaining a supportive communication climate is to resist too rapid a judgment of nonverbal messages. Instead the observer should balance any individual nonverbal message against other such messages, as well as against the verbally conveyed messages of the person observed. In short, because of such messages' imprecision, the observer must take care to place his or her observations in context.

By no means, however, should the communicator disregard nonverbal messages because of their imprecision. Although imprecise, nonverbal messages, as we have discussed, can be most expressive in sending messages. Relatedly nonverbal messages are equally revealing when observed, in part because the sender of the message is often less aware of his or her nonverbal communication than of other outlets of communication, such as the words used.

One means of assessing nonverbal behavior in a manner that would reduce tension and defensiveness is to employ the principles of Gibb's supportive-climate characteristics (1961) described in greater detail in Chapter 2. As we have explained Gibb's approach regarding verbal strategies for establishing a supportive communication climate, the discussion here will only briefly discuss how to modify these strategies to the nonverbal arena. Gibb suggests six categories for establishing a supportive verbal communication environment: description, problem orientation, spontaneity, empathy, equality, and provisionalism. We will discuss the first five as equally applicable to nonverbal communication as well. Gibb's last category, provisionalism, is not discussed in this section, however, as it is manifested primarily verbally and so does not apply to our subject.

Description, for Gibb, is the opposite of evaluation. He suggests that when people believe that they are being evaluated or judged according to how they communicate, they become defensive. Applying this to nonverbal behavior, the communicator should attempt to avoid expressing judgment being passed on the nonverbal behavior of the person observed. The information obtained should be used for the observer but not necessarily shared with the sender, who, Gibb indicates, would likely become insecure or defensive. Indeed this is particularly important for nonverbal messages, since, as we noted earlier, the sender of the message is not always wholly aware of the message he or she sends. Consequently an openly judgmental reception of such messages might very easily make the person observed self-conscious once made aware of this nonverbal behavior. The resultant tension could readily lead to counterproductive conflict.

Gibb writes that problem orientation rather than attempts at control helps to establish a collaborative environment for verbal interaction. To a lesser extent this holds true in nonverbal exchanges as well. Gibb asserts that in the verbal arena, "a bombardment of persuasive 'messages' . . . has bred cynical and paranoidal responses in listeners" (1961, p. 204). Attempts to manipulate and persuade using nonverbal messages may, however, in fact be more effective than their verbal counterparts precisely because people *are* less aware of their presence and so have less of an opportunity to become as jaded by them. Still, Gibb's principle that the attempt to control is in its very nature more likely to provoke conflict than an attempt to solve a problem collaboratively holds true for any communication, including nonverbal.

As discussed in Chapter 2, Gibb explains the difference between strategy and spontaneity as the difference between deliberate manipulation (through feigned guilelessness and other forms of pretense) and genuine responsiveness and openness to a communication exchange. Although Gibb refers to verbal situations, this distinction parallels precisely the difference between interactive listeners and pretending listeners described earlier in this chapter.

Nonverbal behavior is particularly well suited to maintaining the next characteristic in Gibb's supportive communication climate, empathy. Since nonverbal behavior, as we have discussed, is particularly effective in communicating emotions, it is useful in conveying to others that its user feels empathy with them. Empathic listening in particular is useful in encouraging a speaker to continue and in expressing to him or her without interrupting that the listener understands and cares about what is said.

SUMMARY

In this chapter we have discussed various nonverbal communication messages. We have described how appearance, oculesics, proxemics, touching behavior, and body motion communicate messages. We also examined how paralanguage and pauses convey messages.

We noted that although nonverbal behavior communicates messages in every culture, what is actually communicated is culturally determined. Therefore the nonverbal communication discussed in this chapter is limited to the United States. The use of nonverbal communication in other cultures is discussed in more detail in Chapter 5.

Finally, we have shown how nonverbal messages can lead to conflict through unintended disclosure or through misinterpretation. To lessen the chance for undesirable, counterproductive conflict, we have indicated methods for using nonverbal behavior as a supportive communication tool.

SUGGESTED ACTIVITIES

A. FOCUS ON APPEARANCE

Take two photographs of someone you know well. For the first photograph, have that person dress in very formal business attire (a dark suit, for example). For the second photograph, have the person dress very casually (jeans and a T-shirt, for example).

Next, show the first photograph to five people who do not know the person. Ask them to tell you what they think the person in the photograph is like. Ask them to indicate what they think he or she does for a living, his or her relative economic status, intelligence, level of education likely attained, goals, and so forth. Record their answers.

Then take the second photograph and show it to five different people who also do not know the person. Ask them the same questions that you asked of people regarding the first photograph. Record their answers.

Compare the responses. How similar or dissimilar are the responses of those people who viewed the same photograph? How similar or dissimilar are the responses of those who viewed different photographs? To what extent did the appearance and dress affect these people's responses?

Now compare the responses of these people to what you know about the person. How accurate or inaccurate were their first impressions based on appearance? Was one group of viewers more accurate in your estimation than the other? Were attributes you believe to be true noticed by one group and not by the other? Be prepared to discuss your findings and observations in class.

B. FOCUS ON KINESICS

For this exercise a short videotape of two people speaking will be played in class. The volume will be turned off. If this exercise is done at home, a VCR can be used, as long as the viewers watch a film with which they are unfamiliar.

Each student will take out five pieces of paper. Each student will write out the categories of the Ekman-Friesen types of nonverbal communication so that the top of one page will read EMBLEMS, another ADAPTORS, the next ILLUSTRATORS, the next AFFECT DISPLAYS, and the last REGULATORS.

Next, the students should draw a line down the center of each page, forming two columns. The first column should be marked SPEAKER ONE; the second, SPEAKER TWO.

As the students watch the film, they should quickly record the number of body motions they observe on the sheets according to the appropriate categories and for the appropriate speakers.

At the end of the film, the students should discuss how frequently the various types of kinesics were used. They should also discuss which speaker used more or less of each type and what significance, if any, they believe this had.

They should consider as well what, based on kinesic behavior alone, they believe the conversation of the two people in the videotape was about. Was this a conflict situation? Did one speaker appear more dominant than the other? What nonverbal messages were sent between the two communicators? How receptive to these signals did each seem to be?

C. FOCUS ON OCULESICS

Hold a conversation with a friend. Make very direct and unbroken eye contact throughout the conversation, staring very intensely without stop as you speak and as you listen. Observe what your friend's reaction is. What is your *own* reaction?

Now hold a conversation in which you make as little eye contact as possible. When the person with whom you speak is talking, look away. Again record the reactions you observe.

Next, enter an elevator and make strong eye contact with a stranger in the elevator. How did that person seem to react? How did *you* feel?

For each situation, be prepared to discuss whether your behavior causes any tension. If so, could there have been enough tension to have caused a conflict situation? How were the reactions in each situation alike or different?

D. FOCUS ON HAPTICS

Shake hands with a friend. Use a very firm grip and, pumping vigorously, extend the handshake much longer than you normally would.

Next, shake hands with the friend again. This time use a very limp handshake and cut the clasp off quickly.

Ask the friend to evaluate the two handshakes. What message did each communicate?

E. FOCUS ON PROXEMICS

Obtain three male and three female volunteers. Ask two of the male volunteers to come to the front of the room. Have the third male volunteer and the three female volunteers stand outside the room, with the door closed, so that they are unaware of what is happening in the room.

Have one student stand at the center of the room and the other at the opposite side of the room against the wall. Have the student at the center of the room stand still and ask the other student to approach until he feels he has reached a comfortable conversational distance. Mark the spot unobtrusively. Have him return to his seat.

Ask the remaining male volunteer to enter the room. Have him approach the student in the middle of the room in the same manner and to stop when he has reached a comfortable conversational distance.

Did he select the same approximate spot?

Now ask one of the female volunteers to enter the room. Ask her to approach the male student in the center of the room in the same manner and to stop when she has reached a comfortable conversational distance.

Did she select the same approximate spot?

Have the female volunteer replace the male volunteer in the middle of the room. Ask the remaining female volunteer outside the room to come in and repeat the exercise.

Did she select the same approximate spot?

Inform the volunteers of where they stopped relative to one another. Is there a universal proxemics for comfortable conversation? Does this distance shift by gender? By any other factor? Discuss what the differences and similarities of their proxemics signify.

4

GENDER DIFFERENCES

The Impact of Communication Style on Conflict Management

....

Points to Be Addressed

1. Applying the five-step model of conflict management to gender and communication;
2. Assessment: Dichotomizing behavior and its impact on how women and men experience conflict; factors that influence our approach to managing differences;
3. Acknowledgment: Growing up male and female—effects of the home and of education;
4. Attitude: Sex-trait and sex-role stereotyping and their influence on assumptions about, and prescriptions for, male and female behavior;
5. Action: The communication scripts for men and women; verbal and nonverbal communication styles as sources of conflict;
6. Analysis: Perceived and actual differences in how women and men manage conflict.

....

In Chapters 2 and 3 we presented the kinds of effective verbal and non-verbal communication skills required to facilitate both communication and problem solving in conflict management. Without developing such skills, one's ability to manage conflict productively may be impeded.

Societal norms, however, exert an enormous influence on what is regarded as both effective and appropriate communication. A legacy of literature in the fields of communication, linguistics, psychology, and sociology suggests that men and women communicate differently; they attend to different cues and values in their interactions with others (Bem, 1993; Bernard, 1981; Borisoff and Merrill, 1992; Deaux and Major, 1990; Gilligan, 1982; Haste, 1994; Henley, 1977; Kramarae, 1981; LaFrance and Henley, 1994; Lakoff, 1975; Rubin, 1976, 1983; Stockard and Johnson, 1980). Lilian Breslow Rubin observed more than two decades ago that women and men "are products of a process that trains them to relate to only one side of themselves—she, to the passive, tender, intuitive, verbal, emotional side; he, to the active, tough, logical, nonverbal, unemotional one" (1976, p. 116). Although these differences have been somewhat mitigated over time, gender remains a factor that may be a source of conflict and shapes how individuals view and manage differences.

In Chapter 1 we indicated that both personal and professional relationships are fraught with conflict and that gender is one contributing factor. Recognition of the need to address how gender affects the ability of women and men to manage conflict has emerged as a growing area of investigation. As women and men increasingly pursue careers that reflect collegial interactions (as opposed to subordinate-superior interactions), and as both sexes struggle to reconceptualize and to redefine their social relationships, the communicative acts of women and men and, moreover, society's attitudes toward these acts have undergone considerable scrutiny. Such an analysis may result in the ability of women and men to understand more fully their own communication behavior, as well as the behavior of members of the opposite sex. Such understanding can inform the ability of both sexes to manage conflict productively and will, ideally, begin to dispel the misunderstandings between women and men that experts like Rubin have long observed. As we review our model for the process of conflict management—assessment, acknowledgment, attitude, action, and analysis—we will see that the process of recognizing and changing society's views toward the roles and behavior of women and men in U.S. culture is a slow, albeit a necessary, process.

ASSESSMENT

Before engaging in a confrontation, it is important for individuals to (1) assess their individual traits to understand how they may view and be viewed by others, (2) assess the nature of the conflict, (3) clarify their own goals, (4) examine the communication climate, and (5) make a preliminary determination of how they will approach the conflict.

Individual Traits

In his chapter on the subjective dimensions of conflict resolution, Deutsch (1991) contends that whenever there is a propensity to categorize people on the basis of differences, "the differences between each category tend to be enhanced" (p. 29). Often, he goes on to argue, these differences are more a matter of perception than actual divergence, but perceptions exert a strong influence on what people come to expect from others.

The expectations for women and for men reflect a long-standing propensity to regard women and men as different, often as opposite. This propensity is not surprising. It reflects a tendency to view the world and behavior in bipolar terms—a tendency, Borisoff and Hahn (1995) contend, "that can be traced at least as far back as the Pythagorean Brotherhood of the Fifth Century B.C., which embodied their dualism in ten sets of opposites: the limited and the unlimited, the one and the many, odd and even, right and left, male and female, good and bad, motion and rest, light and darkness, square and oblong, and straight and curved" (p. 382).

History undoubtedly has shaped the propensity to view the world in terms of opposites. Included in this tradition is the tendency to divide and to assign behavioral norms and roles according to sex. Thus it is difficult to think about masculine and feminine behaviors without simultaneously conjuring the sex-trait stereotypes that accompany these behaviors. The literature suggests that people persist in using bipolar terms to categorize men as "adventurous," "dominant," "forceful," "independent," "masculine," and "strong-willed" and women as "emotional," "passive," "dependent," "sentimental," "submissive," "feminine," and "nurturing," despite the fact that much has been written identifying other attributes (e.g., "empathic," "sensitive," "cooperative," "assertive") that ought to be equally valued and encouraged in women's and men's communication (Aries, 1987; Arliss, 1991; Bem, 1974, 1993; Borisoff, 1993; Borisoff and Merrill, 1987, 1992; Pearson, Turner, and Todd-Mancillas, 1991; Powell, 1993; Williams and Best, 1982; Wood, 1994).

Implicit in dividing behavior according to sex is that it simultaneously creates expectations about how women and men ought to act and to respond in various contexts and relationships. People make assumptions when the boundaries for these proscribed behaviors are crossed. And, as feminist and gender scholars have argued, masculine and feminine behavior tends to be valued differently. According to Sandra Bem (1993), despite "the profound . . . transformation of America's consciousness . . . over the past 150 years, hidden assumptions about sex and gender remain embedded in cultural discourses, social institutions, and individual psyches that invisibly and systematically reproduce male power in generation after generation. I call these assumptions the lenses of gender" (pp. 1–2).

The lenses of gender to which Bem alludes inform how every facet of women's and men's lives are perceived and assessed. These lenses shape the way women and men talk and how they look, as well as determine how they are supposed to feel. These lenses, moreover, influence attitudes about intimate relationships, child care, politics, and the workplace.

Without exploring here the positive and negative connotations that accompany these stereotypes and expectations for men's and women's behavior (described later in this chapter), it is important for both men and women to assess accurately attributes or labels applied to them on the basis of gender. This is especially important when these labels contrast with how they perceive their own behavior.

Two brief examples illustrate how discrepancies between stereotypes and one's own perceptions may influence behavior. A woman executive, for example, might feel compelled to work harder than her male colleagues to demonstrate her competence to those in the organization who hold deep-seated beliefs that women are more passive than men in a competitive marketplace. A father who takes care of the home and children while his wife works outside the home may feel similarly driven to convince others that his role as househusband does not imply that he is weak or a failure. Both the executive and the parent in these instances feel pressured to prove to others that they do not fit the stereotyped role that society has defined for them on account of their sex. Identifying, then, not only one's own qualities but also the assumptions others might hold about sex-trait stereotypes often shapes behavior. How some of these assumptions might be changed is examined in the sections on attitude, action, and analysis.

Assess the Nature of the Conflict

Earlier we identified several of the sex-trait stereotypes associated with men and women and connected these traits to our bipolar *Zeitgeist*, or world view. Polarizing gender in this way has two important consequences: "First, it defines mutually exclusive scripts for being male and female. Second, it defines any person or behavior that deviates from these scripts as problematic" (Bem, 1993, pp. 80–81).

From the conflict cases submitted by students over the years, it appears that gender-based conflicts often arise when individuals attempt to alter or extend the boundaries of the prescribed scripts that have become embedded in the U.S. cultural psyche (Borisoff, 1992). In her examination of more than two hundred gender-related conflicts (conflicts, moreover, that were either overwhelmingly experienced by women or that were written by men about women), Borisoff found three patterns of gender-based interpersonal conflicts. The first pattern revealed that women, despite the expansion of professional opportunities available to them, often received conflicting messages from their families about their expected roles. Typical comments included all names have been changed):

- "My mom feels that women should get the best education possible and work to establish themselves but that eventually the woman has to get married and give all this up to be a wife and a mother. I wish my parents would be more open-minded and not put limitations on what women can and cannot do" (Karen, nineteen-year-old psychology major).
- "My dad wants me to focus my efforts after graduation on getting married and starting a family. Yet my brother went to work and then to law school and my father supported him. I wish there could be a simple way to persuade my father to alter his old ideas about what is appropriate for girls and what is designated for boys" (Anne, twenty-seven-year-old business major).

Such conflicts of values and attitudes send a potent message to young men and women: Being a parent and taking care of the home are regarded as women's responsibilities and are regarded differently in a monetarily fueled economy. One coed articulates the distinction between women's and men's roles in the homes she has seen: "Women are definitely treated as subservient, and the prime responsibility and reward is in nurturing their family. Their place was in the home, as a support role. The husband was the career person and active in the community" (Jill, twenty-four-year-old communications major).

Conflicts about expected roles for women appeared not only in family-related cases but also in romantic ones. In many instances relationships ended when couples could not agree about what roles they would assume in the home. If we recall the cited messages from parents about homemaking and child care as women's responsibilities, we are not surprised to hear the following voices:

- "Even though my fiancé and I both worked full-time, we couldn't agree on how to handle household chores. He told me that since he worked all day, dinner should be on the table when he got home *just as his mother had done.* When I objected, telling him that I would be working full-time too, he asked me why I was making such a big deal over this. It became clear that we had very different values. I finally broke the engagement" (Susan, age twenty-six; emphasis added).

One couple eventually ended their marriage when they could not reconcile their opposing beliefs about child care. They both had full-time careers to which they were firmly committed. Robin, the wife, believed that both parents should be involved in raising children. When she suggested that she and Richard, her husband, take turns with leaves of absence so that they could each take care of the baby, Richard refused: "He said *his mother stayed home and took care of the children.* He maintained that men were incompetent in this area. Besides *how could he explain this to friends and family?*" (emphasis added). Richard's belief that child care is a woman's role was so firmly entrenched that he was either unable or unwilling to alter his perceptions about fatherhood and his professional obligations. Given some of the familial relationships discussed earlier, it is not surprising that men's esteem, ego, and self-respect are intimately tied to work outside the home.

"If the family initially provides the framework for a set of cultural norms and values, it is hard to walk unfettered into the work place. One cannot simply hang up one's gender-role expectations on a coat hook at the office door" (Borisoff, 1992, p. 17). Assumptions about women's performance, commitment, and place in the work environment form the second recurring pattern of gender-based conflict.

How effectively and successfully one executes job responsibilities is a concern of every professional, regardless of gender. However, when an individual is expected to work harder or is treated differently, the implicit (and at times explicit) message is that the individual is not welcome. In such instances the individual is made to feel apart from the team that defines the organization. The gender-based professional conflicts revealed that women, especially, were sanctioned, or punished, or expected to outperform their male colleagues simply to succeed in the workplace. Many of these cases were submitted by male students who witnessed this differential treatment and were upset by such inequities.

Jim, a paramedic and part-time graduate student, worked with his partner, Patty, for five years. "Many of my colleagues tease me because I work with a woman. And Patty also has problems when she is teamed up with other guys. *She says she often feels as if she has to prove herself to them*" (emphasis added).

Allan writes about his friend, Jan, who expressed the harsh realities of getting a law degree and becoming an attorney:

- "In law school she found the male professors noticeably tougher on women. She periodically receives sexist remarks and treatment from fellow lawyers, judges, and clients, and *finds that she has to over prepare to be accepted professionally*" (emphasis added).

The sexual discrimination leveled against Geoff's sister, Sharon, was more overt. Despite having graduated the number-two accounting student from a major university, being hired by one of the top firms, and doing exceptionally well on the CPA examination, Sharon found that her male colleagues received much more support and mentoring than she did. When Sharon inquired about this, a male colleague explained: "Women coming into this field are not taken as seriously because they are viewed as being 'temporary.' They will eventually leave the firm to have children. *The partners felt that an investment in them in terms of guidance was pointless*" (emphasis added).

Seth, in contrast, is surprised by his own attitude toward professional women. Seth is a partner in a securities firm. When Carole takes over for the previous broker, Seth is troubled:

- "My problem was that *I didn't feel confident about a woman doing this job*. This was shocking to me because I never believed that I had this attitude about women. I started to do things, like test her knowledge about petty issues, double check all her work, and always call her before and after she did anything. *I thought about firing her* and tried to make the phone call but I couldn't do it. This would be a wrong decision. Not only is Carole a very intelligent person. She has made the partnership a substantial amount of money" (emphasis added).

Although we might surmise Carole's reaction to Seth's always checking up on her, this case, especially, reflects how difficult it is for women—even successful women—to break the stereotypical attitudes held about them in certain types of positions. This example is a poignant illustration of why women often feel they have to outperform men. If they don't, they may lose their jobs.

Several writers have suggested that when men or women attempt to enter careers traditionally held by the opposite sex, they often encounter gender-based stereotyped assumptions regarding behavior, competence, and performance (Aries, 1987; Bem, 1993; Blau and Ferber, 1986; Haste, 1994; Jamieson, 1995; Morrison, White, and Van Velsor, 1987; Powell,

1993). Because women have attempted to enter traditionally male-dominated vocations rather than vice versa, it is they, as the previous accounts indicate, who have felt the brunt of negative sanctions for attempting to expand their roles. These same writers contend, however, that as the number of women who enter male-dominated professions continues to climb (e.g., in law, medicine, business, engineering, the computer field, journalism) and, as women and men increasingly work together, the professional climate, and attitudes in that climate, are likely to be redefined.

The third, and final, pattern of gender-based conflicts revealed that women and men have different expectations for and interpretations of their interactions with friends and romantic partners of the opposite sex. In these instances both the content and the process of communication with members of the opposite sex were sources of conflict for men and women.

Typical of female students' complaints were that their male friends and boyfriends did not "really listen" to them, that men were reluctant to talk about their "real feelings," that their conversations with men often felt more like a "verbal competition" than an exchange of ideas and feelings. Male students often voiced frustration about the demands placed on them—especially by their romantic partners—to communicate in specific ways. The following examples were typical:

- "Jennifer and I have been dating for nearly a year. While we have a great relationship, I get upset when she wants me to sit and talk about my feelings. I have no problem listening to her, but *I'm uncomfortable when she expects me to tell her everything I'm feeling. This wasn't how I was raised*" (Mark, twenty-year-old business major; emphasis added).
- "Why do women always need to hear the words 'I love you.'? When I love a woman, I show her that I love her through my actions. It's easy to say words without really meaning them. It's more meaningful to show your feelings through your actions" (Anthony, twenty-four-year-old graduate student, communications major).

One final example, presented by Mike, a twenty-one-year-old prelaw major, reflects an especially sensitive recognition of the different communication styles of women and men that was echoed by numerous students. He writes:

- "I have noticed in my dealings with all of my female friends, there is an open and carefree environment where I readily share my confidences, while with some of my male friends, there is always the need to prove myself. For example, if I talk about sports with my male friends, they'll quiz me about what I've read. *Though this is by all means a rather minor incident, which hardly seems like a gender conflict, I believe that this is one because . . . I have come to the conclusion that my male friends do not talk to me, but at me"* (emphasis added).

Mike's analysis about his communication with male and female friends is significant, for he points to a major gender-based distinction in women's and men's communication styles that is usually noticed by women—the feeling of being talked "at" rather than "to." The feeling of engaging in a verbal "competition" rather than a dialogue is a natural consequence of men having been raised "to learn conversation around competitiveness and dominance while girls learn conversation around affiliation and equality" (Borisoff and Merrill, 1992, p. 75; see also Gilligan, 1982; Maltz and Borker, 1982; Rubin, 1983; Tannen, 1990, 1994).

The other accusations about men as listeners and their inability to talk about feelings may be related more to conversational style and interaction setting than to the actual performance of listening and self-disclosure. (These, along with other aspects of communication as they relate to gender, will be explored more fully later in the chapter.) Several writers suggest that how we study gender (Arliss, 1991; Borisoff and Hahn, 1995; Pearson and Cooks, 1995), identify affective traits for self-disclosure and listening (Bem, 1993; Borisoff, 1993; Borisoff and Hahn, 1995), and measure these traits in prescribed interaction settings (Aries, 1987; Borisoff and Hahn, 1995, 1997; Wood and Inman, 1993) not only privileges one type of behavior (in these instances feminine modes of expression) but also perpetuates stereotypes about men as communicators.

The three patterns of gender-based conflict identified in this section are typical, but by no means inclusive, of all gender-based conflict. However, whether conflicts stem from divergent beliefs and attitudes about expected roles, stereotyped assumptions about behavior, or different modes and processes of expression, individuals who experience conflict share the same dilemma. Each must identify his or her goals, decide whether to confront the other party, and determine what approach to employ.

Goal Clarification

Before individuals can engage in productive conflict management, they first need to identify their goals. Second, they need to overcome their assumption that differences are inherently negative.

In their study on the distinct communication strategies employed by high and low self-monitors to manage conflict, Smith and her colleagues (1990, pp. 92–95) present a typology of ten general goals: to obtain permission, gain assistance, give advice, change opinion, share activity, elicit support, change ownership, enforce obligation, protect right, and change relationship. Implicit in these general goals is that individuals fundamentally seek support, cooperation, acceptance, approval, respect, understanding, and change. These fundamental motivations, moreover, are not mutually exclusive but are often interrelated.

In considering the gender-based conflicts described earlier, we can see how the explicit general goals, as well as the implicit goals, often overlap. For example, when women felt that their professional goals conflicted with their parents' expectations for them, they hoped not only to change their parents' opinions (e.g., not seeing career and family as conflicting goals for women) but also to elicit their support (e.g., by helping to finance their graduate education). They hoped, moreover, to convince their parents to understand why these goals were personally significant to them, to gain both their approval and acceptance for pursuing these goals, and finally, to elicit their respect for holding these values.

In the work-related gender conflicts, similarly, many women and men saw the need to protect women's rights to be productive contributors in diverse professions and to alter the opinions of those in the workplace who retain stereotypical (and often negative) assumptions about women professionals. In these instances they hoped, moreover, to gain the understanding, acceptance, approval, and respect of their colleagues and potential employers. Without such support their success in the workplace could, as the examples illustrated, be jeopardized.

Identifying goals is one step. Overcoming the assumptions that differences are inherently negative is, as was explained in Chapter 1, another matter. Confronting differences implies a risk. The fear of denial and rejection are compelling. Yet it is, according to Barnlund (1979), precisely the different perceptions that individuals hold that make communication not only inevitable but also possible. He explains why this is so:

> *If men saw the same facts in the same way, there would be no reason to talk at all. Certain rituals of recognition or flattery might interrupt the silence, but there would be no experience to share, no occasion for serious talk, no conflicts to negotiate. A simple experiment will demonstrate this idea. At the next conversational opportunity, agree completely, both in fact and feeling, with the person who has just expressed an opinion. . . . In a matter of seconds following this*

restatement, the conversation will grind to a halt, or someone will change the subject. The reason is clear: Where men see and feel alike there is nothing to share. Talk is primarily a means of confronting and exploring differences. Conversation moves from disagreement to disagreement, interrupted only occasionally to note areas of momentary concurrence. *(p. 9, emphasis added)*

Barnlund's observations are especially significant. By situating differences within the communication process, he helps us to recognize, anticipate, and, ideally expect differences as normal rather than as deviant.

Identifying one's goals and accepting the inevitability of difference are critical dimensions of the assessment phase. Examining the climate, or communication environment, in which we negotiate differences is the fourth factor that influences our approach to managing conflict.

Examination of Climate

Many of the students who enroll in our courses have established their professional goals. Often, in fact, they have even identified the specific companies, agencies, hospitals, or educational institutions where they want to begin their careers. Such decisions are based on an organization's reputation, size, and perceived resources. Other students are already employed. All too often, however, these individuals pay little attention to understanding themselves, understanding the environment in which they either hope to or currently work, and reconciling these two very important criteria with their professional aspirations. We frequently hear from students who, several years after graduation, regret the choices they have made, realizing that their hopes and expectations about a particular organization were unmet. We hear similar complaints from those students who are currently employed: All too often they feel stuck in their present positions.

We noted in Chapter 1 that conflicts do not exist in the abstract; rather, they result from divergent and often contradictory perceptions. In Chapters 2 and 3 we explored the kind of oral and nonverbal communication required to facilitate the productive management of conflict using Gibb's (1961) supportive communication climate as a model. Understanding basic concepts about conflict management and about the requisite communication skills that facilitate such management, however, is of little help if one has not attempted to assess the environment in which one will or does interact.

In general, for individuals to integrate successfully within an organization, they need to understand, first, what factors influence organizational conflict. Second, they need to consider the extent to which their own attributes and professional expectations match those of the organization. Finally, they need to examine how the organization treats others like themselves. We turn to a brief examination of these three issues.

In their work on conflict and negotiation, Linda L. Putnam and Marshall Scott Poole (1987, p. 555) identify four general aspects of organizations that interact with communication in organizational conflict. These aspects are

- Actor attributes—the members of the organization and those factors and traits that make them individuals (e.g., personality, culture, race, sex, religion, experience, education);
- Conflict issues—the nature or source of conflicts that typically arise due to incompatible beliefs, goals, and/or attitudes or from scarce resources;
- Relationship variables—the extent to which individuals within an organization feel that they can interact and relate to one another in an atmosphere conducive to communication;
- Contextual factors—the organizational norms, climate, and protocol that influence the way problems, procedures, and communication are handled.

These four factors contribute to the overall environment and shape how individuals will experience that environment. These factors, moreover, are typically learned on the job.

Although it would be impossible for any interviewer to provide comprehensive information about each factor, individuals pursuing positions should actively seek out information that will help them assess how they will fit within a particular work environment. In general, for men and women to integrate successfully within an organization, ascertaining and/or examining the following information will allow them to determine the extent to which a fit is possible and will help those who are employed to assess, manage, defuse, and/or prevent the conflicts that inevitably arise:

1. What will be my role/function in the organization?
2. Does this role coincide or contrast with my personal strengths?
3. With whom (e.g., colleagues, subordinates, superordinates) and how frequently will I be required to interact, and how comfortably do I interact with different organizational levels?
4. What kind of interaction is expected (e.g., one-to-one, working in teams, public communication, oral and written communication), and how effectively can I perform these tasks?

5. What types of challenges is the organization facing (or experienced previously), and how are (were) these challenges being addressed?
6. What has been the typical career path of those who have been successful? Conversely why do employees typically leave (the turnover rate)?
7. What kinds of contributions are generally valued and encouraged (e.g., working independently, developing/initiating procedures)?

At best, understanding a communication environment and one's role in this environment is difficult. Because the work environment has traditionally been established by men, decisions regarding hiring, expectations for behavior, and the evaluation of performance have typically embraced masculine modes of behavior (Aries, 1987; Bem, 1993; Bernard, 1981; Borisoff and Hahn, 1994; Jamieson, 1995; Powell, 1993; Stockard and Johnson, 1980).

As women have endeavored to extend their professional goals, the following additional dimensions of the work environment need to be considered (although these concerns may be equally applicable to any group underrepresented at certain levels of a particular organization):

1. What is the highest position occupied by a woman in the organization?
2. How many women hold high-level positions?
3. What has been the promotion/retention history for women?
4. Are there equivalent salaries for women and men holding comparable positions?
5. Are facilities for women and men comparable?
6. Do benefits include maternity leave?
7. Are there adequate policies regarding child-care and family-care leave of absence? (This policy would apply to both men and women, although presently women utilize such leaves with far greater frequency.)
8. What impact would a child- or family-care leave of absence have on one's position?
9. Does the organization have clear policies on discrimination and sexual harassment, and are these policies enforced?

Bem (1993), we noted earlier, indicated that when individuals attempt to deviate from their prescribed gender roles, these attempts are often regarded as problematic. Sociologist Jesse Bernard (1981) has argued that the professional scripts for women have been pink-collar, that is, service, or low-paying positions. Assessing both the explicit and the implicit policies of organizations is therefore important for those women who wish to alter these scripts. By examining the professional environment, men, and women especially, may avoid future conflicts over professional expectations, practices, and goals.

To this point we have explained how examining the climate in the professional realm can help prevent conflict. Examining the environment of personal relationships is more problematic. Although organizations have written policies and procedures intended both to help and to protect its employees, and although legislation has been enacted to protect all workers, there are no policy manuals for families, friends, and romantic partners. There are no written prescriptions regulating familial values, attitudes, ideas, and beliefs. There are no assurances about a family's resources and how these resources are to be allocated. Nor can individuals change families as they can their jobs if they are dissatisfied.

Much has been written about the development, maintenance, and deterioration of personal relationships (Beck, 1988; Duck, 1991; Fitzpatrick, 1988; Hatfield and Rapson, 1993; Lerner, 1989). But the decision to confront those closest to us and over what issues rests with the individual. As psychologist Harriet Goldhor Lerner (1989) has suggested, only the individual can evaluate the previous events and relationships that have shaped the behavior of others; only the individual can assess the consequences of confronting others. We would suggest, however, that the process of examining the four variables (posited by Putnam and Poole, 1987, and defined earlier in this section) that affect communication in organizational conflict—actor attributes, conflict issues, relationship variables, contextual factors—may be equally valuable when applied to relationships in one's personal life.

Preliminary Determination of Appropriate Conflict Style

In Chapter 1 we presented five modes of managing conflict—competing, compromising, collaborating, avoiding, and accommodating—and indicated the extent to which each of these approaches reflects low, high, and moderate levels of assertiveness and cooperation. The approach used to manage conflicts in personal and professional relationships does not arise in a vacuum but is, as we have explained, influenced in part by personal traits, the nature of the conflict, goals, and the environment in which the interaction occurs.

Because people rely on others to achieve their goals and to resolve differences, the impetus to scrutinize behavior is compelling. James Tedeschi (1990) explains the process of interdependence in this way:

Consider what people want: wealth, status, power, respect, love, security and health. These goals cannot be achieved independently of other people. Others must mediate or provide the money, resources, position, love, and health care that a person desires. . . . Most of us realize that if we want wealth, we must do something to convince people who have or control wealth to give it to us. Similarly, if we want love, we must make ourselves lovable to the relevant target person(s), and if we want respect, we must somehow either earn it or con others into believing that we merit it. The upshot is that most human actions occur in the context of interdependence of outcomes and the desire to affect how these outcomes are distributed. This interpersonal context of social actions makes power and influence salient and probably ubiquitous to human interaction. Actors must either forego seeking to affect outcomes, thereby giving up the realistic possibility of achieving them, or actors must take the bull by the horns, foray out into the social world, and assertively try to influence the course of behavior of significant others. (p. 303)

How people manage the impressions they make and present themselves to others is largely culturally determined (Goffman, 1959). Also determined by culture are the strategies individuals employ to influence the behavior of significant others. Smith and her colleagues (1990, p. 96) call these strategies "message tactics." Smith et al. identify the following six distinct tactics and link these strategies to different goals.

1.   *Rationality.* The use of justification or logic is often employed when individuals endeavor to gain permission from parents (e.g., to borrow the car), to influence bureaucrats (e.g., shape or change an organization's policy or procedure), to give advice (e.g., persuading a friend to stop smoking), to propose a change in a relationship (e.g., turning a hobby with a friend into a business partnership).

2.   *Coercive influence.* The use of explicit or implicit threats is often employed as an initial attempt to protect one's rights (e.g., threatening litigation if one feels that he or she has been passed over for a promotion due to discrimination), and to enforce obligations (e.g., ensuring that a contractual agreement has been fulfilled).

3.   *Compromise.* Individuals' willingness to acquiesce or to cede certain areas of a negotiation generally occurs when seeking assistance (e.g., agreeing to help a colleague with a project if he or she will return the same favor at a later date), proposing a change in a relationship (e.g., one member of a couple agrees to postpone marriage until the partner has secured an upcoming promotion), seeking to protect one's

rights (e.g., a neighbor agrees not to complain if the couple next door ends its weekend parties at a reasonable hour), and enforcing obligations (e.g., a contractor agrees to provide additional work at no extra cost if the homeowner will extend the target deadline by one month).

4.   *Manipulation of positive feelings.* Strategies to ingratiate oneself with others are frequently employed by individuals seeking permission from others (e.g., a teenager hopes that his exemplary behavior will convince his parents to allow him to go on the ski vacation to which they were initially opposed), eliciting assistance from others (e.g., flattering a coworker on her computer savvy in the hope that she will help with a new program), attempting to escalate a relationship (e.g., when a friend lavishes attention on another, hoping to move their friendship into a romantic stage), and trying to influence bureaucrats (e.g., agreeing with and complimenting one's superior in an attempt to secure a positive evaluation and raise).

5.   *Manipulation of negative feelings.* Smith et al. (1990) indicate that these affective displays (e.g., appearing disappointed, pouting, sulking) often are employed when initial attempts to achieve one's goals have failed. In both personal and professional relationships, when requests or permission are denied (e.g., from parents or bureaucrats), personal overtures are rejected (e.g., by potential romantic partners), requests for assistance are denied, and advice is not followed, individuals may overtly demonstrate their displeasure nonverbally. By using these affective displays, they hope to gain the compliance of others.

6.   *Referent influence.* This tactic is often employed when individuals refer to the nature and quality of the relationship as justification for compliance. "We are in this together" and "You're doing this for the sake of the family" are examples of appeals employed to elicit support, give advice, and change the relationship. This tactic, Smith et al. point out, "is almost never used on strangers or bureaucrats" (1990, p. 97).

There are four observations we wish to stress regarding these six message tactics in the conflict-management process. First, these strategies are not mutually exclusive. That is, individuals may employ several approaches when attempting to resolve a conflict or influence behavior. Second, these strategies, with few exceptions, are used in diverse contexts and are employed for both personal and professional relationships. Third, several of these tactics are reflective of collaborating, competing, compromising, and, to a lesser extent, accommodating. Fourth, the language and nonverbal behavior used to communicate these strategies may be employed differently by women and men; the interpretation of these messages may also be influenced by gender.

For example, at a committee meeting Robert, the committee chair, says, "It would be helpful if we could have a record of today's meeting." Turning to the only woman present, he continues, "Ann, I know you're very organized. Would you please take the minutes?" Although Robert believes that he is complimenting his colleague, Ann may construe this request differently. If at previous meetings other members have recorded the minutes, she may willingly accept the responsibility of note taking in the spirit of cooperation. If, however, this is not the case, she may interpret Robert's request as a sex-stereotyped assumption and male bias that women are typically better at secretarial tasks and will willingly undertake these duties. In the latter scenario she may react negatively. Thus the same request (for note taking) may produce two different responses: cooperation in the first case, noncompliance in the second instance.

According to Barry (1970), because the process of growing up is experienced differently by women and men, they learn to perceive acts differently. Since conflict is a function of divergent perceptions, when two parties come to an encounter with different ways of perceiving and interpreting a particular event or situation, the potential for a conflict to occur increases. Thus it is important for both men and women to assess how their own actions may be construed differently by others, to consider whether the source of a conflict is attributable to their divergent backgrounds. To gain an awareness of these divergent backgrounds, we turn now to an examination of how gendered behavior is culturally transmitted.

ACKNOWLEDGMENT

In Ellen Rothman's book *Hands and Heart: A History of Courtship in America* (1984) women's and men's correspondences suggest that throughout the eighteenth and nineteenth centuries, women had greater difficulty adjusting to marriage than did their husbands. The letters indicate that whereas a man's life remained essentially intact, a woman had to leave her home, friends, and family to accompany her husband to where he would work. If she had developed a career, admittedly uncommon during this period, she was required to relinquish her professional aspirations to tend to the hearth and child rearing.

Despite the passage of nearly three centuries, life for the U.S. woman resembles in some ways that of her predecessors. In spite of the increased entry of women into the work force, one career—usually the man's, due to either salary differences or cultural norms—takes priority

(Bem, 1993; Bernard, 1981; Stockard and Johnson, 1980). In addition, the expectations for women, even when they do work—what Hochschild (1990) has labeled the "second shift"—to retain the major responsibilities of caring for the home and for the children remain compelling (Blumstein and Schwartz, 1983; Hochschild, 1990).

In the previous section we indicated that women and men come to events with different perspectives, shaped by their backgrounds and experiences. We pointed out that oftentimes conflicts between men and women may be due to the messages they receive from their families, colleagues, friends, and romantic partners. We further indicated how the same event may be construed differently by women and by men. To foster greater understanding between women and men and to diminish the chances for gender-based conflict to occur, it is important to acknowledge the differences in women's and men's backgrounds that have informed their outlooks.

"Is it a boy or a girl?" The answer to this question will greatly influence how the child will be raised, what kind of behavior will be expected and tolerated, and what kinds of personal and professional achievements will be encouraged. One way to examine how gendered behavior is learned is to consider what anthropologist Edward T. Hall (1961) calls the "formal" (explicit) and "informal" (implicit) transmission of culture. It is through such transmissions that people learn what it means to grow up male or female.

Acculturated Sex Differences in the Family: Cultural Transmission

How is culture transmitted? How do boys and girls acquire what is considered appropriate behavior and gender-linked attitudes? What kinds of gender-linked behaviors are encouraged in children? Hall (1961) has called culture a "silent language" and explained that children learn cultural norms both directly and indirectly; often indirect learning occurs without the child's own awareness. Gendered behavior is one dimension of culture that is transmitted in this way.

Many parents do not consciously set out to sex-type their children. However, beginning in the early 1970s, studies revealed that expectations for masculine and feminine behavior exerted a powerful influence over how males and females are raised and what is expected from them. Through play, dress, household tasks, socialization, and education, girls learn to be polite, expressive, nurturant, compliant, dependent, and pretty and to value sex differently. Boys, in contrast, are encouraged to display aggressiveness, emotional control, independence, competitiveness, and physical strength (Bem, 1993; Bernard, 1981; Borisoff and Hann, 1993, 1997; Broverman et al., 1970; Gilligan, 1979, 1982; Macoby and Jacklin, 1974; Stockard and Johnson, 1980). (It should be noted that most of the data emerges from studies of white, middle-class families, and therefore findings may not be applicable to all members of U.S. culture.)

At an early age children learn what types of toys and activities are acceptable. In Beverly Fagot's (1978) study of two-year-olds, for example, she found that her subjects demonstrated marked toy preferences. Girls preferred to play with dolls and soft toys; boys were attracted to blocks and other objects they could manipulate. This preference, however, was not biologically motivated: The children's parents reinforced this behavior by giving positive responses and negative feedback when the children selected and played with what were regarded as appropriate and inappropriate toys, respectively. In fact, when boys played with the girls' toys, their fathers reacted strenuously to discourage such preference.

Children learn at an early age not only what toys are acceptable but also to display different behaviors when at play. In her study of forty-eight male and female two-year-olds who were pretending to take care of their dolls, Phyllis Berman (1986) found that the parents—all professionals—positively reinforced the girls' behavior when they demonstrated care; they did not encourage this kind of behavior in the boys. These responses led Berman to conclude that the affective display of caring is culturally determined and determined differently for both sexes.

In "Growing Up Female," Graebner (1982) notes the overt pressures placed on young children who attempt to deviate from societal expectations for males and females. He describes how Nancy's predilection as a teenager for playing football with the boys and climbing trees is discouraged: "Several times she overheard her mother and grandmother discussing her exploits, worrying that she was becoming a tomboy. And gradually she learned that a lady could never be a tomboy" (p. 157). As a result, Nancy "tried to be a little more restrained and to act like a lady" (p. 157).

If we compare Berman's (1986) study and Graebner's (1982) account, we note that "restraint" is defined differently for males and females. Whereas young boys are encouraged to rein in their expressions of care, young girls are expected to rein in displays of competitiveness, especially if they are engaged in competition with males. These dichotomous expectations for restraint are experienced differently by children on the playground and later by adults in the bedroom.

In their work on sexual metaphors as a reflection of women's and men's divergent attitudes toward sex, Borisoff and Hahn (1993) trace this development and explain how these differences are manifested in behavior:

> *Historically, sex has been an important commodity. Women used the potential for sex to solidify relationships. In return for being granted sexual favors, men promised lifelong protection and security. Because virginity traditionally was the only way to assure a man that his children were truly his own, women learned to guard their prized treasure accordingly; they learned to withhold sex.* (p. 256)

Attitudes that originated to ensure paternity have had an enormous influence in sustaining cultural values toward sex. Sex, as solely a pleasurable activity, is discouraged for women. As Cassell (1984), Person (1989), and Rubin (1983) argue, women are still instructed not to squander their sex. They are expected to imbue sexual liaisons with feelings of love. Only by releasing sexual impulses in the context of a "commitment," a "relationship," or a "marriage" can women legitimately acknowledge their sexuality. Sex must happen to them; they can yield to sexual impulses only when they are overcome by passion (Fox, 1977) or swept away (Cassell, 1984).

Men learn a different cultural imperative. Whereas women learn that sex is a gift that may be bestowed within the context of love, men, according to Simone de Beauvoir (1952) learn to expect, demand, and pursue sex and love actively. Moreover, whereas sex without intimacy fuels women's ambivalence toward sex, the sex act for men may be a form of intimacy. Philosopher Sam Keen (1991) contends that the act of sex has become the only legitimate way for men to feel, to unleash their emotions:

> *It is not that men are only interested in sex, but that we have been so conditioned to curtail our natural needs for intimacy that only in sex do we have cultural permission to feel close to another human being. . . . Emotionally speaking men are stutterers who often use sexual language to express their forbidden desires for communion.* (p. 78)

Perhaps, he concludes, we can expect no more from a gender that has been trained to be workers, that has been well trained to put on a front of stoic silence.

The home is the initial backdrop where cultural expectations for gendered behavior is learned, where we begin to construct our social selves. Our educational system is the second arena that reinforces gendered behavior and often encourages and instills divergent intellectual pursuits according to sex.

Acculturated Sex Differences in Education: Cultural Transmission

The educational environment is generally regarded as the first formal arena where all students have equal access to acquiring information and to developing and honing critical-thinking skills that will prepare them for life after graduation. Yet according to Myra Sadker and David Sadker (1994), this assumption is not accurate. The doors of education are unequally opened to males and females: "Today's schoolgirls face subtle and insidious gender lessons, micro-inequities that appear seemingly insignificant when looked at individually but that have a powerful cumulative impact. These inequities chip away at girls' achievement and self-esteem" (p. ix). Research indicates that these inequities are especially manifested through student–teacher interaction and through teaching materials and access to subject matter.

Student–Teacher Interaction

Although teachers at all levels of the educational process may believe that they treat their students equally, studies indicate that often they unwittingly reinforce (and thereby perpetuate) sex-role stereotyped behavior. Beverly Fagot and her colleagues (1985) report that this process may begin well before children enter the formal classroom. In their study on teacher interaction with babies, they found no discernible differences in the ways that twelve-month-old girls and boys communicated with one another and with teachers. The differences the researchers discerned, however, were in how teachers responded to these babies. The teachers reinforced the girls for communicating gently and the boys for communicating more aggressively. The teachers, moreover, were unaware that they treated these children differently. By the time these children were again observed twelve months later, the boys and girls displayed the different styles of communication that were initially reinforced. Although the childrens' parents presumably contributed to sustaining these behaviors, this study demonstrated how early children incorporate the preconceived notions of adults into their own behavioral repertoires.

Studies conducted at all stages of schooling—from the elementary through the graduate levels—indicate that education is experienced differently by boys and girls, men and women. In their study of more than one hundred fourth-, sixth-, and eighth-grade classes that included diverse subject areas (mathematics, science, language arts, and English), Sadker and Sadker (1985, 1994) found that educators provided four types of classroom feedback (praise, remediation, criticism, and acceptance) unequally to their male and female students. "While boys received more of all four reactions, the gender gap was greatest in the most precise and valuable feedback. Boys were more likely to be praised, corrected, helped, and criticized—all reactions that foster student achievement. Girls received the more superficial 'Okay' reaction, one that packs far less educational punch" (1994, p. 54). One area for which girls received more positive feedback than boys was for appearance (e.g., dress and hair) (Sadker and Sadker, 1994, p. 54). In another study researchers Virginia Richmond and Joan Gorham (1988) found that 1529 public students in grades 3–12 were taught by teachers who consistently employed masculine generic language in the classroom.

If as young students, girls are "rewarded" for being silenced, or invisible, it is not surprising that lessons initially learned from elementary through high school will follow them into the college classroom and beyond. In their study on the effects of gender on students' willingness to ask questions, Judy Pearson and Richard West (1991) reported that in college classes taught by male professors, female students asked significantly fewer questions than did their male classmates. And at the graduate level, especially when women pursue master's and doctoral degrees in areas still dominated by men (especially the hard sciences), the climate for women may be unreceptive. According to Harvard psychiatrist Katherine Kris, "The expectation [is] that they must choose between their identities as professionals or as women" (cited in Sadker and Sadker, 1994, p. 190).

The classroom environment that educators create for students communicates powerfully about what kinds of behaviors are permissible for males and females. It is important to point out that most teachers studied did not harbor overt biases about gender roles. To the contrary, when the subjects reviewed the materials or tapes that revealed their differential treatment, they were often surprised by the findings. Their behaviors that either perpetuated or reinforced sex-role stereotypes were unintentional. Studies indicate that the unintentional reinforcement of sex-role stereotypes is revealed by not only how educators teach but also in what they teach and in the subjects they encourage their students to pursue.

Gender Biases in Classroom Materials and Subject Matter

Although the reinforcement of gendered behavior in classroom instruction is, as we have seen, often discerned at the microanalytic level, more obvious is the presence or absence of male and female role models in instructional materials, as well as the distinction of achievement between male and female students in certain subject areas.

In her chapter on gender and communication in the classroom, Pamela Cooper (1993) provides a comprehensive review of the literature, which indicates that women are underrepresented in texts; when women do appear, it is often in sex-stereotyped roles. This discrepancy begins with children's literature. In her review of ninety-seven children's books that had received either the Caldecott Medal or the Newbery Award, Cooper (1991) found that over a twenty-year period (1967–1987), the ratio of human male characters to human female characters did decline; in 1987 the ratio remained 2:1. However, in only fourteen of these ninety-seven works were women represented as working outside the home.

The relative absence of women not only emerged in these award-winning books but also appeared at all levels of the educational process and in diverse subject areas. Citing nearly thirty studies that analyzed texts used from the elementary grades through college-level education and covering courses in history, science, mathematics, economics, speech communication, and English literature, women either were conspicuously absent or were represented more in supportive rather than in active roles (Cooper, 1993).

The separate spheres that young girls and boys experience in the classroom and that are represented in the texts they read are reflected as well in their curriculum choices. Despite Title IX and the fact that boys and girls take approximately the same number of math and science courses, Sadker and Sadker (1994) observe that it is only up to a point, and "then their roads diverge" (p. 122) in high school, with male students dominating courses in calculus and physics. In part this disparity stems from dominance of males in the classroom—both in numbers and in assertiveness (Jones, 1990; Jones and Wheatley, 1990). In part this difference may be due to the more positive reinforcement males receive in these classes (Jones, 1990; Jones and Wheatley, 1990). In part this distinction reflects a fundamental assumption: "Girls are supposed to be less good at math, so that difference is incorporated into the way we live" (Gleason, cited in Shapiro, 1990, p. 57).

Even the introduction of computers into the curriculum has not been gender neutral. This stems in part from different at-home instruction in computers that young girls and boys receive (18 percent of female students versus 60 percent of male students, according to Sadker and Sadker, 1994); in part this is due to teaching computer skills in math departments. If young women are not expected to perform well in certain disciplines, and if educators are complicit—either knowingly or unknowingly—in perpetuating and reinforcing separate educational spheres, they are limiting the opportunities for more than half of the population: "When girls self-select out of math, science, and computer technology, they are making decisions that will affect them the rest of their lives. Without the right high school courses, science courses in college are out of reach; and without college courses, females are filtered out of careers that remain overwhelmingly and solidly male" (Sadker and Sadker, 1994, p. 125).

Both at home and in school, growing up male and female is experienced differently. How these experiences reflect attitudes toward women and men and toward their abilities to manage conflict is examined in the following section.

ATTITUDE

At the beginning of this chapter, we discussed the tendency to view the world in bipolar terms. We further explained that included in this dualistic way of thinking are people's concepts of male and female. The process of dividing individuals may be based on several categories, such as sex, race, culture, economics, or religion. Such divisions, however, are not without consequences. According to Michel Foucault (1982), until there is division, there is no need for power. Once division is achieved, however, power is inevitable and becomes legitimized through cultural norms and practices.

According to Sandra Bem (1993, pp. 2–5), this "legitimate power," insofar as it applies to expectations for and valuation of gendered behavior, has been fueled by the acceptance of biological sex differences, or "biological essentialism," as justifications for dichotomizing gendered behavior and roles, or "gender polarization." Bem contends, moreover, that such divisions both reflect and perpetuate androcentrism, or "male centeredness," which upholds men's behavior as the presumed neutral standard or norm against which all other behavior is measured and evaluated.

We concur that if sex is used as one criterion to divide individuals and to prescribe roles and behavior, the roles, along with the "correct" behaviors for these roles, become part of the cultural psyche. People are likely to embrace unchallenged these behaviors and roles. But we would contend that the received wisdom for women's and men's behavior is also contextual: What people accept as "standard" reflects the division of the work and domestic spheres and the channeling of men and women into these separate spheres.

The division of the worlds of work and home has been attributed to the Industrial Revolution. One consequence of this division has been to accept as "standard" the communication styles of whichever sex has assumed primary responsibility over each of these domains. We hasten to point out that although the Industrial Revolution was not the sole cause of distinct styles of men's and women's communication, the division of responsibility according to sex created a climate that allowed each style to become self-perpetuating. Thus the world of work, fashioned after male modes of behavior, became characterized by aggression, competition, independence, action, and so on (Berryman-Fink and Eman-Wheeless, 1987; Davis, 1992; Powell, 1993). Conversely the domestic sphere and modes of behavior appropriate for personal affiliation became associated with women's ways of communicating, characterized by sensitivity, nurturance, affiliation, empathy, cooperation, self-disclosure, and so on (Beck, 1988; Borisoff, 1993; Chelune, Robison, and Kommor, 1984; Duck, 1991; Gilligan, 1982; Hatfield and Rapson, 1993; Wood and Inman, 1993).

Characterizing behavior according to context and sex legitimizes and privileges the prevailing behavior of whoever dominates a particular environment. Such characterizations shape one's expectations and attitudes about others. As explained in Chapter 1, attitudes, once formed, can be used to explain behavior, to justify actions, and to limit the activity of others. When this type of ascription occurs, we call it a stereotype, a dangerous assumption defined in *Webster's Dictionary* as a "standardized mental picture that is held in common by members of a group and that represents an oversimplified opinion, affective attitude, or uncritical judgment." In order to understand how sex-role and sex-trait stereotypes may constrain both women and men, we must first examine the processes and consequences of stereotyping.

Processes of Stereotyping: A Cultural Consequence

How do people interact with others? Is it on the basis of each discrete encounter? To what extent are perceptions based on objectivity? In their work on social perception and appraisal, George J. Simmons and J. L. McCall (1966/1979) contend that the attitudes and values placed on objects, on people, and on behaviors do not exist in any external and objective form. Rather, attitudes and values are arbitrary; that is, they are informed by what one imputes to others. "It is in this sense," they write, "that we can be said to interact, not with individuals and objects, but with *our images* of them. We do not, after all, deal with them directly as physical 'things,' but as *objects* that we have clothed with identities and meanings. We act toward them on the bases of their meanings for us, the implications they have for our manifold plans of action" (pp. 62–63).

As we explained earlier, these "meanings" are transmitted through socialization, which is predicated on the cultural beliefs, norms, values, and sanctions society embraces. Through the socialization process, people develop their own perceptions, expectations, and interpretations of the behaviors of others, or what Jerome Bruner (1958) has termed "expectancy sets." People seek experiences and interactions that will tend to confirm and strengthen these expectations. Individuals tend to be critical or skeptical when others' behavior is not consistent with these expectations.

Because the different "expectancy sets" for women and men are a product of culture, stereotypes about their roles and behaviors are likely to be created and perpetuated. These stereotypes have important consequences for limiting behavior and for managing conflict.

Consequences of Sex-Role and Sex-Trait Stereotyping

Because gender (like ethnicity) is an immutable trait, stereotyping remarks that target gender or race are particularly insidious. Consider the following example: "Most corporate executives are men. Executive tasks should be performed by men. Men are analytical, aggressive, and competitive. Thus women should not assume executive positions in corporations."

This example, sadly, is typical of the kind of justification used to create and to maintain a "glass ceiling" for women in corporations. It is modeled on John Williams and Deborah Best's (1982) syllogism for sex stereotyping. If we examine this example, we see that "sex roles ('Most corporate executives are men') are often "explained" by reference to sex-role stereotypes ('Executive tasks should be performed by men'), which in turn are "explained" by reference to sex-trait stereotypes ('Men are analytical, aggressive, and competitive')" (1982, p. 16). The conclusion one is expected to draw from the example is that because the presumed traits required to perform executive responsibilities are those that conform to stereotypical masculine behavior, men make better executives than do women.

Although the syllogism presented is fallacious, the attribution of qualities to one group of people often is used to exclude qualified individuals from attaining their professional goals. The case of Sharon, the accountant who was denied the mentoring that would help her succeed in her company (described earlier) illustrates how individuals can be marginalized on account of sex-role stereotypes. More than denying individuals access to positions, ascribing attributes to individuals solely on the basis of gender expectations serves to perpetuate gender-linked socialization, which subtly leads women and men in disparate and often limiting directions.

Sex-role stereotyping occurs in part because of the traditional separation of the domestic and work spheres. Sex-trait stereotyping, however, is a significant factor in how "appropriate" roles are construed. The basis for these traits is rooted in communication. Table 4.1 lists several of society's expectations for women and men. Many of these terms have come from our students; others have appeared in the works of Bem (1974), Broverman et al. (1970), Rubin (1976), Williams and Best (1982), and Wheeless and Dierks-Stewart (1981).

The characteristics listed in the table are not a function of biological sex differences. Rather, they result from a legacy of expectations and adaptations to meet culturally prescribed behavior. To the extent that the need to conform to society's expectations is compelling, women and men have been encouraged to adopt and to demonstrate styles of verbal and nonverbal modes of behavior that reflect and reinforce cultural norms. Many of these so-called traits are, in fact, inappropriate, exaggerated, or true for both sexes. How these characteristics have been used to shape attitudes creates formidable barriers to how people interpret and manage conflict, to the attainment of personal and professional satisfaction.

We explained in Chapter 2 that the communication skills required for effective conflict management include openness, clarity, assertiveness, empathy, credibility, flexibility, and the ability to listen. Many of the assumptions about how women and men communicate, however, conflict directly with these skills and cast doubt on the effectiveness of both sexes to manage differences productively. Consider, for example, these limiting assumptions about women's and men's behavior:

Women are compliant and tentative in their assertions.

Men make generalizations and sweeping claims.

Women's speech lacks power and is hyperpolite.

Men's speech is forceful, often offensive.

Women's voices belie weakness and emotion.

Men are inexpressive.

Women are not as effective negotiators as men are.

Women are unable to assert their concerns; they are often silenced.

Men interrupt others as a sign of dominance.

Women and men listen differently: She listens too much; he, not enough.

Women's smiling behavior often masks their true feelings.

Men are unable to express their true feelings and emotions.

Women are better nonverbal decoders because they are less powerful than men are.

TABLE 4.1 Gender-Linked Attributes

Masculine Traits	Feminine Traits
Active	Accessible
Aggressive	Accommodating
Analytical	Appreciative
Assertive	Approachable
Athletic	Compassionate
Blunt	Compliant
Bold	Considerate
Brash	Cooperative
Candid	Correct
Competitive	Cute
Confident	Dainty
Dark	Demure
Decisive	Dependent
Direct	Emotional
Dominant	Enduring
Egocentric	Fearful
Forceful	Feminine
Handsome	Fickle
Harsh	Flowery
Independent	Forgiving
Individualistic	Friendly
Industrious	Frivolous
Intelligent	Gentle
Logical	Gossipy
Loud	Graceful
Macho	Helpful
Masculine	Indecisive
Outspoken	Intuitive
Physical	Loving
Powerful	Manipulative
Practical	Motherly
Rational	Nurturing
Rude	Open
Self-confident	Perfumed
Sexy	Pleasant
Short-tempered	Poised
Shrewd	Pretty
Stern	Quiet
Strong	Refined
Tall	Reserved
Tough	Sensitive
Unemotional	Sentimental
Virile	Sexual
	Sincere
	Submissive
	Sympathetic
	Talkative
	Tender
	Timid
	Understanding
	Warm

These assumptions have been commented on by Aries (1987), Borisoff and Hahn (1997), Borisoff and Merrill (1987, 1992), Dindia (1987), Eakins and Eakins (1978), Hall (1984), Henley (1977), Keashly (1994), Kramarae (1981), Lakoff (1975), Powell (1993), Tannen (1990), Watson (1994), Wood (1994), Wood and Inman (1993).

Several of these works have challenged such assumptions. Despite findings to the contrary, however, stereotyped assumptions about "appropriate" sex traits often influence attitudes about how men and women ought to communicate. Consequently someone who has come to expect that women should be nurturing, polite, and self-effacing may be at a loss to deal with women who demonstrate independent, assertive, and competitive behavior. Thus is created what Linda Putnam has termed a "double-bind" (1983): For women to succeed in a male-dominated context, they often jeopardize their femininity and risk pejorative labels. People may similarly be at a loss to deal with men who openly reveal their personal feelings and problems. To do so conflicts with their image of the man as the strong, silent type (Bem, 1993; Borisoff, 1993; Derlega and Chaikin, 1976; Hatfield and Rapson, 1993; Keen, 1991).

Although historical sex-role divisions may explain the proclivity to cling tenaciously to sex-trait stereotypes, people need to scrutinize their connotations and attitudes toward presumed normative behavior for women and men if they want to break down gender-based barriers in their lives. The extent to which differences in men's and women's communication is based on actual differences or is a matter of perceptual differences needs to be examined. Relatedly how these real or perceived differences are valued needs to be considered. Finally, ways to alter attitudes about gender roles that have perpetuated dividing traits and roles according to sex, that have created a climate in which gender stereotyping has persisted, need to be explored. In the final two sections we examine these issues.

ACTION

In 1976 the French psychoanalyst Hélène Cixous made the following observation about the power of language:

> *Everything is word, everything is only word. . . . We must grab culture by the word, as it seizes us in its word, in its language. . . . Indeed, as soon as are, we are born into language and language speaks us.* (1976/1985, p. 73)

The language into which women and men are born reveals that the language they speak and that "speaks them" reflects divergent styles and patterns. These styles and patterns are valued distinctly. In this section we consider some of the findings about women's and men's communication and relate those findings to the privileging of masculine and feminine styles of communication. Part of this examination includes how both of these styles may either facilitate or impede conflict management.

Gender-Communication and Conflict Management

Effective conflict management depends on shared communication. Individuals need to feel that they can express their concerns and that their voices will be heard. As explained in the section Acknowledgment, boys and girls are encouraged to develop different styles of communication—styles that conform to the masculine and feminine stereotypes. What children are encouraged to reveal and how to do so is also constrained by gender.

Literature on gender and communication suggests that women and men have not had equal access to communication, due in part to how power has traditionally been construed, valued, and distributed (Arliss, 1991; Bem, 1993; Borisoff and Merrill, 1987, 1992; Hall, 1984; Haste, 1994; Henley, 1977; Kramarae, 1981; Lakoff, 1975; Pearson, Turner, and Todd-Mancillas, 1991; Wood, 1994). Because women and men have traditionally had different resources and different amounts of legitimate power, they have been required to use different strategies to obtain their goals. In her work on the psychology of power, Hilary Lips (1981) contends that this power imbalance has forced women to resort to indirect, or hedonic, modes of influence, such as using their appearance and adopting communication strategies that are neither threatening nor construed as too assertive.

If we turn to examples of direct and indirect modes of male and female communicative behavior, we will see that many of the conventions of both sexes can serve as either barriers to or facilitators of effective conflict management. It is important to keep in mind that the "appropriateness" of these modes is informed by the context and by the nature of the relationship (e.g., the workplace versus the home; collegial relationships versus romantic partnerships).

Gender-Linked Verbal Communication and Its Effect on Conflict Management

Qualifiers

Many criteria exist by which to evaluate the effectiveness, credibility, and power of a speaker. How one voices ideas and concerns affects the way that person is listened to and judged. Qualifiers, such as "somewhat," "in my opinion," "maybe," "perhaps," and "sort of," have typically been more indicative of women's speech. These phrases, when interjected into a direct statement, reflect the speaker's uncertainty or tentativeness and weaken the statement.

There are inappropriate and appropriate uses of qualifiers. In conflict situations in which it is important to articulate clearly one's goals, ideas, and feelings, the use of qualifiers may diminish one's assertions and credibility. Statements such as "I'm *kind of* disappointed that I wasn't promoted," "*Maybe* I deserve a raise," and "*Perhaps* we need to organize ourselves better if we want to meet the deadline" may be less effective than the more direct "I'm disappointed that I wasn't promoted," "I believe that I deserve a raise," or "We need to organize ourselves better if we want to meet the deadline."

Because qualifiers soften the impact of assertions, however, their use may be appropriate when the channels of communication between conflicting parties are impeded. In such situations the use of qualifiers may indicate a willingness to talk about a problem. For example, the statements "*Maybe* we should discuss this over lunch" or "*Perhaps* we need a few days to come up with some solutions" allow the other party to participate in the decision-making process on how to address the problem.

It is important for individuals to determine the appropriate use of qualifiers. When qualifiers are employed to soften statements that are intended as assertions, it is especially useful for individuals to understand the message they want to convey and to communicate that message as clearly as possible without qualification.

Disclaimers

A major goal of communication is to share feelings, ideas, and information with others. The use of disclaimers creates a barrier to communication; this type of hedging separates the speaker from the listener, reflecting in part an apology for asserting one's ideas or feelings.

Disclaimers are words or phrases that diminish the speaker's statement or request: "I'm probably wrong, but . . . ." or "I'm no authority, however . . . ." Disclaimers often precede statements for which the speaker does not wish to claim responsibility. In both examples the listener is given the option and power either to accept the speaker's claim ("That's correct, you are wrong because . . . .") or to reject it ("You are as much of an authority as I . . . .").

When individuals are engaged in a conflict, disclaimers may have positive or negative consequences. In Chapter 1 one of the steps listed to ensure effective conflict management was to keep the channels of communication open in a supportive climate. When these channels have been closed, the use of disclaimers to distance oneself from one's assertions may facilitate interaction. Such statements as "I may have misinterpreted your report" or "Perhaps I didn't fully understand your intentions" engage the other party in a discussion about the report and the intentions.

When it is important for both parties to be empowered, we would discourage the use of disclaimers that abrogate responsibility for one's assertions. To the extent that women are thought to resort to disclaimers more frequently than men do, they should be aware of how their authority can be greatly diminished when they disassociate themselves from or apologize for their assertions.

Tag Questions

Like disclaimers, which often reflect hesitancy or diminish the impact of statements, the addition of tags to declarative statements (e.g., "Isn't that so?" or "Don't you think?") may discredit speakers. Such questions may communicate to the listener that the speaker is unwilling or unable to assert him- or herself.

Judy Pearson (1985, p. 189) suggests that tag questions have appropriate and inappropriate application in interaction. They can be used legitimately to (1) clarify information ("He's starting tomorrow, isn't he?"), (2) elicit information ("This is a round-trip ticket, isn't it?"), (3) obtain feedback ("The show was excellent, wasn't it?"), and (4) persuade others ("A camping trip would be fun next summer, don't you think?").

When tag questions are used to avoid asserting one's ideas or beliefs, however, the speaker gives the listener the power to agree, to disagree, and/or to evaluate his or her statements. Research suggests that women employ tag questions more frequently than men do, in ways that diminish their assertions (Kramarae, 1981; Lakoff, 1975; Tannen, 1990, 1994; Zimmerman and West, 1975). It is important, therefore, to monitor one's intentions. Especially in conflict situations, individuals must ask themselves whether they are seeking confirmation from the other party or are attempting to express their concerns or defend their ideas in a forceful and legitimate way.

Compound Requests

A manager tells her subordinate, "If it wouldn't be too much trouble, I would like you to try to complete the report by Friday morning." When Friday comes and the report is not ready, she becomes upset and accuses her assistant of being irresponsible. The assistant defends himself: He assumed that his boss was asking him "to try" to finish the report "if it wouldn't be too much trouble." Because he had other priority work, he thought he could postpone this assignment.

This conflict of understanding occurred because the manager employed a compound, rather than a direct, request, such as, "I'll need the report on Friday. Please make sure to complete it." By being specific, the manager would let her assistant know what is expected. The assistant, in turn, could clarify which priority work is most important.

Compound requests soften statements and make the speaker appear more polite and less assertive. Research indicates that women employ this linguistic form more frequently than men do (Lakoff, 1975; Tannen, 1990, 1994; Zimmerman and West, 1975). Whereas women are described as resorting to compound requests when direct requests would be more effective, men are often accused of being overly direct and terse in their requests. "I need the report immediately" may be intended as a request but may be understood as a command.

When there is disparity between the intention of messages sent and the interpretation of messages received, the potential for misunderstandings to occur increases. When compliance and cooperation are required, we would encourage men and women to consider the words they use to communicate their requests. We would further suggest that individuals reflect on how others may construe their style of interaction.

Interruptions and Overlaps

When individuals are engaged in conversation, certain rules of etiquette are expected. For example, these rules include allowing each participant a voice in the interaction, indicating active listening through appropriate verbal and nonverbal cues, providing feedback, and so on. The quality of interaction is thus influenced by how interaction is regulated. Two of the ways that this regulation is demonstrated is through interruptions and overlaps (cases when individuals speak simultaneously).

As with other verbal strategies, there are appropriate and inappropriate instances for using these regulators. When a message is so important that it can't wait or when an individual is especially excited or agitated, speakers tolerate interruptions and overlaps. However, when speakers feel that others employ these regulators to dominate interaction, they are likely to feel ignored, silenced, muted, their contributions diminished.

Much of the research on mixed-sex dyadic interaction has yielded contradictory findings on patterns of and explanations for interrupting behavior. Several studies indicate that regardless of status, context, and relationship, women are more frequently interrupted than are men (Beck, 1988; Eakins and Eakins, 1978; Mulac et al., 1988; Spender, 1985; Zimmerman and West, 1975). But other findings report no difference in the frequency patterns of interruptions of men and women (Dindia, 1987; Kennedy and Camden, 1983).

Also debated is the attribution of intent for interrupting. Several researchers contend that women employ interruptions as a means of conversational maintenance to indicate interest and support, whereas men interrupt others as a form of conversational control (Aries, 1987; Mulac et al., 1988; Stewart et al., 1990). Different interpretations for why interruptions occur are offered by others. Dindia (1987), for example, suggests that interruptions occur because opposite-sex conversations may be more awkward than same-sex interaction. She therefore compares interruptions in these instances to conversational overlaps rather than to direct attempts at dominance. Also proposed as an explanation for why men may interrupt others more frequently and take up more speaking time is that they are more uncomfortable with silence than are women (Tannen, 1990).

We would argue that although intention is indeed an important component of the communication process, when individuals are denied an equal voice (regardless of how seemingly benign the motive), their attitudes about the interaction may be negatively affected. In conflict situations it is important for all parties to be able to express their concerns, confident that their assertions will proceed uninterrupted. Women and men need to distinguish between the appropriate and inappropriate use of interruptions and overlap. Moreover, when individuals believe that they are being unfairly silenced, they need to develop strategies that will allow their voices to be heard. For example, they could say, "I haven't finished speaking," "Please let me finish," or "You are interrupting me. Let me finish," which are intended to discourage interruptions.

Gender-Linked Nonverbal Communication and Its Effect on Conflict Management

Space (Proxemics)

How space is delegated, utilized, and violated may be potent indicators of entitlement and power. Studies conducted in the United States suggest that the early socialization of males and females leads to divergent expectations about space and differing responses to spatial intrusions.

Julia Wood (1994) has suggested that encouraging young boys "to go out on their own" and young girls "to stay close to adults and home" influences differing levels of entitlement (p. 161). "From these patterns, boys come to expect space for themselves, while girls learn to share space with others" (p. 161). These early expectations may shape attitudes about spatial violations. What constitutes one's personal, or private, space may be construed differently by men and by women. If men have learned to expect their own space, it is not surprising that findings confirm that they respond more negatively when they feel that their space is violated (Fisher and Bryne, 1975; Hall, 1984; Henley, 1977). If women have been expected to share space with others, research indicating that women more readily yield space is also understandable. (Hall, 1984; Henley, 1977; Polit and LaFrance, 1977).

Conflicts may occur when individuals feel that they are approached too closely. Consider the terms that recur in the literature: One feels uncomfortable when others "invade," "violate," "encroach," or "intrude" on one's personal space. What constitutes an intrusion may be influenced by gender. Studies indicate that men enter women's spaces more than women enter men's spaces (Evans and Howard, 1973; Hall, 1984; Henley, 1977; Willis, 1966). Nancy Henley (1977) attributes this behavior to male power.

What has not been reconciled to date, however, are the intentions behind this behavior. If women have been raised to demonstrate more affiliative behavior, which is displayed in part by closer proximity during interaction, others may perceive that they are more accessible and may approach them more readily (Hall, 1984). Conversely if men have been raised to maintain greater distance during interpersonal encounters, individuals may "expect men to keep larger distances, and when they do not, it may be disturbing" (Knapp and Hall, 1992, p. 161).

Although all interaction is shaped by the nature of relationships and the context of interaction, we would encourage individuals to consider how others may interpret physical closeness. What might be regarded as "appropriate" distance for some individuals may be viewed as "aggression," "encroachment," or "harassment" by others.

Body Language (Kinesics) and Eye Contact (Oculesics)

Kinesics, or body language (gestures, facial expression, posture, bodily movements), and oculesics, or eye contact, also reflect cultural variation in women and men. Deportment, the way one acts or reacts toward others nonverbally, speaks volumes about how one feels and may in fact be a more accurate indication of how the person feels than what he or she says (Birdwhistell, 1970; Knapp, 1980; Mehrabian, 1981).

Barriers to effective transactional communication and to effective conflict management emerge when nonverbal behaviors are incongruent with verbal assertions. Moreover, the nonverbal responses received from others may reinforce and sustain sex-trait stereotypes.

At an early age, women learn to smile, tilt their heads, allow others to approach them more closely, condense their bodies, and sustain eye contact when engaged in conversation. Men, in contrast, are socialized to control or monitor these behaviors—behaviors that may be construed as too revealing. The nonverbal behavior of women has been linked to affiliative behavior (Hall, 1984). But it also has been interpreted as a sign of powerlessness in our culture (Henley, 1977). The nonverbal behavior of men, in contrast, tends "to indicate they are reserved and in control" (Wood, 1994, p. 164).

A potential source of gender conflict is that although expressiveness ought to be a reflection of genuine feeling, the cultural expectations for women's and men's nonverbal communication instead may cause them to mask or inhibit how they feel. Studies have indicated that women often display smiling behavior when in fact they are feeling otherwise (Bugental, Loug, and Gianetto, 1971; Halberstadt and Saitta, 1987; Hochschild, 1983). Moreover, the nonverbal feedback women and men receive from others may reinforce sex-role and sex-trait stereotypes that serve to discourage both sexes from extending beyond societal expectations for masculine and feminine behavior.

In their study on responsiveness to leaders, Butler and Geis (1990) found that male and female subjects displayed more positive nonverbal responses and fewer negative nonverbal responses to male leaders than to female leaders. These findings are striking because both the male and the female leaders were confederates of the researchers, delivering identical messages; the subjects were unaware that they had treated the group leaders differently. The findings are important. They suggest that many individuals may have difficulty viewing women in leadership positions, and these feelings are expressed through their nonverbal responses to women in authority positions. Such expressions may, in addition, convey to women leaders that they are less credible, thereby undermining their own effectiveness.

Male subjects also may receive disconfirming responses. In their work on self-disclosure, Derlega and Chaikin (1976) found that women and men were regarded differently when they disclosed personal problems. In male–male and/or male–female dyads, when a male stimulus person disclosed a personal problem, he was viewed more negatively than when he remained silent. The opposite results were obtained when female stimulus persons were evaluated. It appears that even if men want to reveal their feelings and emotions, the negative assessment of such behavior may discourage them from doing so.

Both of these studies indicate that assumptions about, and expectations for, male and female behavior may differ and are informed by the limiting roles society has created for men and women. These studies also reveal that the negative feedback individuals receive when they attempt to alter or to expand societal norms restricts their own behavior and limits the full range of human communication for all individuals.

Haptics (Touch)

There is a strong perception that women receive more touch and are touched more by men because they are generally regarded as weaker and more vulnerable (Henley, 1977). Other studies, however, reveal conflicting information about who initiates and receives more touch and suggest that such factors as context, age, and status may inform findings (Hall, 1984; Jones, 1995; Knapp and Hall, 1992).

Touch has many meanings: warmth, affection, interest, or encouragement versus anger, dominance, or abuse. Whether touch is reciprocal (initiated by both parties) or unilateral (initiated by one party) depends on several factors: (1) the relationship of the parties involved (e.g., parent and child, husband and wife, employer and employee, doctor and patient); (2) the age of the individuals; (3) the context of the interaction (e.g., the home, the workplace, a social or sporting event); and (4) the culture's attitude toward touching behavior.

The act of touching another individual is open to diverse interpretations and can serve to defuse or create conflict. Although touch often belies attempts to affiliate, to encourage, or to empathize with the other party—acts that can be constructive in conflict management—it can also reflect efforts to control or to impose one's will on another.

Stanley Jones (1995) identifies four types of "taboo" touches in the workplace: unwanted sexual touches, touches overly friendly for the relationship or situation, inappropriate power plays, and touches that disrupt or interfere with work tasks (pp. 180–190). Such touching behavior may create a hostile work environment and lead to allegations of harassment.

To avoid these potential allegations, many companies have attempted to formulate policies that would prohibit touch in the workplace. Jones explains why these efforts may be misdirected:

> *Despite such concerns and attitudes, seeing touch in the work place as a problem to be eliminated is not realistic. The impulse to touch simply does not go away when people put on a suit. In fact, in some ways the workplace environment creates special needs for touch. . . . [T]here are numerous legitimate reasons for touching in the office. The awareness of being evaluated on an ongoing basis means that touches of support and encouragement are especially wanted. Touch is also a legitimate and effective way of persuading others, and exerting influence is an integral part of work. In addition, many people see their work activity as an opportunity for social contacts that may carry over outside the office, and friendly exchanges can also enhance working relationships; both of these motivations encourage touching.*
>
> *The question is not whether people will or should touch in the*

*office. They will and they should. The question is, what are the real
barriers to touch, the ones that should not be crossed? (p. 179)*

We would argue that in order to determine "the real barriers to
touch," it is important for men and women to examine carefully both
their motivations for touching and their responses when others touch
them. Such scrutiny can help to dispel the prevalent negative stereotypes about tactile behavior between women and men.

Vocal Cues (Paralanguage)

Judging and being judged by others is influenced largely by the way
people express themselves, by how they sound. Burgoon, Birk, and Pfau
(1990) have identified five variables that correlate positively with perceived credibility, persuasiveness, and comptence: more pitch variation,
greater volume, faster speech, shorter pauses between turn taking, and
nonhesitant speech. These variables, moreover, reflect masculine forms
of expression (Dindia, 1987; Eakins and Eakins, 1978; Kennedy and
Camden, 1983; Maltz and Borker, 1982; Tannen, 1990, 1994;
Zimmerman and West, 1975).

Because the model for effective conflict behavior has been based primarily on male forms of expression, the paralinguistic modes ascribed
to men have gone largely unchallenged. In contrast, women's advancement in the workplace may be impeded by how they sound. When
women are described as sounding too soft spoken and as speaking in a
nonthreatening, high-pitched voice, they may be judged as not sufficiently authoritative to assume positions of power. Similarly, when
women employ rising inflections, they may be regarded as lacking the
self-confidence required to advance professionally.

Two issues need to be raised at this point. First, whether women's
paralinguistic behaviors reflect powerlessness (Henley, 1977; Kramarae,
1981) or attempts to affiliate with others (Hall, 1984), when one is dealing with conflict management, the attributes ascribed to women's voices
become debilitating labels. To the extent that credibility, self-confidence,
and assertiveness are needed in certain conflict situations, it is important for women to communicate in ways that reflect strength and
assuredness. Second, it is important to question the paralinguistic
modes for men as appropriate and effective for all types of conflict situations. To the extent that empathic listening, accessibility, and equal
access to communication are also valued for managing differences, it is
important for men to consider how their own modes of communicating
may serve as barriers to resolving conflicts.

We conclude this section with the following observation. The communication strategies identified in Chapters 1, 2, and 3 do not distinguish between or advocate either masculine or feminine ways of communicating. Rather, the strategies to manage conflict productively are indicative of human attributes that are equally accessible to and appropriate for women and men. The extent to which individuals have achieved these attributes is examined in the next section.

ANALYSIS

In the previous section we considered how the communicative scripts for women and men perpetuate gender polarization. We indicated how both styles of communication may facilitate or impede managing conflict productively. We explained how the masculine and feminine stereotypes for behavior imply that men are more adept at negotiating (especially when competing with others) and that women are regarded as more cooperative and compliant in conflict situations. Whether these assumptions are accurate in professional and personal relationships forms the core of this final section.

The received wisdom that women are less competitive negotiators has resulted in the image of women as weaker and less effective in bargaining situations. Several studies, however, indicate that this image may be inaccurate. In 1977 Rosabeth Moss Kanter suggested that many of the differences observed in men's and women's behavior in organizations were erroneously attributed to gender. Because women at that time were predominant in lower-status positions and occupations, Kanter believed that these findings were a function of status and power differences rather than a reflection of gender socialization.

Carol Watson's (1994) recent review of studies published since 1975 supports Kanter's contention. In studies that included power as a variable in simulated bargaining situations, it was found to be more salient in determining outcomes than was the subjects' sex (Dovidio et al., 1988; Putnam and Jones, 1982; Siderits, Johannsen, and Fadden, 1988; Watson, 1994). These findings led Watson to conclude that "gender differences in negotiation behavior are an artifact of power and status differences between men and women in U.S. culture" (1994, p. 203).

Implicit in these findings is that women and men may be equally successful at competing with others in bargaining and negotiating situations when they are given or are assigned power. Also implicit is that "women are not nicer negotiators than men in terms of being more fairminded or compassionate as some feminist writers should have us believe. . . . Rather, women are likely to accept the rules of interaction as men have written them" (Watson, 1994, p. 206).

The extent to which we ought to accept or to challenge the "rules of interaction" established by men has been an abiding concern of recent scholars (Aries, 1987; Bem, 1993; Haste, 1994; Johnson, 1983; Keashly, 1994; Kramarae, 1981; Powell, 1993). We need to question whether competing with others and beating one's opponent are the only measures for success. We need to examine how other forms of compliance-gaining strategies may be equally, if not more, appropriate and effective for resolving differences. The acquisition of power may legitimize the use of competition when dealing with others, but competition may not be the most legitimate way to develop morale, commitment, trust, and productivity in the professional relationships we forge.

Similarly, we ought to examine the masculine and feminine stereotype for managing conflict in personal relationships. William Cupach and Daniel Canary (1995) indicate that it is generally assumed that women are "more relationally sensitive, engaging, and cooperative" (p. 246) than their male partners; that this difference will emerge in how they deal with conflict.

Contrary to these assumptions, both self-report and observational studies indicate that men and women employ similar tactics in managing conflict. Gender, in fact, was not found to be the critical factor that influenced conflict behavior. Similarities and differences in conflict-handling behavior have been linked, rather, to such other factors as subjects' age (Gayle-Hackett, 1986), level of emotional commitment to the relationship (Billingham and Sack, 1987), behavioral patterns prior to the relationships (Burggraf and Sillars, 1987), couple type (Fitzpatrick, 1988), degree of attachment to one's partner (Baxter and Shepherd, 1978), and access to resources/power (Bell, Chafetz, and Horn, 1982).

If, in fact, studies support the notion that men and women are more similar than they are different in both their attitudes toward and in their strategies for managing conflict, why does the perception of difference persist? Cupach and Canary (1995) suggest that *how* women display anger may account for this perception. Citing several studies indicating that women's anger is more likely to be accompanied by tears, Cupach and Canary explain how such behavior is likely to be misconstrued:

> [F]or women, crying does not replace anger; rather it can be a behavioral manifestation of anger.
>
> Because of the belief that anger is associated with aggressive behavior, a woman's anger may be easily misconstrued when it includes crying. . . . Focussing on the tears, men may misinterpret the woman's anger as hurt, depression, helplessness, or incapacity. If a woman expresses anger through tears, the male partner may fail to

recognize the anger and respond accordingly. The woman may then interpret the man's response as condescension and become even more angry. . . . Moreover, if the woman's tearful anger is in response to the man's anger, then he may interpret the tears in a fashion opposite of what was intended; he may construe the crying as remorse or capitulation, which validates his sense of justice for being angry in the first place. Obviously, such a sequence results in miscoordination, misunderstanding, and escalation or repression of conflict. (1995, p. 242)

This explanation suggests that although the intensity of anger may be experienced similarly by men and women, the behavior of an individual moved to tears ought not be misconstrued. Rather, it legitimizes and expands our understanding of how powerful feelings are conveyed.

The attributes of an effective negotiator include clarity, trust, empathy, openmindedness, confidence, flexibility, fairness, the ability to listen, and equality. These qualities are equally appropriate for professional and personal relationships. These traits, moreover, are the purview neither of men nor of women but reflect what we ought to value for human communication. Although this chapter has indicated many factors that have contributed to differences in growing up male and female, it has also suggested that factors other than gender contribute to how women and men negotiate the differences in their lives.

SUMMARY

In her work on gender inequality, Sandra Bem (1993) makes the following observation:

Gender polarization is the organizing of social life around the male–female distinction, the forging of a cultural connection between sex and virtually every other aspect of human experience, including modes of dress, social roles, and even ways of expressing emotion and experiencing sexual desire. (p. 192)

This chapter examined both the impetus to divide individuals according to sex and to prescribe behavior and roles similarly. Once this division occurs, there is a tendency to ascribe traits to each sex and to value these traits distinctly.

Using the five-step model for conflict management, we identified several conflict patterns and indicated how they may be related to expected gender roles and behaviors. Understanding the nature and source of the conflict, as well as the environment in which interaction with others occurs, influences one's approach toward others. This comprises assessment.

The section on acknowledgment described how gender roles, traits, and behavior are acquired. The transmission of culture often occurs in subtle and "silent" ways. Although cultural norms are reinforced at many different levels, we focused on the home and on the educational system as setting the stage for learning how to behave as a male or as a female.

The process of dividing individuals according to sex and assigning and/or expecting different behavior from them is often accompanied by valuing distinctly these behaviors. In the section on attitude we considered how dividing the worlds of work and the home and relegating men and women to each of these domains not only privileged the behavior of whichever sex was assigned to these spheres but also resulted in stereotypical assumptions about behavior that became embedded in the U.S. cultural psyche.

Expectations about sex-role and sex-trait stereotypes often inform a person's behavior and perceptions of others. The section on action examined the communication scripts for women and men and indicated how many of the verbal and nonverbal strategies associated with both sexes may either impede or facilitate conflict management.

The gendered scripts prescribed for women and men, however, may be reflective more of a person's own expectations than of what actually occurs. The final section, on analysis, considered recent studies on gender and conflict management and indicated that in both their professional and personal relationships, women and men deviate from the prescribed scripts; often how they communicate in conflict situations reflects more similarities than differences.

That the lines between how women and men do communicate are beginning to blur is a hopeful sign. We are still at a point, however, where assumptions about gendered behavior continue to divide rather than to unite the two sexes. Bem (1993) ends her book by indicating that only by depolarizing gender will people be able to view biological sex as a "minimum presence." She writes:

> *Simply put, this psychological revolution would have us all begin to view the biological fact of being male or female in much the same way that we now view the biological fact of being* human. *Rather than seeing our sex as so authentically who we are that it needs to be elaborated, or so tenuous that it needs to be bolstered, or so limiting that it needs to be traded in for another model, we would instead view our*

sex as so completely given by nature, so capable of exerting its influence to those domains where it really does matter biologically, that it could be safely tucked away in the backs of our minds and left to its own devices. In other words, biological sex would no longer be at the core of individual identity and sexuality. (1993, p. 196)

SUGGESTED ACTIVITIES

The following exercises focus on gender and conflict management.

A. FOCUS ON SEMANTIC DIFFERENCES

Consider the following observation: "Men and women speak different languages even when they use the same words. The misunderstandings between men and women are thus much less a result of linguistic and semantic differences but of emotional divergences when the two sexes use identical expressions" (Reik, 1954, p. 15). Working either in groups or individually, identify words or expressions that support Reik's contention and explain what these terms mean to women and to men, respectively.

B. FOCUS ON METAPHORS AS CULTURAL REFLECTIONS

Consider the following: "Metaphors operate as analogies; they offer models for how things work. . . . We take them for granted; they are so embedded that we are not conscious that they are metaphors. For example, we describe male and female in terms of *soft* and *hard*. . . ." (Haste, 1994, pp. 11–12). Either individually or in groups, identify metaphors that are normally associated with women (or feminine behavior) and with men (or masculine behavior). Discussion should focus on the extent to which these metaphors reflect bipolar thinking and on how these metaphors are viewed and valued. If different cultures are represented, what kinds of metaphors emerge?

C. FOCUS ON SELF-EVALUATION OF CONFLICT-HANDLING BEHAVIOR

Write about a recent conflict situation in which you participated in either a personal or a professional context. Address the following:

1. How did you behave (avoiding, competing, accommodating, compromising, collaborating) in the situation? Describe specifically your behavior.
2. Were you satisfied with the way you dealt with the problem? If yes, explain why. If no, how would you act if the same situation were to occur again? What would you hope to do differently?
3. Did your behavior conform to or deviate from the sex-role-related stereotypes assigned to women and to men?

D. FOCUS ON GENDER-RELATED ISSUES IN PERSONAL AND PROFESSIONAL INTERACTION

Following is a list of several issues that affect men and women. These issues, as well as others, may form the core of research projects or discussions.

1. The "glass ceiling" is the image that has been evoked to describe barriers to women's making it to the top in certain professions and organizations. To what extent does the "glass ceiling" still exist? What changes, if any, have occurred to shatter this barrier?
2. Technology has changed people's ability to communicate with others. In what ways does communicating on line affect or sustain gender differences?
3. What role does physical appearance play in professional life? In what ways does it affect women and men?
4. Many institutions have implemented policies on sexual harassment and hostile work environments. In what ways do such policies influence how a person communicates with others?
5. What impact does taking child-care leave have on individuals' employment? Is the impact the same or different for men and for women?
6. What are some of the current definitions of leadership? Do these qualities apply equally to men and to women? Has the concept of leadership changed in recent years? In what ways?

5

CROSS-CULTURAL AWARENESS IN CONFLICT MANAGEMENT

Points to Be Addressed

1. Assessment: The need for intercultural communicative competency; what we mean by culture;
2. Acknowledgment: Why intercultural misunderstanding occurs;
3. Attitude: Language, place, thought processing, and nonverbal communication as major sources of intercultural conflict;
4. Action: A twelve-point process for minimizing the potential for intercultural conflict;
5. Analysis: Strategies to ensure effective intercultural communication.

> *"The most universal quality is diversity."*
> —*Montaigne,* Essays, Book II, *Ch. 37*

ASSESSMENT

In this chapter we deal with those conflicts rooted in cultural differences in the way people communicate. To the extent that all parties involved are fully aware of one another's cultural differences, these differences may themselves be the source of conflict that is unresolvable. As attention in this book is directed toward that conflict for which one can effect change, the focus of this chapter is primarily on pseudoconflict, which Miller and Steinberg define as conflicts emerging from disagreements created by inaccurate communication (1975, p. 267).

In actual conflict the concerns of two or more parties are incompatible. In pseudoconflict these concerns do not *actually* exist but instead are *perceived* as existing. In cross-cultural pseudoconflict the mistaken perception that a conflict situation exists derives from cultural differences in how people process information and communicate. Although certainly not all conflict in a multicultural setting derives from misunderstanding culturally determined behavior among the parties, a great proportion of what passes for actual conflict in cross-cultural situations is tied to the pseudoconflict of such misunderstandings. This chapter discusses ways for understanding and reducing the causes of the cross-cultural pseudoconflict.

Before we can assess adequately the sources of pseudoconflict stemming from cross-cultural differences, it is necessary to define two broad areas. First, we should recognize the importance of intercultural communication. Second, to assess the nature of cross-cultural conflict, we must be familiar with what is meant by culture. Only then is it possible to understand the climate in which communication-based cross-cultural conflict takes place and, relatedly, the means to manage conflict situations likely to occur in such an environment.

Need for Intercultural Communication

Before an individual can successfully eliminate pseudoconflict that arises from misunderstanding of cultural differences, it is necessary to understand the importance of intercultural interaction in the first place. The need for cross-cultural awareness and the skills needed to communicate effectively across cultures are not always a given for all people. Cross-cultural pseudoconflict, however, is difficult to eliminate unless one believes that it is necessary. Therefore the first step in the assessment of intercultural conflict management is the establishment of the *need for* and *value of* such cross-cultural communication skills.

The importance of intercultural communication is important precisely because, as Christopher Moore (1993) observes, "all decision-making and conflict management procedures are not necessarily universally applicable or appropriate" (p. 5). Moore, who is a partner in an international dispute-resolution firm, goes on to indicate that professionals in conflict management must undertake "significant exploration of cultural dynamics and constraints prior to designing or implementing a process in a specific culture" (p. 5).

Admittedly the issue of intercultural awareness as a factor in conflict management is not new. But the awareness of the need for intercultural communicative competency in conflict management has arguably increased in the last quarter of the twentieth century, due to such technological breakthroughs as satellite broadcasts, facsimile machines, e-mail, and the Internet. When this is coupled with an increase in the reach and quantity of air travel, the likelihood of intercultural interaction increases correspondingly. Yet as Halina Ablamowicz warns, potentials for misunderstanding occur when

> *people from the farthest corners of the globe are brought close together. The new communication technologies allow for efficient information exchange and closer contact among people from all parts of the world. However, having these means does not make communication better or more satisfying. They do not bring people closer psychologically. While technology makes this contact possible, it does not guarantee success. Forcing together people with different values and lifestyles may turn a vision of global village into a nightmare.* (1993, p. 13)

The comparatively rapid awareness of the importance of cross-cultural communication has been particularly dramatic in the United States. Unlike Singapore or the Netherlands, which have long been export-driven economies, historically the United States has held a relatively insular view, often relegating intercultural expertise as something limited to the academy or possibly to a handful of expatriate executives selling U.S. products to foreign markets. Since the 1960s, however, the United States has grown steadily more integrated both into the world economy and into a culturally more pluralistic society as a whole. As Louise Fiber Luce and Elise Smith have noted, "Global interaction, whether political, economic, or educational, has intensified so dramatically that, as a nation, we have begun to understand the significance of cultural pluralism and its impact on national affairs and daily life" (1987, p. 3).

Nor is this increase in the awareness of intercultural competence limited to the United States. As Susan Vonsild (1995) observes, speaking of Europe in general and Denmark in particular

An international outlook is no longer the reserved realm for man-agers—or international sales staff—alone. In fact few employees are left untouched as geographical dispersion and multiculturalism char-acterize all parameters.

The internationalization which in the past was reserved for a few multinational companies is now common for every company. . . . This trans-global strategic orientation forces the company to manage cul-tural diversity within the organization as well as between the organi-zation and its network of suppliers, clients and alliance partners. Attention to cultural differences becomes critical for managing both the firm's international organizational culture as well as its external relationships. (pp. 133–134)

Moreover, even greater cross-cultural interactions are taking place among the multinational corporations, which have—even in the most ethnocentric eras of the most insular nations—by nature had to involve their staffs with cultures different from that of their home base of opera-tions. Employees of multinational corporations are increasingly subject to what Magoroh Maruyama (1992) calls "cross-national career advancement," or the promoting of foreign employees from one coun-try to another (p. 88). This is already a widespread practice, Maruyama points out, noting, for example: "Electrolux, a Swedish firm, had a French director in its factory in Singapore. Thomson, a French elec-tronics firm, had German, Irish, and Japanese engineers working together in its laboratory in Singapore. A manager of Hyatt Hotel in Jakarta was Danish, who subsequently was transferred to Egypt. The head of Michelin-Okamoto in Japan is a German, even though Michelin is a French firm" (p. 88). In all such cases, Maruyama observes, "A manager can work more satisfactorily if he/she under-stands the cultural differences and adapts his/her management to the culture of the host culture" (1992, pp. 89–91). To interact with others in this integrated global arena, the individual must be able to communi-cate across cultures and with other minority subcultures within his or her own culture.

To this point we have touched only on interactions between mem-bers of different national settings, but, as Varner and Beamer (1995) point out, it is important to "emphasize how often many cultures are represented within the borders of one nation: this is true of all countries that have developed, or are rapidly developing, a high technological expertise. In fact all large city centers, from Delhi to Detroit, from Caracas to Canton, are peopled by members of cultures from all over the world" (p. 9). In short, cross-cultural conflict management is not a factor limited to the international arena but is necessary for addressing cultural diversity in a wholly domestic setting. In turn, as Taylor Cox defines the term, "*cultural diversity* means the representation, in one social system, of people with distinctly different group affiliations of cultural significance" (1993, p. 6). This includes people who have immigrated into another national setting, as well as nonimmigrant minority groups already present in the society.

Thus to be fully competent in conflict management to interact with others in both a globally integrated environment and a diverse domestic setting, one must become adept at intercultural communication, "the sending and receiving of messages within a context of cultural differences producing differential effects" (Dodd, 1982, p. 9). How an individual handles these differential effects of culture clearly influences the way in which one manages conflict. As several writers have observed, conscious awareness of the cultural factors will better equip the individual for handling conflicts that occur from cross-cultural differences in understanding the values or expression of issues at the heart of the conflict situation (Chaney and Martin, 1995; Cohen, 1991; Gudykunst and Kim, 1992; Ting-Toomey, 1985; Victor, 1992). Chaney and Martin (1995) suggest that understanding "the social system and cultural values of other negotiators will help you identify the signs of conflict or prevent the conflict from forming" (p. 181). Consequently the need for U.S. businesspeople to be skilled in intercultural communication has become increasingly important. Of course, intercultural misunderstanding occurs in any number of fields, not just in business.

What Is Culture?

At this point it would be prudent to define culture. First, it should be noted that few experts agree as to exactly what they mean by culture. More than forty years ago, Alfred Kroeber and Clyde Kluckhohn reviewed almost three hundred definitions of culture without reaching a general consensus as to the term's meaning (1954). Since then, the term has only broadened. Still, we might agree to define culture in a broad sense as it affects communication. Kluckhohn's own definitions of culture are informative here: the "patterned ways of thinking, feeling and reacting" (1951, p. 86) and "the total life way of a people, the social legacy the individual acquires from his group" (1964, p. 24).

In the view of many experts, culture and communication cannot be separated (Porter and Samovar, 1982; Ronen, 1986; Ruben, 1977; Singer, 1987; Victor, 1992). As Condon and Yousef note, however, although "we cannot separate culture from communication . . . it is possible to distinguish between cultural patterns of communication and truly intercultural or cross-cultural communication" (1985, pp. 34–35). We can, in other words, identify specific dimensions of what Hofstede has called the "collective programming of the mind" (1984, p. 21). In the next two sections of this chapter—on acknowledgment and attitude—we present an overview of some of the most prominent of these dimensions in the context of conflict management.

ACKNOWLEDGMENT

After having assessed the general influence of culture underlying the communication process, we can next place in cultural perspective how conflict can stem from communication-based cultural differences. To do this we need to analyze why cross-cultural misunderstandings occur. This section examines the general causes of cross-cultural misunderstanding. The next section—on attitude—analyzes those specific aspects of cross-cultural communication variables most likely to create a perceived conflict.

Why Does Culturally Caused Misunderstanding Occur?

Misunderstanding, and from this counterproductive pseudoconflict, arises when members of one culture are unable to understand culturally determined differences in communication practices, traditions, and thought processing. Jone Rymer Goldstein has objected to the view of the many communication experts who hold that "language could serve as a window or direct conduit to an objective reality about which there could be perfect agreement by all who apprehended it rightly" (1984, p. 25). Although the experts she cites believe that if the sender is careful enough in designing the message, the receiver will understand it without interference, Goldstein herself argues that such a communication window is unlikely to allow a message to pass through unhindered. Her objection holds particularly true for cross-cultural communication. Indeed, in communicating across cultures, we might say that the message in the same situation is being transmitted through a stained-glass window. To understand how people from another culture perceive the message sent to them, it is first necessary to understand to what extent their culture has tinted the window of communication.

Meaning, in intercultural communication, must not be seen as an objective constant. As G. A. Kelly has argued:

Meaning is not extracted from Nature but projected by people upon it. People's behavior can be understood only in terms of their own constructs: that is, from their own internal frames of reference. Even people's most familiar constructs are not objective observations of what is really there; they are instead inventions of personal and group culture. (cited in Singer, 1987, p. 9)

Although communication across cultures can in some cases proceed smoothly without any particular awareness of cultural differences, many authorities in fields as varied as business, communication, sociology, anthropology, foreign-language instruction, and linguistics strongly argue that the likelihood of effective communication diminishes when that awareness is lacking (Bass and Burger, 1979; Black and Porter, 1991; Condon and Yousef, 1985; Dodd, 1982; E. Hall, 1961; Hoecklin, 1995; Hofstede, 1991; Janssens, Brett, and Smith, 1995; Miller and Kilpatrick, 1987; Nostrand, 1966; Seelye, 1984; Terpstra and David, 1985; Varner and Beamer, 1995; Victor, 1992).

Ethnocentrism

At the most fundamental level cross-cultural pseudoconflict may come about when one or more of the people involved cling to an ethnocentric view of the world. Ethnocentrism may be defined as the "unconscious tendency to interpret or to judge all other groups and situations according to the categories and values of our own culture" (Ruhly, 1976, p. 22). Ethnocentrism manifests itself in many ways in intercultural communication:

A U.S. executive, for instance, who considers English to be the "best" or the "most logical" language will not apply himself to learn a foreign language which he considers "inferior" or "illogical." And if he considers his nonverbal system to be the most "civilized" system, he will tend to reject other systems as "primitive." In this sense, ethnocentrism . . . can lead not only to a complete communication breakdown but also to antagonism, or even hostility. (Almaney, 1974, p. 27)

In such situations, the ethnocentric party views culturally derived variations in communication as *wrong* rather than as simply *different*.

Conflict due to misunderstanding in cross-cultural communication, however, may affect even enlightened communicators. "Being aware," as Ronen writes, "does not necessarily mean that one can eliminate one's own ethnocentrism" (1987, p. 104). Ethnocentrism is deceptive precisely because members of any culture perceive their own behavior as logical, since that behavior works for them. Thus to see beyond the ethnocentric boundaries of one's own culture is difficult even when one is aware that one's own behavioral patterns may not be universal.

Indeed, some experts assert that much of what the communicator bases his or her assumptions on derives from perceptions below the conscious level (Berelson and Steiner, 1964; Key, 1968; Singer, 1987). Although the degree of importance of subliminal perception in communication is open to debate among these experts, the very possibility that the framework of values and perceptions on which the communicator's message rests is subconcious has great ramifications for the intercultural communicator. If the communicator's assumptions derive from subliminal perceptions, "It becomes particularly difficult to get people to establish different perceptual frames, precisely because they do not know—consciously—what caused them to establish those frames in the first place" (Singer, 1987, p. 77). To reduce communication-based conflict across cultures, people must strive to be conscious of their own culturally imbued ways of viewing the world.

The effective communicator is one who understands *how* the perception of a given message changes depending on the culturally determined viewpoint of those communicating. To this end the next section of this chapter—on attitude—provides a set of guidelines for communication between members of different cultures.

ATTITUDE

This section discusses ways to recognize how people can shape their attitudes toward individuals from other cultures and approach specific sources of cross-cultural pseudoconflict. Again, pseudoconflict is defined as conflict that arises out of misunderstandings based on perceived rather than actual opposing views or goals in which the misperception is rooted in cultural differences.

This chapter presents a four-point checklist designed to provide a more open attitude toward communication in a multicultural setting by helping communicators be aware of the most prominent factors causing pseudoconflict and misunderstanding in cross-cultural communication. By understanding the factors most likely to shift in the perception of people from other cultures, communicators can prepare themselves to lessen the likelihood of pseudoconflict related to intercultural differences in communication.

In studying factors likely to shift across cultures in a cross-cultural setting, Victor (1992) identified and discussed seven elements at length:

language, environment and technology, social organization, context-ing, authority conception, nonverbal communication, and temporal conception. These seven elements were collectively referred to with the acronym of LESCANT. In the discussion that follows, we have simplified the LESCANT model to four culturally derived influences on communication in perceived conflict situations: (1) language, (2) place, (3) thought processing, and (4) nonverbal communication. Although all four elements are to some extent interdependent, they are not examined here as a system. Instead, they are intended to be used as a checklist of major considerations in cross-cultural communication, offering specific suggestions for evaluating each variable.

Admittedly these four variables alone do not provide a thorough knowledge of another culture. Moreover, they are not intended to represent the *only* cause of intercultural pseudoconflict. These guidelines do, however, provide an underlying foundation on which the average communicator can construct a framework for understanding the culture in question. They also provide a way to maintain an open attitude toward those differences that may produce real anxiety in individuals whose own outlooks and beliefs may seem to be diametrically opposed.

By asking the right questions, the communicator should be able to manage more effectively pseudoconflict that arises from the most significant cultural differences. In her classic study, *Patterns of Culture*, Ruth Benedict argues that the only way one can know the significance of a selected detail of behavior is against the background of the motives and emotions and values that are institutionalized in that culture (1934, p. 55). The four points of this checklist are intended as a guide for the person wishing to construe an overview of that background.

Language

As discussed in Chapter 2, even when all parties use the same language with equal familiarity, the very nature of language provides a source for misunderstanding any attendant conflict. Among the most often cited barriers to conflict-free cross-cultural communication is the use of various languages and dialects.

Accent Differences

How one pronounces, enunciates, and articulates words falls under the general category of accent. Within nearly every language, standard and variant pronunciations exist for each word. A host of social and cultural factors influence how listeners react to these variations. Most variations are tied to geography and the social class of the speaker and therefore remain cultural factors affecting communication.

Such differences in pronunciation and articulation are compounded by dialectic differences in actual word choice (the effect of which is discussed in more detail in Chapter 6). An entire field of study—sociolinguistics—is devoted to the study of the perceptions of these variations from standard dialects of each respective language. Briefly, though, listeners judge speakers on their enunciation. If the speech is strongly Northumberlandish in accent, the Northumberlandish listener may feel more comfortable but may also be aware that the speaker is less likely to be educated than one who uses standard British English—the dialect of the educated upper class, which varies very little despite its speakers' geographical differences. The relative social class of those from Northumberland as a whole vis-à-vis the rest of Britain is also assessed in such a case, often negatively so against the accents of the generally more wealthy populace of southern England.

Not all accents possible in a given language are judged the same by all of that language's speakers, however. To stereotype speakers sociolinguistically, the listener must first be familiar with the culturally learned associations of the appropriate accents. Thus in the United States the distinctions described about Northumberland may be entirely lost, as no familiarity with Northumberland exists. Consequently the Northumberlandish accent is undistinguished from other accents from England and is usually judged according to U.S. stereotypes of those from England. This is not to imply that speakers of U.S. English do not divide themselves into dialect categories based on social class and geography, which they do; U.S. English speakers are usually unable to judge many non-U.S. English accents according to their place in a sociolinguistic continuum.

Foreign accents are also judged according to cultural stereotypes within each language group. These sociolinguistic prejudices often reflect the cultural biases of the host culture. Thus in the United States listeners place a great deal of emphasis on speaking English without the accent of a foreign language. It has been shown, for example, that those born in the United States rate Europeans speaking English with the accent of their native language more negatively than U.S.-born speakers using a recognizably U.S. accent (Mulde, Hanley, and Prigge, 1974). It is possible to argue that this prejudice derives from numerous cultural factors: U.S. global insularity and views of Europeans or the use of standard English as a sign of assimilation in a nation composed primarily of immigrants or immigrant stock. One might also argue that the use of a non-U.S. accent prevents the U.S.-accented English listener from accurately determining sociolinguistic cues about the speaker. Without the help of such cues, the listener cannot determine the speaker's social class and so attributes the lower social class until proved otherwise.

Linguistic Differences

It is difficult to underestimate the importance that an understanding of linguistic differences plays in intercultural communication. Indeed the proponents of the so-called Sapir-Whorf hypothesis believe that language shapes the culture that uses it, affecting the way that its users think (Gumperz and Hymes, 1964; Hoijer, 1982; Hymes, 1972; Lander, 1966; Niyekawa-Howard, 1968; Pike, 1971 Romney and D'Andrade, 1964). To quote Edward Sapir: "No two languages are ever sufficiently similar to be considered as representing the same social reality. The worlds in which different societies live are distinct worlds, not merely the same world with different labels attached" (cited in Mandelbaum, 1962, p. 162).

Similarly, for Benjamin Whorf, "the linguistic system . . . of each language is not merely a reproducing instrument for voicing ideas but rather is itself the shaper of ideas" (1952, p. 5). Thus even if one can approximate the meaning of a message through translation, it is at best difficult to convey the ideas connected to the translator's choice of words in that language. This can be a source of pseudoconflict. Since language shapes thought, those speaking different languages understand the world around them—including the messages they communicate—in a way that is essentially linked to the language used. For anyone not using that language, the message received will, by nature, be only approximate.

It should be noted at this point that considerable criticism against linguistic determinism exists. In part this stems from the difficulty of proving or disproving the hypothesis definitively. More significantly, though, the theory was weakened in academic circles when it was discovered that Whorf had used some questionable evidence to make his point. When Whorf's scholarship was convincingly drawn into question (Martin, 1986; Pinker, 1994; Pullum, 1991), so was the theory he helped popularize. Still, the founding work of Sapir, and later studies of unquestioned integrity—by, for example, Alfred Bloom (1981)—have done much to continue to validate the concept of linguistic determinism.

The premises of linguistic relativity are ultimately unprovable and highly debated. Harry Hoijer, expressing the general argument against the Sapir-Whorf hypothesis, warns that it is "easy to exaggerate linguistic differences of this nature and the consequent barriers to intercultural understanding. No culture is wholly isolated, self-contained, and unique. There are important resemblances between all known cultures—resemblances that stem in part from diffusion . . . and in part from the fact that all cultures are built around biological, psychological, and social characteristics common to all mankind" (1982, pp. 211–12). Still, as Noam Chomsky argues: "The existence of deep-seated formal universals . . . implies that all languages are cut to the same pattern, but does not imply that there is any point by point correspondence between languages" (1968, pp. 29–30).

Language itself reinforces cultural associations contained within the group that speaks it. As Robbins Burling observes, "the terms of one language carry a burden of irrelevant connotations that interfere with our grasp of the terms of the other" (1970, p. 13). Yet although it remains ultimately unprovable that language shapes reality, at the very least one can assert that "the lexicons of different languages do indeed suggest different conceptual universes, and that not everything that can be said in one language can be said (without additions and subtractions) in another, and that it is not just a matter of certain things being easier to say in one language than another" (Wierzbicka, 1992, p. 20).

Bernd-Dietrich Mueller (1995) illustrates this in practical terms. He explains that

> there are a considerable number of words which from a superficial point of view, mean the same thing, such as:
>
> *Spanish:* familia; *French:* famille; *German:* Familie; *British English:* family
>
> In spite of common Latin roots, these words have different social meanings. They comprise different groups of people (parents/children plus grandparents, uncles, aunts, etc.). Different relationships between, responsibilities towards and degrees of protection one can expect from the family members and the family as a whole exist. "Family" does not become the topic of conversation in exactly the same ways in the above mentioned cultures. Finally, the different social value of each of the concepts produces different connotations and different attitudes. (pp. 90–91)

As Jonathan Slater notes, "Lexicons may differ so radically between languages as to prohibit reaching equivalence" (1987, p. 37). Harvey Daniels has written that "each language allows its speakers to easily talk about whatever is important to discuss *in that society*" (1985, p. 31, emphasis added). Daniels is careful, however, to point out that "this does not mean that every given language will work 'perfectly' or be 'equal' to any other in a cross-cultural setting." The resulting inaccuracy in the message can lead to misunderstanding and, consequently, to perceived conflict.

To avoid pseudoconflict, one must determine the degree of error probable in translating whatever communication is exchanged. To do so the communicator should remain sensitive to the degree to which the environment in which he or she operates is similar to that of the person into whose language any given message is communicated. As Mary Douglas has argued, where experiences in the culture of one linguistic group roughly match, language is less an impediment to communication; however, "where there is no overlap, the attempt to translate fails" (1975, p. 277). For the cross-cultural communicator the main purpose of translation ought not to have as its main goal an exact equivalence but "to prevent any confrontation between alien thought systems" (Douglas, 1975, p. 277). To this end, the other variables discussed in this chapter can help the communicator determine how "alien" the "thought systems" are between people of different cultures.

Translation Difficulties

Aside from the effect of language on actual thought processing, one might argue that difficulties with the translation of language fall basically into three categories: gross translation problems, the conveyance of subtle distinctions from language to language, and recognizing culturally based variations among speakers of the same language.

Gross translation errors, although frequent, may be less likely to cause conflict between parties than other language difficulties, for two reasons. First, they are generally the easiest language difficulty to detect. Many gross translation errors are either ludicrous or make no sense at all. Thus the General Motors standard slogan "body by Fisher" was embarrassing but readily caught when it was translated into Flemish in its Belgian campaign as "corpse by Fisher" (Ricks, Fu, and Arpan, 1974, p. 11). Only those translation errors that continue to be logical in both the original meaning and the mistranslated version pose a serious concern. Thus although "this is not available" and "this is now available" differ by only one letter in writing or one mispronounced word in speech, the meanings of the two phrases are diametrically opposite, although both versions may be perfectly logical in any number of situations.

Nor do such mistranslations need to actually cross languages in cross-cultural situations. Dialectic differences within the same language often create gross errors. One frequently cited example occurred when a U.S. deodorant manufacturer sent a Spanish translation of its slogan to its Mexican operations. The slogan read, "If you use our deodorant, you won't be embarrassed." However, the translation, which the Mexican-based English-speaking employees saw no reason to avoid, used the term *embarazada* to mean *embarrassed*. This provided much amusement in the Mexican market, as *embarazada* means "pregnant" in Mexican Spanish (Ball and McCulloch, 1985, p. 199).

Even when easily detected, gross translation errors waste time and wear on the patience of the parties involved. Additionally, some such errors imply a form of disrespect for the party into whose language the message is translated, because it may be construed that the individual who made the error did not consider the foreign language (or people) important enough to ensure accuracy. These feelings and perceptions in turn can produce an unnecessary and easily avoidable conflict.

The subtle shadings that are often crucial to negotiations are also weakened when both parties do not share a similar control of the same language. In English, for example, the mild distinctions between the word *misinterpret* and *misunderstand* can prove significant in a sensitive situation. To a touchy negotiator, to say that he or she *misunderstands* may imply that he or she is not prepared or not fully competent to handle the negotiation. To say that the same negotiator *misinterprets* a concept, by contrast, allows the negotiator a way to save face, since all interpretations are arguable. He or she has reached an understandable, although inaccurate, interpretation of the matter. In such a situation the term applies more objectively to the matter at hand than to the specific negotiator. To a nonnative speaker with inadequate control of the language, however, such subtle distinctions might be lost. When other parties with full control over the language with whom the nonnative speaker communicates assume that knowledge of this distinction exists, it is likely that classic pseudoconflict, as defined at the beginning of this chapter, will derive from misunderstanding.

To reduce the risk of inaccurate translation, the communicator should take great care to find a qualified translator. The choice of translator should not rest on chance. A friend who has lived in Rotterdam for a year or two, for example, may have rudimentary knowledge of Dutch but hardly has the requisite skills to ensure that the sorts of translation errors described earlier are avoided. To some extent one may be protected by employing translators who are certified or who work with a respected translating firm.

The rise in reliance on electronic communication media has brought the question of translation and second-language use even more to the forefront in recent years. Despite recent advances in character-conversion programs, the use of the keyboard for e-mail and telex use, for example, still necessitates the use in most cases of a letter-based language. It is, in short, difficult to compose with character-based languages such as Chinese or Japanese.

Moreover, much of our present communication technology—the fax, the telex, and e-mail over the Internet—requires a special form of English. The lack of awareness of this may not even be evident for native speakers, especially of English as the predominate second language of choice for the electronic media among character-based languages (and many letter-based languages as well). This is made even more problematic for second-language users, since the adaptations to English needed for the telex are not the same as the truncated form of English used in fax cover sheets. As Chad Hilton (1992) observes regarding the Japanese concerns for this issue: "Japanese international trade has long relied extensively on communications technology, the telex and now the fax, to facilitate overseas business. The telex requires a special adaptation of English. . . . [T]he fax, though, requires 'standard' English writing skills, a subject largely neglected by corporate trainers in favor of spoken, 'communicative' English" (p. 255).

The "standard" English writing skills, if somewhat underdeveloped, can in turn lead to sources of miscommunication and conflict as well (as detailed in Chapter 6). Finally, beyond the fax and telex, the Internet is still predominately in English. Communication through the Net—even in the form of search engines and home pages alone—is predominately written in English, nonetheless reaching a much wider scope than the relatively small pool of native English speakers. Even those other languages found more or less commonly on the Net (French, German, Spanish) represent only a fraction of the languages used as first languages by the Net's users. This means that information placed on the Net should be written with the needs of the second-language speaker in mind.

Probably the greatest source of potential language-based conflict derived from the Net, however, rests in e-mail. The language of e-mail is in yet another style, with a more standard written style than the telex but one that arguably blends speech and formal written styles. Moreover, especially in direct online exchanges (such as chat rooms), the Net becomes fully conversational in tone and thus requires an immediate need to respond. Time pressures usually prevent one from using a translator and preclude the second-language writer from a dictionary or grammar checker. One writes online communication with all of the lasting impact of the written message but none of the ability to use nonverbal signals to indicate intended meaning. Moreover, this takes place with all of the demands of immediacy in conversational oral communication coupled with a predominate tone of informality. The result is a medium primed for conflict derived from miscommunication.

Nevertheless, it is important to stress that even when one eliminates linguistic barriers, one still faces numerous other obstacles to clear cross-cultural communication. As Lennie Copeland and Lewis Griggs note: "Learning the language is no substitute for learning the culture and appropriate behavior. People who are fluent in a language but not sensitive to the culture can make worse mistakes, perhaps because the locals expect more of them" (1985, p. 114). The remaining three factors in the checklist—place, thought processing, and nonverbal communication—provide a foundation on which the communicator can build an understanding of the "culture and appropriate behavior" to which Copeland and Griggs refer.

Place

Factors of place may be defined for our purposes as (1) the physical environment in which one lives and (2) existing technology, or the way in which one manipulates that environment. These two factors of place profoundly affect the way one views the world. The differences in this world view in turn are prime sources for pseudoconflict.

To some extent the environment and technology of a culture are interrelated, forming a cultural system. The interrelationship of environment to technology may be defined as that "cultural system concerned with the relationships between humans and their natural environment" (Terpstra and David, 1985, p. 148).

The way in which people use the resources available to them often shifts notably from culture to culture. "The environment in which a communication occurs," Singer observes, "can be a major factor in determining how effective one can be in intercultural communication" (1987, p. 58). Culturally engrained biases about the natural and technological environment can create communication barriers. The communicator accustomed to certain ways of looking at the environment and the use of technology particular to his or her culture may find it difficult to adapt to those views. This in turn can create misunderstandings and pseudoconflict.

These place-related communication differences manifest themselves on a wide spectrum of subjects. Many of these differences are relatively easy for the communicator to overcome as sources of pseudoconflict. This is because many place-related differences are based primarily on lack of *knowledge* rather than on culturally intrinsic *values*. These can be eliminated or at least reduced by acquiring an understanding of differences in transportation and logistics, health care and sanitation, accident prevention and occupational safety, settlement and territorial organization, and energy cost and availability (Seelye, 1984; Victor, 1992). Even the role of weather and the climate in general are subject to drastic change from one culture to another (Seelye, 1984).

To illustrate how such knowledge-based differences may cause a communication-based pseudoconflict, consider how the standard means of transportation and logistics in one culture may seem patently absurd in another. The manager of a Canadian company doing business in South America might never think to ship goods from Chile to neighboring Argentina by the circuitous route of the Panama Canal. Because Canada is relatively flat and has an excellent network of railroads and highways, the Canadian manager might assume that the overland route would be the easiest way to transport goods for any short distance. Indeed, the Canadian might well specify this preference in any relevant communication. What the Canadian might not understand, however, is that the rugged physical environment of the Andean terrain and the related absence of cross-Andean railroads and freeways would make such an option unreasonably expensive or even impossible.

Not all place-related sources of pseudoconflict, however, are so easily resolved. Many place-related issues go beyond mere knowledge-based differences, embracing actual cultural values. For example, as we saw in Chapter 3, the perception of living and working space—whether office space or the use of space in domestic housing and buildings in general—can carry distinct meaning within any one culture. The way one interprets the messages inherent in the use of space is, however, subject to great cross-cultural variation that is often imbued with deep-rooted cultural associations. Simply being aware of differences may not reflect these value-linked differences and therefore might affect how one communicates matters relating to the notion of space.

Thus some have argued that in Germany the use of space reinforces extended social distance (compared to the United States) through greater emphasis on such environmental features as soundproofing, physical barriers such as double doors and a preference for heavy curtains, and the use of shrubs and barriers to shield yards from neighbors (Condon and Yousef, 1985; Hall, 1966).

Pseudoconflict in turn may result when someone from a culture that places less emphasis on these qualities—such as a North American—interprets the German emphasis on privacy and use of space by standards other than those actually held in Germany. In such a situation the North American might view the German behavior as intentionally isolating, cold, or standoffish, creating a possible source of irritation, resistance, and consequent misunderstanding. Pseudoconflict can easily escalate into true conflict when the North American shows signs of irritation and the German has no idea of its source. The German would naturally assume that the irritation arose elsewhere and respond accordingly, the misplaced response leading to more negative reactions from the North American until both parties become engaged in a full-scale conflict cycle.

In Japan, by contrast, people are accustomed to living and working in much closer and less private quarters. Indeed, a European Community Report—which at least in part reflects a German frame of reference—claimed that the "Japanese lived in rabbit hutches" (Fields,

1983, p. 27). Although such a claim in Europe (or the United States) would have represented a deep insult, the Japanese, as one marketing expert observed, took the comment as a reinforcement of their own cultural self-perception as "underprivileged self-achievers" (Fields, 1983, p. 27).

The difference (vis-à-vis Europe and the United States) of Japanese emphasis on space creates a similar difference in the way people interact with one another in a "rabbit hutch" environment. The physical environment of the standard business office, for example, varies drastically from that in the German example described. Unlike the German manager, who places great emphasis on the physical separation of his or her office—emphasized by size, location, soundproofing, and the use of doors—the Japanese *bucho*, or department chief, generally has no separate office at all. Instead, the *bucho's* desk is simply one of many desks in a rectangular-patterned arrangement in a large open area. The *bucho's* desk is usually farthest from the door, often near a window, and offers an easy view of the department. Although workers within the box-shaped arrangement are often strictly postioned by rank as to where in the box they have their desks, the open environment is more conducive to greater visibility and to greater ease of access and communication. As Japanese business expert Boye DeMente has observed:

> *Within each of these basic boxes, responsibility and activity is more or less a team thing, with work assigned to the group as a whole. Members of each section are expected to cooperate and support each other. . . . The effectiveness of a particular section is strongly influenced by the total morale, ambition and talent of the whole team.* (1981, p. 70)

Although teamwork and ease of access for communication in the Japanese system are perhaps more emphasized than in the German situation as described, a German entering such an environment may well misinterpret such a system—from its physical appearance judged by German rather than Japanese standards—as egalitarian. The German reflecting this in his or her communication, however, would be making a serious error. The Japanese are strictly ranked by importance within this seemingly (by German standards) open seating and are very concerned not only about their placement in the seating box but also to which box they belong (DeMente, 1981, pp. 69–70).

Another environmental and technological factor affecting communication that is likely to differ across cultures in a value-related manner and thus result in cross-cultural pseudoconflict is the *human* climate, that is, the nature of a culture's human resources. The literacy rate and the role of mass media, for example, may change greatly from one culture to the next. Thus using written warnings to notify a largely illiterate population of a potential hazard with a product is unlikely to serve its purpose. In a well-known case of such conflict, a Swiss corporation provided only written instructions for the safe use of its baby formula. To large numbers of the baby formula's illiterate users in the Third World, such a written warning proved useless and, when coupled with other factors, was ultimately fatal to the children to whom the formula was fed.

Finally, value-based misunderstanding and pseudoconflict may arise when people do not adapt their world views to the technological level of sophistication of a given group of people or work force. For example, among those from the more industrialized nations, a common assumption is that the way people in less industrialized nations use their resources results not only from an inferior level of technology but also from an inherently inferior culture. Such a view is particularly dangerous when one considers the power available to cultures with a high level of technological sophistication to impose a cultural dominance over those to whom they introduce that technology (Ellul, 1964; Illich, 1977; Rybczynski, 1983). Technology may break down cultural barriers but may create enormous resentments if all its ramifications are not carefully considered. As one expert has observed:

If in one sense technology—particularly communications—no longer permits the "separate state," in another sense technology that confers these powers also makes possible—at any rate, for the favored few—a policy akin to autarchy. (Tucker, 1977, p. 99)

Not only pseudoconflict but also a very real conflict may derive from how technology is shared. If one nation depends on another for the technology needed to sustain its economic viability and is unable to maintain that technological capability on its own, communication dealing with that technology is likely to be charged with negative sentiments. Conflict arises because, as David Blake and Robert Walters have noted, "outright resentment toward foreign sources of technology are likely to arise" (1976, p. 145). Such an attitude is not limited to the so-called lesser industrialized world but, as Blake and Walters describe, is prevalent wherever such disparity exists: "Europeans, particularly the French, took note of the seemingly unassailable scientific and technological predominance of the United States" (1976, p. 145). Similarly, as the strength of Japanese technology increased, so too did U.S. concerns and resentment (Brooks, 1985; Feigenbaum and McCorduck, 1983; Gregory, 1986; Hofheinz and Calder, 1982; Vogel, 1979).

A relatively low level of technological sophistication, however, may be a quite deliberate choice of a specific country. "Existing sets of priorities defining what is good, proper, desirable, or important in a society may set limits on the kinds of technology that can successfully be introduced in a society" (Terpstra and David, 1985, p. 152). One extreme example of a nation reacting against the kinds of technology introduced into it from outside the culture is the revolution in Iran in the late 1970s. The revolution overthrew the shah, who had rapidly introduced many technologically based changes into Iranian society. The shah conceived of these changes as advances. He, however, remained unaware of the mass resentment these changes produced among his subjects, who believed that such changes were tearing away the fabric of traditional Iranian values.

A culture need not feel threatened, however, by high-level technological innovations to reject them in favor of a lower level of technology. A nation may use the lower technology available because it makes good sense to use it in that fashion within the context of that culture. For example, the halberd was developed in Switzerland in the Middle Ages. This weapon was, for its day, of a technologically low level, consisting of a long spike with a hook and cleaver attached. Swiss farmers used the halberd as a means of defense against marauding German and French barons, who used the high-technology weapon system of horse and armor. For the Swiss, the halberd was cheap, as compared to horses and armor. Second, this simple weapon involved little training. Unlike equestrian combat equipment, the halberd consisted of farm implements (hook and hatchet) with which the Swiss farmers were familiar, and its use was elementary: the central object being to hook the armor of the attacking knight and, using the cleaver, hack the grounded horseman immobilized by the weight of his armor. Yet despite its significantly lower scale of technology, the halberd was used extremely successfully by the Swiss, with at least one expert (Rybczynski, 1983) asserting that it helped bring an end to the era of the armored knight.

Significantly the halberd did not develop among the German or French peasantry. This was not because they were free from attacks by knights or because the farm technology from which the halberd was born was unavailable in France or Germany, for the hook and cleaver were as common to the peasants there as to the farmers in Switzerland. Rather, the halberd was a culturally inappropriate weapon for them. As serfs to the barons who raided their lands, the German and French peasants actually accomplished little in holding off the marauding nobles, as the land itself was already owned by the attackers. Thus it made little sense to risk great bodily harm or even death in defending the land. "While the halberd did not require great skill, it demanded considerable bravery. . . . The halberd involved close combat, and until the halberdier, who wore no armor, was able to unseat or incapacitate the charging enemy, he was at great risk" (Rybczynsk, 1983, p. 170).

For cultural reasons, however, the Swiss farmer had the needed bravery his French or German counterpart did not. In contrast to the French or German peasant, the Swiss farmer fought for his own land: "a free man fighting for home and family—neither a serf nor a slave—a necessary prerequisite for the bravery required to use this kind of weapon" (Rybcznski, 1983, p. 170). Thus Swiss farmers in the late Middle Ages used with highly favorable results the lower technology available to them because it was culturally better suited to their needs.

The attitudes that a particular society may hold toward technological innovations and its overall effect on the cultural values of that society are often at variance with those from other cultures. To the extent that the level of technology is determined according to preexisting cultural values, the attitudes toward its use will most likely be reflected in any communication regarding that technology. In the United States, for example, technological innovation is generally regarded as positive. U.S. communicators therefore would most likely reflect this outlook by seeing technology as generally good for its users. Indeed, the average individual from the United States might well be expected to believe that all those *without* an equally sophisticated level of technology would of necessity *want* to acquire it, with only lack of access or ability impeding such acquisition.

This view would fall far from the mark for many other cultures. Even in Japan, the country with the greatest emphasis on research and development (R&D) after the United States, the U.S. penchant for technological innovation has been considered extreme. Naohiro Amaya, an influential senior official of the powerful Ministry of International Trade and Industry and among Japan's greatest planners, has been recorded as questioning the value and extent of U.S. emphasis on technological innovation: "The Americans seemed to him to have reached the outer limits of inventing devices of use to the average citizen. Machines that opened cans and machines that polished shoes were different from heavy domestic machines like washers and dryers, they were less basic, less necessary" (Halberstam, 1986, p. 39).

It is, however, not from the Japanese or other technologically sophisticated cultures that the United States and other technology-centered cultures diverge most notably. Rather, it is with those cultures in which such technology—at times by choice—is not so prevalent that a difference in the view toward technology is most likely to affect communication and to create conflict. Thus in prerevolutionary Iran highly sophisticated technology had been imported as a showpiece. The pervasive influence of much of that technology was viewed, however, as contributing to the undermining of traditional values. This led, at least to some extent, to that nation's revolution and strongly anti-Western stance. Thus some governments find that acquiring state-of-the-art technology is inappropriate:

> *They often find that their factor proportions of labor and capital and their consumer demand patterns are at variance with the product and process technology. . . . These host nations also look askance at . . . product technology, finding it inappropriate to local income levels and the basic needs of low-income levels and the basic needs of low-income earners. (Rugman, LeCraw, and Booth, 1985, p. 288)*

To incorporate such technology would be disruptive to the society as a whole.

In countries emphasizing the need for employment, labor-saving devices can be seen as wholly counterproductive. In such cases the best level of technology is not necessarily, as in the U.S. view, a positive good.

For communicators the danger of such a difference in the perception of technology is the industrialized world's deeply ingrained bias toward technological innovation as beneficial. Thus even if a person from the United States were aware of this variant view, he or she might well hold such a view as a sign of an inferior culture, at least when communicating about technology. This in turn would contribute to a sense of arrogance and ethnocentrism that would not go unnoticed. Such a position would likely contribute not only to misunderstanding and pseudoconflict but also to real conflict if the variance between the two views were left unreconciled. The communicator must remain flexible to the choices a culture may make regarding the appropriate level of technology, keeping in mind that those choices may not reflect the usual technological presuppositions common in the communicator's own culture.

Finally, in multinational corporations or international nonprofit organizations and relief organizations, the possibility arises that there will be no main central concept of place at all. Observing this trend in multinational corporate situations, Rosenzweig and Singh (1991) describe the emergence of organizational structures comprised of "a set of differentiated structures or processes, and each of these structures and processes, in turn, are affected by a variety of environmental forces . . . [T]hey face, at the same time, a pressure for conformity to conditions in the local environment and an imperative for consistency within the multinational enterprise." (p. 344)

This may prove even more clear in such nonprofit multinational organizations as the United Nations. In many of the UN's multinational efforts, multiple subunits may coexist both in the cultural frame of reference of its participants and in the locales to which their activities take them. The United Nations may be physically based in New York, but arguably many under its umbrella are unlikely to be influenced at all by the concepts of place attached to that locale as a headquarters site.

Thought Processing

The third conflict-causing factor in our cross-cultural communication checklist is thought processing, which may be defined as the way in which people interpret the world around them. The entirety of thought processing goes far beyond what we will discuss here. We may, however, limit this term for the purposes of this discussion to the way in which four specific variables likely to shift across cultures affect how a person understands what is communicated. This is assuming that a common understanding exists of environmental and technological factors and of the verbal and nonverbal means of communication used.

The four variables are (1) social organization, (2) contexting, (3) authority conception, and (4) temporal conception. (For a more complete discussion of these factors, see Victor, 1992.)

Social Organization

Social organization, as it affects communication, is often culturally determined. "Culture," note Jaesup Lee and Fredric Jablin, "inevitably shapes the way that people interact with one another in social environments . . . since different cultures promote unique sets of values, norms and expectations" (1992, p. 204). Pseudoconflict is likely to occur when an individual assumes as universal his or her views on issues reflecting the social organization of his or her culture.

Social organization has been defined as "the common institutions and collective activities shared by members of a culture" (Victor, 1992, p. 64). Social organization affects the sender and receiver in communication, since it sets the "roles played by individuals and groups in a society and the relationships between these individuals and groups" (Terpstra, 1982, p. 36). A society defines reality through the relationships it imposes on the members of its cultures. Those relationships most likely to affect communication in a cross-cultural situation are "familiar, religious, economic-occupational, political and judicial, educational, intellectual-aesthetic, recreational, the mass media, stratification and mobility, social properties . . . status by age group and sex, ethnic/religious and other minorities" (Seelye, 1984, p. 41).

Social organization shapes the most fundamental beliefs of members of a culture. Indeed, such beliefs are likely to be taken by members of a culture as a given. Speaking specifically of U.S.–Japanese business communication, John Condon warns that the most notable differences are often of less importance than the more subtle differences that reflect "some unseen or unstated meaning which is usually not pointed out but that everybody is supposed to know" (1984, p. 6). Similarly, in describing the experience of people placed in a foreign context in general and of ethnography in Denmark in particular, Lisanne Wilken (1995) writes:

> *Part of culture everywhere is unconscious for the people living in it. Or at least conceived of as so "normal" that it is seen to be natural. Through observation—and participation—the ethnographer can notice what is taken for granted in a given social setting, since this may not be the least important aspect in the study of culture.* (p. 85)

Arvind Phatak observes that "social institutions—whether they be of a business, political, or family or social class nature—influence the behavior of individuals" (1983, p. 30). The influence of a culture's social organization on that behavior translates directly into the field of communication in many areas. For instance, the nature of praise and personal or employee motivation is socially determined (Adler, 1986; Haire, Gheselli, and Porter, 1963; Hofstede, 1984; O'Reilly and Roberts, 1973; Reitz, 1975). The communicator must be aware that what may be motivating, convincing, or persuasive in one culture may not be so in another.

For example, many East Asian cultures' deeply ingrained feelings toward face saving, seniority, and the maintenance of harmony in the workplace would be likely to affect what motivates workers differently than in northern European and North American cultures, where those feelings are less marked. Thus in Japan praise is likely to be as disruptive to employees as blame would be in the United States or Canada. The promotion of a single member of a traditional Japanese work group may cause the productivity and morale of both the group and the promoted employee to fall:

> *Japanese can be as embarrassed when they are singled out for praise as for blame. . . . Although more subtle, it is an act of giving exceptional attention to one individual, of separating one from the group. Also . . . failure to include people who expect, as members of the organization, to be included can cause a loss of face.* (Condon, 1984, p. 32)

A similar promotion in the United States, by contrast, might be seen as a reward for the promoted employee and might even be viewed as encouraging the remaining members of the group to work harder for a goal that they too might attain. Thus to communicate such a promotion openly may prove to be a poor policy in Japan but a good policy in the United States. As Boye DeMente (1993) explains, this also contributes to the Japanese disapproval toward changing companies or lateral moves from non-Japanese subsidiaries or partners, both common practices in the Americas and Europe. DeMente explains:

> *In such a system it is virtually impossible for anyone to enter a group except at the bottom or at the top, and those who enter at the top are almost never fully accepted by those below them. If the newcomers are not extremely careful in dealing with the group, submerging most of their own personalities and individualistic tendencies, the group will reject them the same way the human body rejects the invasion of incompatible matter.* (1993, p. 87)

As early as 1989, James Lincoln demonstrated in his empirical study contrasting U.S. and Japanese work attitudes: "Younger Japanese are much more likely to share American-style values of leisure, consumption, and affluence" (p. 92). The case remains, however, that "rewards and opportunities are more likely to be explicitly tied to age and seniority than in the American workplace" (p. 91). Conversely Japanese managers of U.S. or European work forces face similarly offsetting difficulties in managing people who do expect differential treatment from their group or place in the organization (Graf et al., 1995).

Because the influence of social organization on behavior determines to a large extent the value system of a given culture, individuals wishing to avoid misunderstanding and pseudoconflict must take particular care to remain nonjudgmental when the values determined by their own social-organizational patterns clash with those with whom they communicate. For example, in many parts of the world, including the majority of the cultures of central Africa, Latin America, southern Asia, and the Arab world, it would seem highly inappropriate to suggest to employees that you expect them to skip over hiring their relatives to hire a stranger. For people in these cultures, nepotism both fulfills personal obligations and ensures a predictable level of trust and accountability. In such societies familial ties are presumed to be more reliable than, for example, the legal and contractual ties to which the cultures of northern Europe and North America generally adhere. The fact that a stranger appears to be better qualified based on a superior resume and a relatively brief interview would not, as it might, for example, in the United States, affect that belief. In such a cross-cultural situation employers would need to adapt how they expressed their own culturally determined views on hiring employees. In the example discussed here, whether hiring practices were based on an employee's resume or on the

strength of his or her family connections, the cross-cultural communicator wishing to avoid pseudoconflict would need to adjust the way in
which this preference were communicated, so that what was indicated
would accommodate those who would find such a preference distressing.

Although it is the goal of the communicator to avoid pseudoconflict
whenever possible, differences in social organization often create a situation in which the individual experiences a very real, rather than a perceived, conflict. It is often difficult to rid communication of a judgmental bias when social organization varies markedly.

For example, whose founding principles as a nation were based on
egalitarian values, people from the United States may find it difficult to
remain neutral on class and role structures that prevent upward mobility. The formerly socially inferior role of nonwhites in apartheid South
Africa, of women in much of the Islamic world, or of lower castes in
India—just to name a few—may prove particularly disturbing to those
from the United States. A U.S. communicator who cannot eliminate the
attendant condemnation from his or her communication, however, cannot expect to function effectively in that society. As James Livingstone
has observed about communication in the workplace, "A society preventing upward movement may in time come apart at the seams, but in
day to day terms it can make difficulties for the enterprise in limiting its
choice of executives to those which will be acceptable in the role to the
rest of the community" (1975, p. 199).

Contexting

The next area of thought processing pertinent to communication is contexting, which we may define as the *way* in which one communicates
and especially the circumstances surrounding that communication.
Virtually all communication depends on the context in which it is set.
The more information sender and receiver share—the more homoge-
neous their shared experience and world view—the higher the context
of the communication and the less necessary to communicate through
words or gestures.

In a highly contexted situation much of what the communicator
chooses *not* to articulate is essential to understanding the transmitted
message. The communicator, however, expects that which is not said to
be understood already. Thus a spouse or longtime friend would be more
likely than a stranger to know when a person was upset without that
person's actually saying so. Clues in the person's behavior or conversation would be more apparent to those who knew that person well,
because their greater familiarity and shared set of understandings
would better allow them to place that person's behavior and communication in its proper context.

In cross-cultural settings those from the same culture would have more common experiences and shared understandings than those from different cultures. In such cases the seeds of unintentional conflict are often planted. For example, in the United States it is not particularly uncommon for someone to invite a business associate to dinner. Once there, the host and guest might well expect to mix some business discussion with purely social small talk. In France, by contrast, an invitation to dine at someone's home is considered an honor and is extremely rare. Once there, the guest and host would go to great extremes to avoid discussing any business matters, as the dinner would be considered a strictly social occasion. Therefore the French business executive visiting the United States who received an invitation to dine at his or her U.S. business colleague's home might entirely misunderstand the context of the invitation. The French executive would feel highly honored when, in fact, the host intended the dinner as nothing more than an attempt to introduce a measure of genial informality into the situation. Once the French executive arrived, she or he would be shocked if, as is fairly common in the United States, someone else had also been invited without the knowledge of the French guest. Moreover, the French businessperson would almost certainly be insulted were the U.S. host to raise business matters, when that may have been the actual reason the U.S. host had invited the French guest home to dinner. A pseudoconflict based on such misunderstanding could easily escalate to a real conflict because the U.S. host and the French guest did not realize the context in which each understood the invitation. They lacked an adequate set of understandings to place the communication in that context.

Such a shared set of understandings acts to reduce the inherent uncertainty present in all communication. As Berger and Calabrese have indicated, "When strangers meet, their primary concern is one of uncertainty reduction or increasing predictability about the behavior of both themselves and others in the interaction" (1975, p. 100). The degree of uncertainty among them is reduced to the extent that those within the same culture share more information in common than with those from other cultures; that is, they approach their communication with a more greatly shared context. Numerous cross-cultural communication experts have observed that the degree of uncertainty among them remains strong to the extent that they cannot predict or explain the differences among them (Gudykunst and Hammer, 1988; Gudykunst and Kim, 1992; Hofstede, 1991).

Moreover, the level of contexting *within* a culture depends on the nature of the culture itself. Seminal works on contexting (Hall, 1961, 1966, 1976, 1983; Hall and Hall, 1990) have observed that some cultures rely more heavily on context than others do. These cultures determine most or even all of the meaning in a message not from the actual words the sender uses but from how it is delivered and under what circumstances it is conveyed. Other cultures, by contrast, rely more heavily on what is actually said or written than on the circumstances surrounding the delivery of the message. In effect, one can actually rank cultures along a context scale:

> *It appears that all cultures arrange their members and relationships along the context scale, and one of the great communication strategies, whether addressing a single person or an entire group, is to ascertain the correct level of contexting of one's communication.* (Hall, 1983, p. 61)

Thus there are high-context cultures whose members rely heavily on inferred meaning, and in low-context cultures whose members rely heavily on literal meaning. Additionally, evidence suggests that members of low- and high-context cultures differ markedly in how they seek information to reduce the uncertainty that contexting attempts to eliminate. As William Gudykunst observes:

> *While members of high-context cultures reduce uncertainty in initial interactions, the nature of information they seek and their level of attributional confidence appears to be different from the typical pattern . . . for a low-context culture like that of the United States.* (1983, p. 50)

In high-context cultures, such as Japan, Mexico, or China, much of what is not actually said must be inferred through what seems (to those from low-context cultures, such as Germany, Sweden, and the United States) to be indirection. To people from low-context cultures those in high-context cultures may seem needlessly vague or incomplete. Conversely those from high-context cultures may view their low-context counterparts as impersonal and confusingly literal. It is important for those people to assess the level of contexting inherent in the communication of the culture in which they conduct business to understand clearly what has been conveyed and to avoid conflict.

Additionally, contexting can be linked to issues of formality, face saving, and respect (Fisher, 1988; Victor, 1992). Cultures that place greater value on face saving or respect tend to be higher contexted precisely because high-contexted communication allows for greater ambiguity than does low-contexted communication. The personal relationship developed in high-context culture allows one to store enough information regarding the other party's potential weak spots, allowing one to avoid raising the issue by circling around it. Speaking around a subject or reading into what is not said can provide a means of allowing another party to save face or to maintain respect.

This circumlocution is apparent in a wide variety of high-context, high face-saving cultures. For example, Bryan Husted (1993) describes how compared to North Americans, "Mexicans are more indirect, often taking digressions to reach the point they want to make. Related to this tendency is a possible significant Mexican tendency to emphasize 'face-saving' over profits" (pp. 226–227). In discussing the Korean concept of *kibun* (literally "feelings," or "mood"), Boye DeMente (1988) suggests that Koreans "are extraordinarily sensitive to slights and setbacks which damage their *kibun* and upset the harmony of their existence, and they go to what appears to Westerners to be extreme lengths to maintain their own *kibun*" (p. 26).

Several strategies exist among high face-saving cultures to sidestep the potentially damaging tear in the fabric of surface harmony. Some of these are fairly culturally specific. For example, as Joseph Page (1995) discusses:

> *Brazilians characteristically seek subtle ways to circumvent difficult situations. Instead of resorting to confrontation, they prefer to use what they call the* jeito *or* jeitinho, *a difficult to translate term referring to . . . a rapid, improvised, creative response to a law, rule, or custom that its face prevents someone from doing something. The jeitinho personalizes a situation ostensibly governed by an impersonal norm.* (p. 10)

At the other extreme from the Brazilian personalizing strategy of the *jeitinho*, the Japanese have refined *de*personalizing strategy involved with *tatemae* and *honne*. *Tatemae* and *honne* can be roughly translated as "surface reality" and "one's true thoughts and feelings," respectively, and are at the core of Japanese communication and conflict management. Robert March (1988) explains that

> *the deeply ingrained habit of behaving in a* tatemae *way is critical to the Japanese ideal of social harmony and to the realities of maintaining harmony among people who are raised to pursue, first and foremost, social acceptance. . . . The interpersonal relationships or identity they [the Japanese] achieve are, for the most part, determined by their jobs or social roles. These are all on the* tatemae *level, often attained at the expense of denying their true feelings. . . . In other words, Japanese society tends to make people depend on others for psychological satisfaction, values, and identities.* (pp. 143–144)

The chasm between the need to communicate in a *tatemae* way is so great that many Japanese organizations are employing what Nobuyuki Chikudate (1995) describes as "communication network liaisions" to act as cultural translators even in situations in which all parties speak English or Japanese.

Although few cultures demand as highly formalized a face-saving system as that which the Japanese must practice to maintain the dichotomy of *tatemae* and *honne*, people in many high face-saving cultures do communicate in highly formalized ways, particularly with those they do not know very well. This formality, in turn, allows social buffers in cultures that place great attention on face (James, 1995).

The use of silence, too, allows for saving face. Although silence still communicates, the absence of words allows for less direct conflict. Not only the Japanese use the tactic of silence as a strategy in conflict situations. Writing of the stereotype of the "reserved Finn," for example, Hilkka Yli-Jokipii (1994) explains how Finnish silence is a response to "the aversion from challenging *other*" through what she describes as "non-intruding, detached behaviour" (p. 252).

Varner and Beamer (1995) suggest several strategies employed in high face-saving cultures that people from lower face-saving cultures must interpret:

> *In cultures throughout Asia, as well as Africa, losing face is a terrible thing to suffer. Besides expressing agreement, various other ways of communicating diminish potential loss of face also, such as laughing to discount the significance of some word or act and therefore diminish its ability to cause loss of face. Simply choosing not to hear is another ploy.*
>
> *The profound desire not to be the cause of someone's losing face results in many cultures in a great reluctance to say no or to bear bad news. When the unspoken objective of every transaction is to create and nurture harmony so the relationship can thrive, bad news is a serious threat to that objective. Or to be precise, the* communication *of bad news is a serious threat. (pp. 100–101)*

Being aware of the importance any given culture generally places on contexting will help the communicator determine how much of the message he or she is likely to receive directly. Still, as even the lowest-contexted cultures use contexting to some extent, the communicator must be sensitive to its effects and not simply to the message as if in isolation.

In oral communication one must observe nonverbal signals closely. But this is not always readily possible. The communicator must become familiar with the nonverbal behavior of those from the culture with whom he or she speaks.

In written communication contexting is even more difficult. The communicator must seek out the underlying message from the writer's choice of words alone. The reader must then place these words within the context of whatever it is possible to construe from the larger range of existing interaction between the message's sender and its receiver.

Authority Conception

One fairly common form of conflict grounded in communication is linked to how people view authority. Conflict in such cases often occurs when a person from one culture does not understand clearly the relative ability or inclination of an individual from another culture to act on his or her own initiative. For example, in cultures with a high respect for authority, such as the Philippines, a subordinate may never point out to his or her boss that an idea seems impossible to carry out. Instead the subordinate will undertake the project and fail. Additionally, the Filipino boss would be surprised and even displeased were the employee to bring up this concern. Conversely in a culture in which people are more likely to question authority, as in the United States, the subordinate might be more likely to share his or her concerns with the boss before undertaking the project. The U.S. superior, in turn, would in many instances *expect* the subordinate to raise these concerns. In a cross-cultural situation conflict would likely occur when a Filipino boss received the unexpected feedback from a U.S. subordinate. Similarly, conflict might occur when a U.S. manager did *not* receive such feedback. Such conflict has its roots in an aspect of communication that could be called *authority conception*.

Different cultures often view the distribution of authority in their society differently. Depending on one's perspective, authority can be seen as differing thought, opinion, and behavior. Here we will focus only on behavior, which is the only one of these areas the communicator can clearly recognize. Those in authority over others therefore can be said to have the power to influence or command behavior. Authority in any given culture is determined by the roles the individuals within that culture assume relative to one another. That system of roles may be called an *authority hierarchy*. *Authority conception* may be defined as the degree to which individuals believe that those higher up in the authority hierarchy have the power to influence or command behavior.

Authority conception varies from culture to culture. In his study of managers in twelve countries, Andre Laurent (1983), asked for the managers' views of authority conception. Laurent queried the managers regarding their reaction to the following statement: "The main reason for all hierarchical structure is so that everybody knows who has authority over whom." The responses varied greatly. The percentage of agreement with Laurent's statement in the United States was the lowest of those polled, with only 18 percent, whereas the percentage of agreement with the statement was highest among Indonesian managers, with 86 percent. Laurent also asked the managers to what extent they agreed that it was necessary to bypass the hierarchical line to have efficient work relationships. Again the managers showed great cross-cultural diversity in their responses. For example, 75 percent of the Italian managers disagreed with Laurent's statement, as compared to 32 percent of U.S. managers and a low rating of 22 percent disagreement among those from Sweden.

Laurent's findings, though admittedly limited to the workplace, have significant ramifications for all communicators. One can infer from Laurent's findings that people in the United States could communicate on a much more informal basis than would be appropriate in many other cultures. This is because those from the United States would feel much less need for an authority hierarchy than do those from nations that have a much stronger authority conception, such as Indonesia. Consequently most people—or at least most managers—from the United States would be likely to believe that they can work in an organization with little or no formal authority hierarchy. Communication, therefore, could be assumed to be less formal, since people in the United States would be more likely than people in most other cultures are to view one another as colleagues and relative equals rather than as superiors and subordinates in the authority hierarchy. The exact opposite, in turn, could be inferred regarding the level of appropriate formality in communicating with Indonesians.

Likewise Laurent's study would imply that the flow of communication would vary greatly from culture to culture. The communicator, one can infer, would be much more able to communicate *directly* with his or her superior in Sweden than in Italy. Relatedly a communicator should probably be prepared to receive considerably more requests for approval from subordinates in Italy than in Sweden.

Another dimension of how authority conception affects communication that varies across culture is *power distance*. Geert Hofstede, who coined the term (based on the work of M. Mulder, 1976, 1977), defined power distance as "the extent to which a society accepts the fact that power in institutions and organizations is distributed unequally" (1980,

p. 45). The flow of communication in those cultures with a greater power distance is more highly centralized in their authority hierarchy than in those with a lesser power distance.

Hofstede twice surveyed employees of a major multinational corporation in forty countries on a number of issues, including power distance (1984, 1992). He found significant differences in the power distance common in various cultures. Using a power-distance index on a scale of 1 to 100, with lower scores representing less power distance, Hofstede discovered an enormous variance. In the 1980 study most countries fell in the range 30 to 60—Greece (with 60), Italy (with 50), and the United States (with 40)—but there was enormous overall variation. The Philippines with a score of 94 and Mexico and Venezuela (both with 81) topped the list; Austria (with 11), Israel (13), and Denmark (18) were at the bottom of the list. When Hofstede repeated the study in 1992, the degree of variability in power distance across cultures remained equally dramatic, although with a few mostly minor individual shifts for specific nations. In this later study most nations again fell in the range 30 to 60. The United States, for example, held a score of 40, ranking at 38 out of 53. At the top of the list was Malaysia, ranking first with an adjusted score of 104. Again the bottom of the list was carried by Austria at 11, Israel at 13, and Denmark at 18 (1992, p. 26).

Relative power distance in a given culture markedly affects communication and thus the likelihood that pseudoconflict will occur. Power distance shapes the view of how a message will be received, based on the relative status or rank of the message's sender to its receiver. Thus in Austria or Israel, which have low power indexes and are therefore fairly decentralized, people would generally pay attention to a person based on how convincing an argument he or she puts forth, regardless of that person's rank or status within the organization or society at large. By contrast, in Mexico or Venezuela, which have high power indexes and are consequently highly centralized, that which a relatively high-ranking individual communicates is taken very seriously, often overriding one's agreement or disagreement with that which is being communicated.

Similarly, in working with Israel and Austria, which have low power distances, we might anticipate at the outset more acceptance of a participative communication model. Conversely, in working with the Philippines with its large power distance, one might anticipate at the outset relatively less use of participative communication styles and more concern with who has the relevant authority.

That a culture has a centralized authority conception or large power distance does not necessarily, however, indicate that its members *prefer* one-way downward communication. As Bernard Bass and Philip Burger have shown in their twelve-culture survey, "Participants tended to favor two-way over one-way communication everywhere. . . . [T]hey viewed two-way communications as less frustrating, more preferable, and more satisfying" (1979, p. 162). Rather, the cultures differed in the *degree* of preference, frustration, and satisfaction implicit in one-way communication.

Temporal Conception

The final area in the checklist of thought-processing factors affecting cross-cultural communication is temporal conception, or how people view time. "A culture's concept of time," as Richard Porter and Larry Samovar have defined it, "is its philosophy toward the past, present, and the future, and the importance or lack of importance it places on time" (1982, p. 41). Those philosophies and assignments of importance regarding time are subject to great variation across cultures. In any communication, as Carley Dodd observes, "Time is a potent force, communicating as powerfully as verbal language" (1982, p. 236). Moreover, Dodd notes, "In intercultural communication encounters, an individual's sense of temporality, or that person's concept of time, may influence communication behavior" (1982, p. 236).

Arguably no factor in communication thought processing is more likely to create conflict based on misunderstanding rooted in cultural differences than how people conceive of time. Before proceeding, it might prove useful to provide an example that has been repeated in various forms on thousands of occasions in cross-cultural interaction.

A U.S. automaker's representative is sent on a sales trip to Saudi Arabia. The prospective Saudi client has set an appointment to meet with her, but when she arrives at exactly the preappointed time, she is asked whether she would mind waiting. She is made comfortable, but after waiting for over an hour, she demands to know how much longer she must wait. She does not receive a definite answer but is assured that her Saudi contact will meet with her as soon as he is free. She accepts this answer with an edge of irritation in her voice that she makes no effort to conceal, since she sincerely believes that she has been treated shabbily. To her amazement she waits an additional two hours before she is finally admitted to meet with the man she has come to see. Her problems, however, continue. The Saudi, for reasons beyond her ken, simply will not get down to business, even though they are running so late: He inquires about various people in the United States whom he knows and with whom she works. Next, he discusses the entire history of his relationship with her company, a relationship that she not only knows already but also takes almost an hour to recount because of his annoying habit of sidetracking his narration onto what she feels are all sorts of irrelevant details about the people with whom he dealt at each step. Moreover, the entire time they are meeting, various people interrupt them either in person or on the telephone, and while he handles each interruption relatively quickly, she resents the lack of his undivided attention after having waited so long herself. Finally, before they have even discussed the sale for which they had set the meeting, the Saudi observes that it is getting very late and suggests that they meet again the following day. Even then, he only hints that he will buy the cars she has come to sell.

By now, the U.S. businesswoman is certain that the Saudi has intentionally snubbed her. Frustrated and angry, she tells him that he has not treated her professionally. She is confused by how sincerely surprised he seems at her response.

Back at her hotel, the U.S. auto executive ponders why she would have been treated so rudely. First, she thinks that perhaps the Saudi was treating her so poorly because she is a woman; she has been told that women may not be treated as equals in some cultures, including Saudi Arabia. Still, she is aware that the Saudi seemed to go out of his way in his conversation to assure her that he both respected her and understood the important role women played in the company she represented. Indeed, in the many stories he related of the various people he knew from her company, she was aware that several had been about other women executives, and in all instances he had seemed to show very little overt sexism. Next, she thought, she had been snubbed because he was not interested in the product. He did hint, however, that he was going to buy the product before she left, although much to her irritation, he did not say so directly at the time. Moreover, she could not figure out why he would have invited her to fly all the way to the Middle East to meet him if the product did not interest him. She concluded at last that she had not been snubbed at all but instead, based on the many interruptions and the rambling conversation, that the man was simply very disorganized. Still, she could not help but wonder how a man could be so disorganized and attain so important a position in so well respected a company. In fact, none of these reasons seemed to explain the Saudi's behavior.

What the U.S. executive did not consider was that the reason the Saudi acted the way he did was that he handled time differently than she did. To the Saudi, it would be wrong to cut short a meeting with a person simply to adhere to a schedule. Regarding people as more important than schedules, he had no choice but to finish his discussion with his previous appointment before he could meet with the U.S. businesswoman. He felt that, as would most people in his culture, she would understand that this was the reason why she had to wait but that she, in turn, would not be cut short by his next appointment. In fact, he ended the day with her, sending the person with the next appointment home before they could officially meet. Of course, to be able to spend this much time with her, he needed to handle the various pressing issues that accounted for the various interruptions in the meeting. He also believed, as is common in many cultures, that time spent developing a good personal relationship is more valuable than rushing into the details of business or the like. Unless one has a good personal relationship with a business partner—or anyone, for that matter—one could never fully trust that person. Relatedly, if one had trust, one need not go over details of a deal too closely, since a person whom one trusted would not likely betray that trust. This is why the Saudi spent time telling the U.S. businesswoman the long history of his ties to her company and all the people at her company with whom he had developed a good personal relationship. In fact, he was shocked when at the end of the day, the auto executive told him that she felt he had treated her poorly. He was distressed that he might lose his ties to the U.S. company and thought perhaps her outburst represented the company's official stance. After all, it had chosen to send a virtual stranger to see him rather than any of those people with whom he had spent so much time establishing a good personal relationship.

This example is hypothetical, but the difficulties described have been experienced regularly in U.S.–Saudi interactions (Almaney and Alwar, 1982; Snowdon, 1986). Moreover, although it is dangerous to oversimplify, this example could have taken place in varying degrees in any number of configurations: a German in Peru, a Canadian in Nigeria, a Swede in Portugal. How one uses time, consequently, may profoundly affect the way in which one needs to communicate with those from other cultures and can be a cause of considerable conflict (Hall, 1983).

The cause of the conflict is rooted in two different forms of temporal conception. In general, most people from the United States, Canada, and northern Europe regard time as inflexible, a thing to be divided, used, or wasted (Hall, 1983; Victor, 1992). For people from these cultures, "[T]ime can be manipulated. It can be used as a tool: to communicate information; to inspire fear; to invoke uncertainty; to create anger; or to demonstrate power" (Borisoff and Merrill, 1992, p. 67). These people (to use Hall's terms, 1983) are said to have a *monochronic* temporal conception. The U.S. businesswoman in our example was demonstrating what we could call classic monochronic behavior. This is not, however, a universal view. Throughout most of the Arab world, Latin America, and central Africa, people are more likely to conceive of time as fluid, ranking personal involvement and completion of existing interactions above the demands of preset schedules. These people are said to be *polychronic* (Hall, 1983). The Saudi in our example could be said to have demonstrated classic polychronic behavior.

Charles Hampden-Turner and Fons Trompenaars (1993), in their discussion of *synchronous* (monochronic) and *sequential* (polychronic) workplace views of time, observe that "both approaches are valid and useful. But cultures tend to be far more comfortable with one way of working than the other" (p. 24). Neither view is right or wrong, better or worse.

Admittedly, not all cultures can be so easily divided into monochronic and polychronic systems. Often certain subsets within a society function monochronically, whereas others within the same culture function polychronically. For example, the employees of most major corporations in the United States follow a strictly monochronic system. Many physicians in the United States, however, follow a comparatively polychronic system. Still, on the whole, one might generalize that U.S. culture follows a monochronic conception of time.

Because people generally complete tasks at the expense of scheduling in polychronic societies, people in high authority may become easily overwhelmed with multiple tasks. To prevent overloading people in positions of high authority, those in polychronic societies often use subordinates to screen for them (Hall, 1983). Once a person can get past those screenings, the person in authority will generally see the task through, regardless of the comparative importance of the task.

Because a polychronic system encourages one-on-one interaction, such cultural organization usually allows for highly personalized relationships to flourish between the person in authority and the task bringer. The flow of information is open in both directions at all times. Indeed, for the system to work smoothly, it is to the advantage of both superior and subordinate to stay fully aware of all aspects—professional and personal—of each other's lives. This personal involvement makes it even more difficult for the person in authority to refuse to carry out a request once the task is presented. In such situations being able to break through those who screen for the person in authority is often the most difficult part of having the person in authority assist in a task.

One's communication strategy in polychronic cultures therefore centers in large measure on simply *reaching* the appropriate individual. No direct barriers exist between the leader and the subordinate; the superior will almost always welcome the subordinate. This develops a system in which influence and close circles of contacts among those screening for those higher up creates an informal and unofficial communication hierarchy.

In a monochronic system personal feelings are rarely allowed to flourish on the job. This is precisely because personal involvement must not be allowed to disrupt preset schedules if the system is to function smoothly. Personal relationships are prescribed by the terms of the job. Multiple tasks are handled one at a time in a prescheduled manner. People in authority are, in contrast to those in polychronic cultures, available by scheduled appointments. In such a system time, rather than the authority figure's subordinates or the personal relationship among the people involved, acts as a shield or screen for the authority figures.

Pseudoconflict is likely to occur when those from polychronic and monochronic systems meet. The monochronic person, for example, feels that the polychronic person is making him or her wait needlessly for a scheduled appointment. The polychronic person, in turn, feels slighted by the monochronic individual's ostensibly cold use of time to end a meeting to adhere to that schedule even though more discussion between the parties may be warranted.

The communication strategy for the individual facing a generally polychronic system of temporal conception would differ significantly from that of the individual facing a monochronic one. First, in a polychronic system one should be aware that people distinguish between insiders and those outside the existing personal relationships. Moreover, the accessibility of the person in authority is often a function of this relationship. One must therefore try to establish an inside connection to facilitate the effectiveness of his or her message. By contrast, in a monochronic society one needs only to schedule an appointment with the appropriate people. The communicator should not expect people in a monochronic system to prefer those they know over strangers. The outsider—at least in the sense of having access to those in power—is treated in a similar fashion as the close associate.

Second, the communicator should be aware of the relatively large amount of information shared among those in a polychronic culture that is not necessarily related to the job at hand. As J. Hall has observed on this point: "Polychronic people are so deeply immersed in each other's business that they feel a compulsion to keep in touch. Any scrap of a story is gathered in and stored away. Their knowledge of each other is truly extraordinary" (1983, p. 50). One should expect, therefore, to keep in continual communication with those in a polychronic system. The communicator diminishes the effectiveness of his or her communication if such contact remains limited to times of direct need. Moreover, the monochronic belief that one must keep to the task at hand and avoid straying from a given subject is likely to clash with the polychronic need to stay informed of all aspects of the people with whom one communicates. The monochronic individual will likely insist on limiting communication to one subject at a time. The polychronic individual approaches communication holistically, handling numerous and often ostensibly unrelated subjects simultaneously.

The influence on communication of temporal conception is extensive. This is further complicated by the fact that no culture is exclusively polychronic or monochronic. Members of any culture lean to one direction or the other, although the cultures as a whole often organize their thoughts and conceive of time more one way or the other. The central issue here is to remain alert to communication differences that would indicate that one culture was more monochronic or polychronic. Armed with this awareness, the individual can adapt his or her communication strategies to avoid the pseudoconflict that the clash of these two temporal systems often creates.

Nonverbal Communication Behavior

As discussed in Chapter 3, nonverbal behavior plays a key role in interpersonal communication. As might be expected from that discussion, one of the most markedly varying dimensions of intercultural communication is nonverbal behavior. Because the topic has already been examined in depth the discussion that follows represents only a brief overview of some of the more prominent cross-cultural aspects of nonverbal communication.

Knowledge of a culture conveyed through what a person says represents only a portion of what that person has communicated. Equally important to full communication is, in the words of Edward Hall, "the nonverbal language which exists in every country of the world and among various groups within each country. Most Americans are only dimly aware of this silent language even though they use it every day" (1959, p. 10).

Although the subject of nonverbal communication as a whole is broader, much of this "silent language" in cross-cultural situations may be broken down into six areas: dress; kinesics, or body language; oculesics, or eye contact; haptics, or touching behavior; proxemics, or the use of body space; and paralanguage. Any one of these areas communicates significant information nonverbally in any given culture.

The fact that individuals from different cultures may have different interpretations for identical nonverbal clues can easily lead to conflict based on misunderstanding. In the arena of dress, for example, a European or North American may interpret as somewhat less than civilized and competent an Arab or Malaysian in traditional garb. Conflict could arise in this case if the European or North American were, based on the difference in appearance, to patronize his or her Arab or

Malaysian counterpart. Conversely, an Arab or Malaysian may well consider as flagrantly immoral the bare face, arms, and legs of a European or North American woman in a standard business suit. Conflict in such a situation could arise if the Arab or Malaysian were to indicate a sense of disdain or even refuse to deal with her because of this perceived affront to social and religious standards.

Differences in kinesics are often more subtle. Still, how people walk, gesture, bow, stand, or sit are all to a large part culturally determined. Thus the various interpretations of day-to-day gestures, for example, may well not prove valid when people communicating are from different cultures. Ruesch and Kees (1964) have asserted that not only do the types and frequency of gestures that people use vary from culture to culture but also that even the underlying purposes for using gestures are culture bound. Thus they suggest that

> *gesture among the Americans is largely oriented toward activity; among the Italians it serves the purposes of illustration and display; among the Germans it specifies both attitude and commitment; and among the French it is an expression of style and containment.* (p. 22)

Kinesics appear to be linked to the language of a culture as well. As Genelle Morain (1987) has noted, those who viewed Fiorello LaGuardia in newsreel films in which the soundtrack was off were able to tell whether New York's trilingual mayor was speaking English, Italian, or Yiddish, based merely on the culturally linked kinesics he used while speaking.

In many cases a kinesic sign or emblem well understood in one culture is totally unknown in another. In Indonesia and in much of the Arab world, for example, it is offensive to show the soles of one's feet or shoes to another. This often clashes with behavior in the United States, where foot crossing is common, and no attention is paid to where one's sole points. In Japan a relatively elaborate system of bowing at varying degrees is common but has no counterpart in Europe or the Americas. This entire system of very expressive nonverbal communication is therefore lost in much Japanese interaction with those from other cultures.

Conflict deriving from misunderstanding can occur in instances when a person from one culture expects an individual from another culture to understand the message he or she delivers nonverbally and the person receiving that message does not respond as the sender expects. Much more serious conflict can arise, however, when sending a nonverbal message that is recognized but that means something quite different in the culture of the person receiving the message. One rather famous example took place during the cold war between the United States and the Soviet Union. The Soviet head of state, Nikita Khruschev, visited the United States on a state visit. When he was met at the airport, he clasped his hands together and raised them over his shoulder. This gesture was duly shown over the television and in papers and readily misinterpreted. To the U.S. audience, Khruschev's gesture looked like that of a victorious boxer, with all its connotations. As a Russian, however, Khrushchev intended the nonverbal message to symbolize the clasping of hands in friendship. Thus in the 1987 Leningrad concert of the U.S. musician Billy Joel, the crowd of Russian youths filling the concert hall almost all clasped their hands over their heads in a similar gesture.

Haptics, or touching behavior, also reflects cultural values. For example, in a generally nonhaptic society such as Japan, touching another person for any reason in public is traditionally avoided. Thus when non-Japanese shake hands with the Japanese, the Japanese are using an essentially unfamiliar practice. Conflict can occur when a non-Japanese interprets the limp or stiff handshake of a Japanese as a sign of weakness or formality rather than merely as a sign of unfamiliarity or lack of practice. The southern U.S. practice of friendly back slapping or exchanging hugs would likely be even more unfamiliar and because of its increased use of touch, might prove distasteful to the Japanese or persons of other less haptic cultures. The United States itself is a fairly nonhaptic society, particularly among men. In many cultures that behave more haptically, expressive men often walk with arms interlinked or hold hands, behavior that to U.S. males might appear effeminate or overly intimate.

The use and meaning of eye contact, or oculesics, also varies significantly, depending on the culture involved. In several cultures, for example, it is considered disrespectful to prolong eye contact with those who are older or of higher status. In many cultures it may be considered improper for women—regardless of age or status—to look men in the eye. By contrast, studies have shown that eye contact in the United States has less to do with age or rank (Beebe, 1974; Ellsworth and Ludwig, 1972)—although not necessarily so with gender (Henley, 1977)—than with a person's sense of belonging or credibility. Although fairly steady eye contact in the United States may indicate the listener's interest and attentiveness, intense eye contact may provide anxiety or imply a threat because we have learned to interpret a stare in such ways.

What is important for the communicator to recall is that such an interpretation is culturally determined. Edward Hall notes, for example, that "Arabs look each other in the eye when talking with an intensity that makes Americans highly uncomfortable" (1966, p. 151). Similarly, Jensen observes that "the educated Briton considers it part of good listening behavior to stare at his conversationalist and to indicate his understanding by blinking his eyes, whereas we Americans nod our head or emit some sort of grunt, and are taught from childhood not to stare at people" (1982, p. 265). By contrast, Dodd observes that Cambodians believe that meeting the gaze of another is insulting—something akin to "invading one's privacy" (1982, p. 14).

The degree to which eye contact in these examples is either greater or lesser than the amount considered appropriate according to the culture perceiving it is often misinterpreted. A culture with relatively more eye contact would be considered overly aggressive or threatening by an individual from a culture with less eye contact. A culture with relatively less eye contact, in turn, may be stereotyped as aloof, bored, or cold by an individual from a culture with more eye contact. Such misinterpretation may serve as barriers to effective cross-cultural interaction.

Finally, how far apart people stand from one another—proxemics—carries significant information to people who share the same culture. Here, too, as with other nonverbal behavior, such information is likely to be misinterpreted or misunderstood across cultures (Hall, 1961; Mehrabian, 1981). Copeland and Griggs have observed that "Americans are most comfortable when standing a little over an arm's length apart" (1985, p. 17). In many Latin American, southern European, and Middle Eastern cultures, however, a comfortable distance would be much closer. Indeed in many parts of the world friendly or serious conversations are conducted close enough to feel the breath of the speaker on one's face.

Conflict based on misunderstanding can arise from these proxemic differences when distance considered too far or too close in one's own culture is interpreted erroneously as being either too intrusive and aggressive or too distant and formal. For example, a U.S. or Norwegian communicator unaware of a different individual use of spatial distance among Greeks or Algerians will face a very discomforting situation with the Greeks or Algerians literally backing their Norwegian or U.S. counterparts into a corner, as one party continues to move closer to the other party, who in turn continues to retreat.

ACTION

We have now established that conflict deriving from misunderstanding often occurs when communicating across cultures. We have established that such misunderstanding are likely to occur from differences in language, environment and technology, thought processing, and nonverbal communication behavior. Merely recognizing and acknowledging such differences, however, is not enough to prevent the attendant pseudoconflict likely to occur.

The course of action for diminishing the possibility of pseudoconflict deriving from intercultural communication differences can follow the twelve-point procedure described in the action-interaction portion of Chapter 1.

1. *Establish credibility.* As Triandis (1976) implies, the ability to understand and acknowledge the similarities and differences between cultures leads to mutual respect and credibility in dealing with people from that culture. Armed with knowledge of the appropriate culture, one is best able to establish credibility with those from that culture. To obtain that knowledge one should seek out as much information as possible on the culture in question not only through reading or films but also through asking those from that culture or those who are familiar with it. It is important to stress that rather than approaching a culture with a list of "do's and don'ts," it is best to ask questions along the lines of cultural differences in language, environment and technology, thought processing, and nonverbal behavior. This way one approaches the culture from a foundation of understanding on which to build a recognition of likely behavior. A catalog of differences may tend to reinforce foreignness, undermining the fact that people behave as they do precisely because it makes sense within their culture to act in that manner.

2. *Establish trust.* Understanding differences and similarities between cultures is the essential first step on which all cross-cultural communication-conflict containment should rest, but understanding itself is not enough. One must at all times work to establish trust in intercultural interpersonal interaction. Singer has pointed out that particularly in intercultural situations, "people who attribute a statement to someone they trust are likely to believe it, while if they attribute the same statement to someone they distrust they tend not to" (1987, p. 152). The difficulty is that that which conveys trust is itself often culturally determined. Thus in a low-context society a signed contract may provide evidence that an individual can trust another. In a high-context society, by contrast, a contract is only as valid as the relationship between the people involved—if the people do not know each other enough to trust each other before signing the contract, the contract itself will do little to offset that inherent lack of trust. Thus to establish trust in a multicultural setting, it is necessary to recognize and then act on the principles that convey trust within the specific cultures involved.

3. *Express problem.* Although one needs to express the existence of a problem enough to recognize that a problem needs solving, it is important to remember that not all cultures respond identically to having a matter directly stated. The way a problem is expressed may prove difficult as well. As Stewart points out, "The conceptualization of the world in terms of problems" (1987, p. 55) to be solved in a rational way is a cultural tendency among those from the United States that is not widely shared. Although the United States is not the only culture to emphasize rational, means-oriented problem solving, it is important to remember that in dealing with other cultures—for example, those in East Asia and the Middle East—other perfectly acceptable means for conceptualizing conflict exist.

Thus the need to save face or the willingness to bow to the hand of God or fate may well prove more important than rational analysis. As Graham and Herberger (1987) observe, the standard U.S. approach to problem solving is to "lay your cards on the table." This approach demands a straightforward statement of points of view on a seemingly immutable truth. New conflict can easily arise from trying to solve existing conflicts if such a problem-solving style is not adapted to the way in which problems are raised in other cultures. As Gudykunst and Kim (1992) observe: "[P]eople in collectivistic cultures prefer indirect styles of dealing with conflict, which allow all parties to preserve face. They tend to use obliging and smoothing styles of conflict resolution or avoid the conflict altogether" (p. 85). For example, being intentionally deceptive about the facts of a matter or making another person expend a great deal of effort merely to determine the accurate facts of an issue are both considered abhorrent in the United States. Indeed such behavior may be enough to bring conflict negotiation to an end. However, as Graham and Herzberger note, "in Brazil, being tricky is a less serious transgression of negotiation ethics. It's even expected if a strong personal relationship between negotiators does not exist" (1987, p. 80).

4. *Accurate communication.* "The more culturally different the individuals are," Marshall Singer writes, "the more likelihood there is of distortion" (1987, p. 145). The problem in communicating across cultures is twofold. First, as with any interpersonal communication, a degree of error exists between what the sender of a message believes he or she has communicated and the way the person receiving that message interprets it. Here the principles described in Chapter 2 on verbal communication should be applied. This problem, however, is compounded in communication across languages, as discussed earlier, by the inexactness inherent in any translation. We can offset this by choosing a translator or interpreter with great care. Thus we would not trust an acquaintance with some high school French to translate an important letter. Nor should such a person with a few phrases of Vietnamese be viewed as particularly qualified to act as a crisis-center interpreter for a substantial Vietnamese-speaking community. Although some language knowledge is better than none in many instances, the importance of finding the best-qualified translator or interpreter in any situation in which accurate communication is important should not be underestimated.

5. *Recognizing status.* The role of status has a great deal of variance across cultures. For example, the United States as a culture places far greater emphasis on egalitarianism than do most other cultures (Adler, 1986; Fisher, 1980; Graham and Herberger, 1987). This takes the form of using first names, downplaying titles, and viewing status-related ceremonies as a waste of time. Such behavior, much to the amazement of people from many other cultures, actually places people from the United States at ease. However, as Nancy Adler notes, "Most countries are more hierarchical and more formal than the United States, and most foreigners feel more comfortable in formal situations with explicit status differences" (1986, p. 163). Thus people in Japan exchange business cards on meeting each other not so much to keep in touch, as in the United States, but to allow each other to know their official status. People in Germany would no sooner call each other by their first names in a business meeting than they would show up to that meeting in beach attire. The use of formal titles and the following of ceremony are not the only means to confer status, however.

Cultural values toward age, gender, and the social class into which one is born all play a strong role in many cultures' view of status. Although such characteristics cannot be changed to accommodate another culture's values, it is possible to substitute others who are older, male, of a different social class, and so forth. Accommodating a culture's different beliefs on these characteristics, however, in itself raises ethical issues likely to create other types of conflict. What is important to the communicator hoping to lessen the possibility of avoidable negative conflict is to be aware that such status-linked differences exist for various cultures and to try, through recognition, to offset to whatever degree possible the conflict arising between differing views of these variant values. Thus a young person representing her university at a conference in China, which confers greater status on those who are older, would be advised to emphasize those areas of status—rank, accomplishments— qualifying her to represent her university. At the same time, she would be advised to show respect for those Chinese older than her and not to diminish their values even though by her very presence as university representative she does not adhere to those values.

6. *Establish goals.* In the cross-cultural arena, as with the other forms of communication-based conflict management discussed in this book, the establishment of goals is necessary to work toward objectives for overcoming the conflict at hand. In cross-cultural communication, though, the form that those goals may take is shaped by the process a culture prefers in reaching those goals. The way in which a culture processes thought, as we have discussed, influences the way in which its members communicate. Thus although members of different cultures may agree to the same end goals, the way in which those goals are understood may prove to be so dissimilar that the identical goals may not be *perceived* as being the same. For example, if a person from New York were working with someone from Moscow and someone else from Tunis on how to solve world hunger, all three might agree on the end goal of eliminating hunger, but in the process of articulating the belief in that end goal, they might convince one another that they actually disagree.

Adler (1986) has chacterized North Americans as factual, Arabs as affective, and Russians as axiomatic. In an admittedly oversimplified version of this situation, the New Yorker might stress the factual: the number of hungry, the amount of money it would take to feed them, the system needed to transport the food, the organization of the people administering the program, and so forth. The Muscovite, in turn, might more likely appeal to the ideals at issue: Would all the hungry receive equal shares of food? Would the food be used as a means of one group to impose its will on another? What would be the long-term ideological consequences of feeding the hungry? The Tunisian, in turn, might choose to stress the affective details of the situation: the hardship the hungry experienced, the importance that the hungry not be forced to lose their essential human dignity in accepting the food, the long-term relationships and bonds that such a program would initiate. Moreover, disagreements on these issues could arise only if the three could reach a consensus to work together at all. Thus the New Yorker with a factual bias might feel justified in knowing in advance how much each of the others would contribute and when. The Tunisian, in turn, could conceivably interpret the demand for hard figures as a lack of good faith. The Muscovite might feel suspicious as to the asserted ideals behind such a request. This triangle of misinterpretation could take almost endless permutations as well.

Consequently the communicator should establish goals to reach consensus in conflict resolution. The communicator must, however, in the process of establishing those goals remain aware of the cultural factors discussed in this chapter already.

7. *Anticipate reactions.* As in all communication, it is important in intercultural exchange to assess the likely reaction of the audience with whom one communicates. The less one knows about the culture to which another belongs, though, the more difficult it is to anticipate that individual's likely reactions. In addition to acquiring as much information as possible before entering into an intercultural communication situation, one must actively attempt to seek out information even as the communication occurs. It is helpful to generalize about probable reactions, but such anticipated responses can easily transform into stereotypes if they are not continually modified. A broad range of behavior exists from person to person within the parameters of any given culture. One should therefore make generalizations regarding anticipated reactions with the express intent of disproving them.

8. *Give and receive feedback.* Several experts (Couch and Hintz, 1975; Ruben, 1987; Sarbaugh, 1979) suggest that among the most important dimensions of successful cross-cultural communication is the willingness to give and receive feedback. Ruben (1987) indicates two benefits of taking turns. First, reciprocity in communication implies interest in and concern for the other party, which contributes to building both the credibility and trust discussed earlier. The second benefit is the opportunity that giving and receiving feedback allows the communicator for collecting more information about the other party's culture, way of thinking, and communicational framework.

9. *Maintain adaptability.* To accommodate cultural differences, the ability to adapt to unfamiliar ways of doing things and of thinking of the world is necessary. Flexibility and the ability to remain nonjudgmental are keys to open and effective cross-cultural communication.

10. *Seek out creative means of problem solving.* Creativity is generally a useful attribute in attempting to resolve any conflict situation; in cross-cultural problem solving the need to seek creative solutions is particularly important for two reasons. First, seeking creative solutions to perceived conflict allows for greater opportunity to detour perceptual difficulties blocking a common solution. That is, by seeking nonconventional approaches to conflict resolution, it is possible to work around those pseudoconflicts that are based less on the facts of the situation at hand than on the culturally based differences in the *perception* of those facts.

Second, agreeing on common solutions in problem solving is important, but approaching a problem from one's own perspective is often unacceptable in reaching consensus with those from other cultures. The culture to which one belongs directly affects the manner of thinking about, outlook toward, and way in which problems are solved. The strategies a culture uses, as well as its institutions for dealing with conflict, reflect the basic values of that society (Likert and Likert, 1976; Moran and Harris, 1982). Seeking creative approaches to conflict management and problem solving allows for the members of all cultures concerned to create a new method of handling the situation at hand drawn from the principles on which the various cultures involved are based but not bound to any one culture's way of handling the problem. The creative combination of culturally divergent approaches to the same problem reduces the risk of antagonizing members of any of the cultures involved, because their own cultural input has been respected and in part used. Moreover, this creative combination of culturally divergent approaches to the problem allows for the opportunity for cultural synergy, in which the contributions of the various cultures involved in a problem create a stronger solution than any existing solutions to similar problems within a single culture (Adler, 1986; Moran and Harris, 1982). In such cases the sum of the parts is greater than the whole, as in the cultural synergy that came about in Japan in the 1960s by creatively combining aspects of U.S. and Japanese management approaches to create the so-called Theory Z management style (Ouchi, 1981).

11. *Maintain open channels of communication.* In all conflict management keeping the channels of communication open is important. In cross-cultural situations, however, as we have seen, this may at times prove to be particularly difficult. How to keep the channels open is itself culturally determined. For example, many cultures—most notably in Asia—do not value the airing of ideas and the expression of feelings; in the United States and much of Europe such behavior is often considered the *only* way to keep the channels of communication open. Similarly U.S. communicators tend to think in individualistic terms when keeping the channels of communication open. Indeed the central role of the individual has been suggested as being the most quintessentially characteristic of U.S. culture (Hofstede, 1992; Rogers, 1964; Stewart, 1987). Yet such an outlook may actually close down communication channels in collectivistic cultures that would not define problems in individualistic terms (Gudykunst and Kim, 1992; Ting-Toomey, 1985). Nevertheless, no matter what the cultural norms, it is possible to maintain open channels of communication once the communication process has been adjusted to accommodate those cultural norms.

12. *Summarize decisions.* Once conflict solutions have been decided, it is important to summarize those decisions for clarity and to ensure agreement. This would hold true whether dealing within a single or a multiple cultural setting. In a multicultural setting, though, summarizing decisions is particularly important, since the odds for inexact communication are higher. Just as pseudoconflict can occur when parties from different cultures perceive an irreconcilable difference where none exists, so too can *pseudoagreement* occur when those parties incorrectly perceive that a common solution exits. Summarizing decisions increases the opportunity for discovering such cross-cultural pseudoagreement.

ANALYSIS

To increase one's skills at communicating in a cross-cultural situation, it is necessary to analyze what has transpired once the twelve points of the action phase have been implemented. By reexamining what occurred in any given cross-cultural interaction, the communicator can adjust his or her behavior in future encounters.

The analysis process may be divided into three steps. First, the communicator should review the expectations he or she held before the cross-cultural encounter took place. By examining the expectations that were met and those that did not materialize, the communicator can gain valuable insights into how he or she stereotypes those from the culture in question.

Second, the communicator can sharpen his or her skills in communicating with those from the cultures in question by noting in the cross-cultural encounter any behavior that was unexpected both on his or her own part and on the part of the person from the other culture. Moreover, the communicator would do well to try to determine why the behavior he or she has observed has taken place. Communicators should also remain aware of their emotions and feelings regarding the cross-cultural encounter. Even though these emotions and feelings may not surface as observable behavior, they provide valuable clues to analyzing how one approaches cross-cultural interactions.

Finally, the communicators are advised to record their observations in writing. Then immediately before and after future cross-cultural encounters, they should review these notes not only to determine how much they have remembered but also, more important, to establish to what extent their views may have changed. They can further understand their thought processing by establishing why these views have altered. They should try to determine whether these changes are due to the distancing effect of time or through reading or through other cross-cultural experiences and why factors affected their beliefs.

By analyzing their cross-cultural experiences in this manner, communicators can learn to adjust behavior in future encounters. This way they can develop a truly multicultural understanding and in so doing greatly reduce the risk of future culturally based conflict.

SUMMARY

In situations involving parties from two or more cultures, the differences in those cultures can seriously affect communication. This chapter has discussed the role misunderstandings and perceived conflict—or pseudo-conflict—play in cross-cultural communication. Ways to reduce the negative effects of communication-based pseudoconflict derived from cultural differences were also discussed.

Several steps need to be followed in managing cross-cultural misunderstandings. The first step is assessment of the unique features of cross-cultural communication. This involves both the recognition of the importance of culture in communication and basic understanding of culture in the abstract. Only then is it possible to see the climate in which communication-based cross-cultural conflict takes place clearly enough to manage conflict situations likely to occur in a multicultural setting.

The second step is acknowledgment, which involves examining why culturally caused misunderstanding occurs. To do so, the communicator must grapple with his or her own ethnocentrism and develop empathy for the other party. Understanding the other party's perspective reduces the level of uncertainty in any cross-cultural communication.

The third and most difficult step is attitude adjustment. This step involves analyzing the possible sources of cross-cultural pseudoconflict in both the communicator's own behavior and the behavior of the culturally different parties with whom he or she interacts. To this end a cross-cultural communication checklist was discussed, covering the four main factors likely to create pseudoconflict in such situations: language, place, thought processing, and nonverbal communication behavior. To some extent all four of these factors appear to be deceptively universal albeit changing—often dramatically—from culture to culture.

A fourth step, action, was discussed next. The twelve-point plan of action for reducing communication-based conflict was adapted to meet the needs of the cross-cultural communicator. Applying this plan of action will not necessarily eliminate all culturally derived pseudoconflict but is nonetheless a means to actively reduce the barriers to cross-cultural communication that cause pseudoconflict.

Finally, a last step—analysis—was suggested. By analyzing what occurred in each cross-cultural interaction to reexamine what transpired, the communicator can learn to adjust behavior in future multicultural encounters and, through this, lessen the chance for future culturally based conflict.

SUGGESTED ACTIVITIES

A. FOCUS ON STEREOTYPING

Students or seminar participants are each given a piece of white chalk taken from a box of chalk in which the pieces look as much alike as possible. The students are then given five minutes to examine their particular piece of chalk closely, selecting features that give it its own unique characteristics. Then the students are asked to write down their observations regarding their piece of chalk. Selected students read their observations aloud. The class should discuss the differences observed in the chalk pieces. A comparison between chalk and people should lead to a discussion of stereotyping and to the power to observe differentiating details among seemingly like elements.

The instructor should next collect the chalk, taking care to note where the chalk pieces belonging to two or three students have been placed. Laying the chalk pieces out on a table or desk, the instructor should call on the students who laid down the chalk pieces whose placement he or she had noted. A discussion may then follow, depending on whether the students were able to pick out the pieces they had studied.

B. FOCUS ON SELF-AWARENESS

Each student or seminar participant should be asked to recall an encounter with a person from another culture. A student who does not know someone from another culture should be asked to recall such an encounter with a person from another ethnic group. Students should then divide a piece of paper into three columns, as follows:

Before	During	After
1	1	1
2	2	2
3	3	3
4	4	4
5	5	5

Students should next record in the *before* column five expectations they remember having had before their encounter regarding people from that culture. They should then record in the *during* column their thoughts while the encounter occurred regarding that expectation. Then the students should indicate in the *after* column their current feelings toward each of the expectations they listed regarding the culture in question.

Students should then discuss or write a short analysis about why their expectations changed or remained constant. They should also comment on how those expectations might have created or avoided possible points of conflict, depending on the inconsistency or consistency of those expectations.

An illuminating extension of this exercise is to have the students share these observations with someone from the culture in question. Does the person from that culture share the views of his or her culture that the student's evaluation suggests?

C. FOCUS ON LANGUAGE AND CONTEXT

Students or group participants should be broken into an even number of small groups. Each small group should be instructed to select three nonsense phrases to replace three common expressions. For example, the nonsense word *quibblezip* might be used to replace the phrase *Do you know what I mean?*

The small groups should then be paired off. The class should be given a subject to discuss, perhaps the ways in which language and contexting may create pseudoconflict in cross-cultural communication. In the discussion group members should use the common expressions they have selected, replacing the expression with the nonsense phrases they have selected.

The discussion should be allowed to run at least five minutes or more so that adequate time has been allowed for the expression to be used several times. At the close of the discussion, students should see whether they were able to identify the meaning of the nonsense phrases from context alone.

The class should then be polled as to how many people were able to identify all three phrases. A discussion should then follow on several subjects:

1. How did the students feel about the use of the nonsense phrases? Was it disruptive? Annoying? Stupid?

2. In what way could the way students felt about the use of the nonsense phrases lead to conflict?

3. What role did contexting play in determining the meaning of the non-sense phrases?

D. FOCUS ON ENVIRONMENT

Provide students or group participants with a photograph of a typical U.S. kitchen, a typical Japanese kitchen, and a typical German kitchen. (These may be obtained from advertisements, from photographs, or from books on interior design or architecture.)

Students should answer several questions to determine that the role the environment plays in shaping the outlook a person holds to be universal or at least normal:

1. How big is each kitchen compared to the others?

2. What sorts of appliances or objects do the three share? Are any of these appliances or objects different in any notable way? Why or why not?

3. Would cooking in the three kitchens differ? Would eating in the kitchens differ?

4. How would the differences in the three kitchens affect an advertising campaign for a microwave oven? For a dishwashing machine? For plastic storage containers?

5. Could differences in how the kitchen environment is used create a conflict between advertising executives determining the appropriate promotional campaign for these three cultures? For guests from one of these cultures in the homes of the other cultures? For others?

E. FOCUS ON SOCIAL ORGANIZATION

Students should select several magazines from the United States and several magazines from another country of their choice (obtainable through the library or an international magazine vendor). Students should examine advertising in the magazines for major items affecting the family (life or medical insurance, savings accounts, financial planning, and so on).

A discussion should follow regarding what these advertisements imply about the social organization of the culture from which they are taken. Students should answer questions such as the following:

1. Do the advertisements show pictures of a single man making a decision for his family? Are they shown with a husband and wife jointly making the decision? What does this say about the role of men in the society? Of married couples?

2. Are there children in the advertisements? If so, what role do they play? What does this say about the role played by family in these cultures?

3. Do the advertisements use animation or humorous pictures, or is the subject handled seriously? How much of the advertisement is devoted to printed material? How much is devoted to illustrations? Are they pertinent to the information, or are they intended to set a mood? What might this say about how the subjects of these advertisements are viewed in their respective cultures?

4. Could what the differences implied in these lead to conflict in other situations? Explain.

F. FOCUS ON NONVERBAL BEHAVIOR

Have participants or students watch a foreign film. What differences from the United States do they observe in kinesics? In proxemics? In eye contact? In touching behavior? A discussion should follow on how these differences could lead to misunderstanding and pseudoconflict.

G. FOCUS ON TEMPORAL CONCEPTION

Students or participants should divide into groups of three and hold a conversation on a topic of their choice, perhaps on the role temporal conception plays in communication. One person in each group should be instructed to count silently to twenty-five before responding to any comment or question. The other two members of the group should speak normally.

Following this conversation, students should examine how they felt about the delayed response time. Specifically they might find it useful to discuss some of the following questions.

For the students who employed the delayed response time:

1. Did you find it difficult to participate in the conversation?

2. Did you find any advantages to employing a delayed response time?

3. In the United States many people consider a quick response time a sign of high intelligence. This belief is not universally held. How does this make you feel about a culture that values a slower response time? Why do you think, based on your experience in this exercise, people in some cultures would think that a slow response time was favorable?

4. How might a delayed response time, when used in the United States, create conflict, particularly in a pressured or tense situation?

For the students who did not employ the delayed response time:

1. Did you find it difficult to converse with the person employing the slow response time?

2. What disadvantages did you observe about a person using a delayed response time? Did you see any advantages?

3. How might conflict result when people from the United States deal with someone from a culture in which a delayed response time was customary in pressured or tense situations?

6

HOW WRITING STYLES CAN CREATE CONFLICT

Points to Be Addressed

1. Written communication as a potential source of conflict;

2. Assessment: The importance of identifying the appropriate aim of written communication to minimize unnecessary conflict (conceptualization);

3. Acknowledgment: Anticipating the reader's expectations and capabilities (reception);

4. Attitude: Vocabulary variation, language misuse, and semantic unclarity as potential sources of pseudoconflict (transmittal);

5. Action: Three checklists to help the writer minimize, defuse, and/or avoid conflict.

Few communication tools serve to manage conflict as effectively as an appropriately chosen writing style. Unlike speech, writing allows the luxury of one-sided communication—a monologue weighted in the writer's favor. Writing, however, is not an easy task.

> *Writing is an unnatural activity. It must be taught formally and studied deliberately. And many of the problems that arise in learning to write are simply problems in finding the proper written equivalent for*

the materials of speech. The spelling of our words is a clumsy attempt to reproduce the sounds of our voices. The punctuation of our sentences and setting off of paragraphs is designed to give some approximation of the pauses and intonations we use automatically to give shape and point to our speaking. . . . If there were no compensations for all these disadvantages, then communicating with other people through the medium of squiggles on paper would be as unsatisfactory as trying to wash your feet with your socks on. Fortunately, there are compensations (even though that word are has to be printed in italic type in order to capture an intonation that would be conveyed effortlessly in speech). (Scholes and Klaus, 1972 p.)

Although writing well can prove to be among the strongest of tools to reduce the likelihood of conflict, inappropriate writing styles may not only increase existing levels of conflict but also often create conflict. How effectively a writer increases or reduces conflict is based largely on the tone and style the writer chooses, the situation at hand, and the perceived needs of the reader.

As discussed throughout this book, not all conflict is nonproductive. Controlled conflict that increases resourcefulness, competitiveness, or the testing of alternative viewpoints can provide an important managerial tool. However, conflict deriving expressly from the way in which something is written rather than from an underlying, intentional, and controlled source of conflict is almost always negative in its consequences. Such conflict arises from chance rather than choice and frequently escalates into damaging interpersonal relationships. Consequently many authors—particularly in the field of business— have stressed the importance of clear and accurate writing as a means of avoiding negative conflict (Munter, 1992; Murphy and Hildebrandt, 1984; Thill and Bouvee, 1996; Wolf and Kuiper, 1984).

To avoid the adverse consequences of unclear or unintentionally inflammatory writing style, it is important to take into account the three basic steps of writing: conceptualization, transmittal, and reception (Victor, 1986). Writing-style conflict comes from a misjudgment of one of these steps.

ASSESSMENT: A MATTER OF CONCEPTUALIZATION

The conceptualization process parallels the assessment step in the five-step model described in chapter one. Conceptualization requires that the writer firmly assess the purpose of his or her writing. Unless the writer clearly understands at the outset which objectives he or she wishes to accomplish through the piece of writing, it is unlikely that the reader will be able to understand fully what the writer intended to convey. The transmittal step is the process of putting words on paper. Several difficulties inherent in language itself may undermine, at times, even the best intentions. Finally, unless those words are chosen with the reader in mind, no matter how clearly the writer understands the message and its objectives, the reader may not receive them in the manner the writer desires. The writer who gives insufficient attention to any of these basic steps—conceptualization, transmittal, or reception—risks creating nonproductive writing-style conflict.

At the core of a great deal of conflict deriving from writing style is the writer's failure to conceptualize the purpose of the piece of writing. Unless the writer clearly understands the precise purpose of what he or she writes, the chance is greatly reduced that the reader will act in the intended manner after reading the message. The difference between the desired action and the actual outcome creates unecessary and nonproductive conflict.

When the written communication attempts to solve a problem, it might seem that the purpose of the piece would be obvious—to resolve the problem. Yet often before writing, the writer fails to anticipate precisely the nature of the problem.

For example, a company president may observe an increase in absenteeism in a certain company division. The president may then send a memorandum requesting a report from the division head. This might read: "Please summarize the performance of the personnel in your division." This request, in turn, could prove inadequate because it fails to explain the president's underlying purpose of gauging absenteeism. If the division head does not understand *why* the president has asked for the report, the report may inadequately describe, or even ignore, the absenteeism problem. Indeed, in attempting to place the division in the best possible light, the division head may not address the absenteeism problem at all, focusing instead on the division's increased production over the last quarter. Without direction from the president, the division head can only surmise the purpose of the report. Consequently the report does not solve the problem, and the president, by failing to specify a purpose, has wasted the division head's time and cost the company an unnecessary expense, and he still has no solution to the absenteeism problem.

Conceptualization, however, often goes beyond determining the purpose of the communication. Generally writers attempt to maintain a certain attitude in their writing. They may wish to persuade a reader to follow a certain suggestion, as in a sales letter, or they may wish simply to inform the reader while appearing as objective as possible, as in a financial statement. In other instances a writer's primary purpose may center on avoiding blame and give only secondary importance to explaining fully the facts of a situation.

Further difficulties may arise when writers fail to balance the content of their communication. Indeed writers may lose sight of the ostensible purpose of what they write if they become overly concerned with a secondary aim or with a purpose that for them is more important than it is for their readers. In turn, by attending only to the ostensible purpose, a writer may alarm the reader.

For example, the company president in the preceding example could have written a direct request for information regarding absenteeism in the division: "Please provide a report to me on the high rate of absenteeism in your division." In such a memorandum the president makes clear that the absentee rate in the division is of concern. In response the division head may well have written a different report but not necessarily one that would prove any more useful to the president. The division head, for instance, may have felt threatened by the president's inquiry. As a result, a large part of the report might attempt to deny direct responsibility for the absenteeism or to divert the president's attention from the problem of absenteeism to some positive aspect of the division, such as the increased productivity. The ostensible purpose of the report in such a case would be to inform the president about absenteeism in the division. The division head's primary purpose, however, is not the same as the ostensible purpose. Indeed the division head's primary purpose most likely is to avoid blame for the problem. If the division head were to concentrate too heavily on the attempt to deny responsibility, the report might still not contain the information the president needed. Ideally the division head would have balanced the need to inform the president against the need for protection. The president, however, could have saved time and might have received a more direct reply had the request indicated that no blame would be assigned or that the report should contain information only regarding the absenteeism rate.

When writing in a potentially explosive situation, writers must identify and address the potential conflict in the least antagonizing manner possible. Although anger or other strong emotional entrenchments often characterize a conflict situation, the expression of such feelings should rarely serve as one's purpose for writing. In particular, a number of experts have shown that threats or attempts to intimidate others through hostile or antagonizing statements reduce the ability to achieve consensus among parties in conflict (Bales, 1970; Burke, 1970). Rather, writers in potentially explosive situations should attempt to maintain as objective a tone as they can. To do so, they should stress objectively concrete goals or suggestions. William Brooks and Philip Emmert note:

"When messages are orientational and substantive, when they clarify and emphasize expectations, procedures, sanctions, and promises of reward, then cooperative behavior is likely to be facilitated" (1976, p. 230). Bearing this in mind, the writer may have to alter the very nature of the content (that is, the ostensible purpose) of the message if one of the primary purposes for writing is to avoid or to manage conflict.

In any case, for the writer to write as if no factors outside of the ostensible purpose mattered in a conflict situation will increase the inherent tensions needlessly. Only after adjusting the tone and focus of the message to reduce as much as possible any inherent tension can the writer safely address the ostensible issue at hand.

ACKNOWLEDGMENT: RECEPTION

To reduce effectively the possible tensions inherent in a message, the writer must thoroughly analyze how the reader may receive the message. To analyze the way a reader receives a given message is to acknowledge or to attempt to understand the reader's perception. Arguably the most dangerous conflict-causing error a writer can make is to write a message as if it were intended for the writer alone, without consideration for the reader. At the source of such an error is the writer's failure to recognize that writing is only as effective as its ability to influence the message's reader in the manner the writer envisions. Unless the writer *anticipates* the message's reception—that is, the likely reaction of the reader—the ability of the writing to influence the message's reader in the desired manner will rest on chance rather than on choice. In short, writing that does not consciously attempt to accommodate the likely reactions of its recipient seriously diminishes its reliability and may provoke conflict.

For example, a letter to a union's membership regarding a less than favorable collective-bargaining agreement with an employer may read as follows: "The following letter details the results of our union's recent collective-bargaining session. Though all our demands were not met, we believe that the members will find that the key issues are addressed." By contrast, the same letter directed to the employer's management team might read: "The following letter details the results of the negotiation with Local 123 of the XYZ Union. Unfortunately, several points had to be conceded to reach a settlement. The consequences should be mitigated by avoiding a lengthy strike that may have severely affected production and long-term profits."

Although the content in both letters is essentially the same, the writer has adjusted each letter's tone and format to account for the fact that one audience would read such information as bad news, whereas the other would see it as potentially good news. Still, writers in such situations all too frequently consider only their purpose at hand—to indicate the results of the new labor–management collective-bargaining agreement.

The need to analyze and to acknowledge one's audience before actually writing, however, holds even when dealing with less obviously inflammatory situations than that just described. By attempting to visualize a specific picture of the recipient of their communication, writers can reduce many potential conflicts inherent in a one-sided communication medium such as writing, which does not allow the reader to respond quickly.

Those writers least likely to create unproductive conflict among their readers visualize their receivers in detail—a process we can call *audience analysis*. They acknowledge the attitudes, rank, age, gender, experience, area of expertise, or whatever pertinent data they can accumulate about those to whom they write. Even if they send a message of some sort to an unknown recipient, such writers attempt to construct a concept of a plausible recipient. If the piece of communication is written for a group, an effective writer will focus on as specific a representative sampling as possible and write for that particular audience. Above all, those writers least likely to create unproductive conflict among their readers attempt to anticipate and adjust their writing for the possible response their communication is likely to provoke.

ATTITUDE: TRANSMITTAL

The analysis of purpose and audience addresses what may well be possible sources of true conflict. The interim step in the communication process in which the conceptualization (purpose) is *transmitted* to the recipient (audience) often does not represent a true conflict at all, however. To the extent that conflict-free transmittal of a message hinges on the consideration of behavior and perspective from the point of view of both writer and reader, it parallels the "attitude" step of our model. Transmittal problems in writing often represent perceived disagreements or pseudoconflicts on the part of parties who actually do agree.

Although such superficial conflict may initially appear easy to control, frequently it remains deceptively difficult to contain at the simplest stage. As Miller and Steinberg observe, "pseudoconflicts are quite difficult to manage effectively. People frequently jump to conclusions about the reality of the perceived conflict and never think to verify their perceptions" (1975, p. 267).

These assumptions or false conclusions may readily escalate to the level of what Miller and Steinberg term ego conflict (1975, p. 267). Ego conflict is the state in which conflicting parties become so involved emotionally in their perception of the conflict that they can no longer divest themselves of inherently hostile relational transactions without losing face or feeling deep resentment. Ego conflicts often occur in contract negotiations in which each party represents his or her interests. Fees and terms offered may be viewed as an affront by the potential contractee, whereas the contractor may be attempting only to make the best possible deal for the organization, without considering how his or her actions may affect the quality of the work of the contractee. Even if a neutral arbiter points out that the difficulty is only a pseudo-conflict based on a misunderstanding, the parties are often too deeply involved at that point to allow cooperative communication to resolve their differences.

In writing, pseudoconflict normally arises from two causes. The first derives simply from errors in writing style, *unrecognized linguistic communication conflict*. The second cause, tonal error, rests not in the misuse of the language but in the miscalculation of the wording required to best address the reader's needs while fulfilling the purpose intended.

Transmissional—or linguistic communication—conflict has at its root the fact that language is itself a faulty means of communication (Bloom, 1981; Whorf, 1952). As discussed throughout this book, all languages are at best approximate media for conveying information. Three basic factors contribute to the inability to communicate in differing degrees: vocabulary variation, language misuse, and semantic unclarity.

Vocabulary Variation

Vocabulary variation takes two forms: dialect differences and professional jargon. Both tend to limit the number of readers who can understand fully what is written. A reader's inability to follow the meaning of a message due to vocabulary variation can in itself cause conflict through misinterpretation. Moreover, preconceived attitudes toward particular variants may isolate or even antagonize those who do not share those variations.

Dialect Differences
Of the two forms vocabulary variation takes, dialect differences in formal writing are less likely to produce conflict through actual misinter-

pretation. Regional slang or colloquialisms, however, are still often limited enough to mislead or alienate those who do not belong to the group, and consequently most writers should take care to avoid such phrasing.

Nevertheless even though most readers can understand dialect differences, conflict often arises from their use, for a secondary reason. Sociolinguistic biases regarding certain uses of the language often encourage some groups to look down on those using forms they consider substandard (Chaika, 1982; Trudgill, 1974). Thus a reader accustomed to standard American English may look down on the language of a writer using an Appalachian or other nonstandard dialect. Although the reader understands what the writer means, the reader may not give full credit to the writer's ideas, because the dialect of the writing may not appear educated enough to merit full credibility.

In return, emotional defensiveness might arise on the part of those groups whose dialects may have been viewed, for whatever reason, in a negative light. The consequent emotional investment could then easily lead to ego conflict based on the variant-dialect users' indignation. Similarly the standard-dialect user is likely to view the variant dialect as wrong (rather than different) and so may become emotionally invested in maintaining what he or she perceives to be correct usage.

Professional Jargon

Vocabulary variation does not manifest itself most problematically in dialect differences but rather in the use of professional jargon. In an age of increasingly specialized labor and complicated technology, many professions have developed their own vocabulary variations, a sort of occupational dialect.

As with all vocabulary variation, jargon risks confusing the reader who is unfamiliar with it. Worse than this, jargon often acts as a profession's passwords to exclude those who do not belong to the group. Thus jargon often intimidates those unfamiliar with it, especially newcomers to the profession or those outside it. This in turn may lead to open conflict if the readers unfamiliar with the jargon feel patronized, isolated, or less intelligent. In turn, they attempt to equalize the perceived power imbalance by, for example, making the jargon user feel incompetent. Similarly, uninitiated readers may believe that their lack of understanding diminishes their credibility in the organization or in the specialized field that uses the jargon. Subsequently they may react rashly to protect themselves and, by failing to take the necessary time and care in their actions, unnecessarily create conflict situations. Finally, readers may feel hostile toward the writer who uses jargon, as they believe—often justly—that the writer deliberately uses such language either to belittle or to confuse them. For example, house buyers may grow irritated with a mortgage company that has written the mortgage agreement in language they cannot understand. This sense of irritation is likely to stem from a feeling that the company is deliberately obfuscating the agreement to take advantage of them. The resultant ego conflict involved in such a reaction may be very difficult to overcome.

Language Misuse

Language misuse, the second element in written linguistic communication conflict, falls into either usage ignorance or ambiguity. Many writers, even successful politicians and executives and respected educators and scientists, are ignorant of the basic rules governing their language. They misconjugate verbs or vary their verb tenses without reason. They misspell words (some classics are "seperate" rather than "separate," "definate" rather than "definite") or choose words that do not mean what they intend. They use double negatives or indecipherably entangled syntax. To compound the matter, many of these people are wholly unaware of their errors. Like vocabulary variations, errors due to ignorance of grammar may lead to conflict when the writer's words become so unclear as to be incomprehensible. Similarly, readers who catch the writer's mistakes may consider themselves superior to the writer and either disregard or look down on the content of the message.

Conflict arises because the grammar errors reflect only on the writer's ability to handle the language and not on the reasoning behind the message. Such emotional overtones and prejudice, as with dialect differences, are deeply rooted in the reader's preconceptions about education, language, and competency. Still, the reader must attempt to see beyond such superficial difficulties to the actual message at hand. Only in this way can the reader prevent escalating the situation from one based on inaccurate communication (but one in which both parties essentially agree) to real conflict, potentially involving the emotional entrenchment of both parties.

Ambiguity is language misuse that is technically correct but carries more than one acceptable meaning. As language itself is an imperfect medium to convey ideas, such situations are relatively common. At times ambiguity adds power to the language. Ambiguity is a favorite device of poets. For example, in Wallace Stevens's famous poem "Anecdote of the Jar," he opens as follows:

I placed a jar in Tennessee
And round it was, upon a hill.

Here the phrase "And round it was," can refer both to the poet, who stayed "'round" the jar, and to the shape of the jar itself. The ambiguity adds resonance to the poem and makes it amusing to read. Imagine such ambiguity in a business situation, however, and the results can become disastrous.

Suppose that an employee wrote in a memorandum: "I have discussed planting the landscape with managers." Like the ambiguous line in the poem, this statement carries more than one meaning. Had the employee discussed *using* the managers—rather than gardeners—to plant the landscape? A reader might even read such a statement as meaning that the employee intends to plant the landscape *with* managers (rather than bushes or trees). Still, as these two meanings are somewhat nonsensical, most readers will understand that the writer had discussed with managers ideas regarding the landscape. The writer will be understood but will likely lose credibility as an effective communicator.

Unfortunately many ambiguities are not so clearly unraveled. For instance, readers would more likely feel confused if the same employee had written: "I discussed running the program with the temporary workers." As in the previous example, the reader may infer more than one meaning from this sentence. In this case, though, both meanings make sense. On the one hand, the writer might have meant that she had discussed with the temporary workers a way to run the program. Just as plausibly, though, a reader might interpret her to mean that she had discussed a way to use temporary workers for running the program. As readers have no way of knowing which interpretation is correct, they may act in a manner that the writer did not intend. The resulting misinterpretation, depending on its seriousness, could easily escalate to open conflict, as both writer and readers would feel fully justified in the actions they took.

Semantic Unclarity

The last category of linguistic communication conflict is semantic unclarity. Semantics, the meanings or connotations of words, vary in the emphasis different words have for different readers. As discussed earlier, readers bring their own experiences to bear when interpreting any communicative act. Different environmental, social, and cultural influences shape each reader's understanding of the world. These different views of the world, in turn, tend to influence the subtle variations different readers associate with the same word. The word *pet*, for example, may mean a dog to one reader or a cat to another or may bring to mind first a rabbit, horse, hamster, or any other tame animal kept for companionship or affection's sake. Such different conceptions on first reading any given word reflect the different perceptions of reality each person brings to bear in any communication process. Such a process, admittedly, is not particularly problematic when dealing with the semantics of such a word as *pet*, as this word is relatively concrete.

By contrast, when words do not describe something that can be understood through the senses—when they must be understood in abstract terms—the difficulty of semantics increases. When words describe concepts that the reader comprehends only through comparative analysis, the reader's experience with the range of comparison for that term dictates his or her feelings regarding its meaning. Such terms as *efficient* or *expensive* vary according to the reader's experience. Managers who have transferred from a division of the company accustomed to completing its inventory of supplies over a three-week period to a division that customarily completes the same task in one week will find that their conception of the word *efficient* is highly subjective. Similarly an executive whose travel budget averages over $2000 each trip may regard a month's business trip costing $1500 as comparatively inexpensive, whereas a worker whose annual travel budget is only $500 may see such a trip as impossibly expensive.

To some extent the subjectivity of the meaning of words described here holds true for all communication, spoken or written. In spoken communication, however, the speaker may be cued to misunderstanding by nonverbal signals or by the immediate response of the listener. In writing the word stands by itself, with no external clues regarding interpretation. Consequently the chances for such miscommunication and attendant conflict increase with written communication.

If writers recognize the inherent conflict involved in comparative terminology, they can attempt to surmount such impediments to accurate communication by stating their ideas more concretely. Rather than ordering an employee to perform a job more effectively, the writer would do better to specify what constitutes effective. To do this the writer must spell out in precise terms that degree of impact regarding time, audience reaction, or amount of profit expected from the employee for the given job.

Semantic misunderstandings increase even further when the abstract terms the writer chooses lack even a comparative base. Such terms as *liberty, friendship, morality*, or *happiness* have vastly different meanings for each person, with little or no common base of comparison. Assuming that others automatically share one's understanding of a comparative or abstract term openly invites conflict. As discussed earlier, such abstract terms depend largely on culturally learned attitudes and values as well. Consequently semantic difficulties in dealing with abstract terms are compounded when interacting with those from different cultures. A Japanese, a British, and a U.S. concept of such a term as *politeness* would vary extensively, depending on its cultural milieu. Because no absolute notion of politeness exists, the writer must carefully gauge the meaning of the word within its cultural context.

A final reason that semantic difficulties often lead to conflict, even when readers share an essentially similar conception of reality, is that many words carry more than one meaning. For example, the English word *sensitive* has varying shades of meaning, depending on the context of the sentence. An employee reading his company file may understand a report calling him a *sensitive person* to mean that his superiors viewed him as one who is alert and considerate about other persons' feelings. At the same time, the superior who wrote the evaluation may have viewed him as one who becomes easily hurt or offended. The former meaning would usually be recognized as a positive statement; the latter, a negative one. Even in the same context this subtle but important shading of the word could connote two contrasting meanings. The result of reading the positive evaluation of *sensitive* in the more negative sense of the word might well produce a pseudoconflict with enough emotional overtones to escalate readily to a state of ego conflict.

Tonal error is the other factor that frequently contributes to pseudoconflict in writing style. Tone in writing may be roughly defined as the manner of expression of character prevailing in a given piece of writing. If that manner of writing antagonizes the reader, even if both reader and writer agree on the issue at hand, pseudoconflict will arise and can easily escalate into full-scale interactional opposition.

Tone generally rests in choosing the best use of emotion for a particular situation. All writing carries within it an emotional balance. Even writing that might be considered wholly objective holds its place on the emotional spectrum as disinterested or lacking in feeling. Were a letter expressing closeness to be written in a purely objective tone, for example, it might appear cold or distant. Contrast the effect of these two, termination letters:

- "We no longer have use for your services. You may pick up your final check this Friday."
- "We cannot renew your contract at this time. Your services have been highly valued by this firm, but economic realities have caused us to cut back and to eliminate all but essential services. We wish you the best in your future endeavors and hope to join forces again at some more prosperous time."

No formula exists for choosing the best tone. It must be selected to match each situation. To best choose the right tone, one should judge it as the ideal spot on a scale between two opposites. Thus to determine how accepting a tone one should adopt, it would be best to estimate the most appropriate degree between openly hostile and uninhibitedly happy. Similarly one must gauge on such a scale of opposites the best tone for all emotions that seem pertinent to the situation.

Conflict arises from tone when the emotions intended do not match the emotions for which the situation calls. Certain tonal stances, however, are more likely than others to produce resistance or to plant the seeds of conflict in readers.

Immoderation in word choice, for example, is generally provocative. Calling a new marketing scheme *putrid* or *disgusting* would create so much hostility on the part of the designer of the scheme that the designer would likely ignore whatever reasoning supported such a conclusion. Even if the writer could have convinced the scheme's originator that problems existed in the plan, the antagonism of the immoderate *tone* would produce an ego conflict even though the *substance* of the objections provided no such impediment.

Similarly, patronizing tones often produce ego conflict where substantive disagreements may not have existed. For instance, such phrases as "of course" or "obviously" mildly imply that the reader should know something he or she may not know, since the writer would not have stated the material if it were already understood. The patronizing phrases, inserted usually because the writer has failed to gauge accurately the knowledge level of the audience, may easily make the reader defensive. If such phrasing is combined with immoderate language—"obviously, as any fool would know"—the defensiveness is compounded and can produce an explosive conflict situation.

Finally, overly general or simplified tones commonly cause conflict. Generalizations such as "always," "every," or "all" frequently inspire resistance unless empirical evidence supports them. Similarly, oversimplification, although effective in rapidly conveying a complex idea, often antagonizes those who feel that the subject merits fuller discussion because the simplified handling does not clearly apply to their situation.

ACTION

The factors of tone and types of linguistic communication that may produce conflict are admittedly numerous. Still, one must remember that the factors together comprise only one of the three steps in the communication process, transmittal. Transmittal in turn should be weighted equally in importance with the conceptualization and reception steps that it connects.

To avoid undesired conflict, the writer should carefully consider the points raised thus far in this chapter. Still, the writer may wish to employ as guidelines the following writing checklists, which reflect a consolidation of the conceptualization, transmittal, and reception stages discussed earlier.

To remain conflict free in the conceptualization process or assessment step, the writer should answer the following four questions:

1. What is my *ostensible* purpose for this message?
2. What are my *underlying* reasons for writing?
3. How do I want the reader to react?
4. Is there a possibility of real conflict here rather than pseudoconflict?

To reduce the chance of negative conflict in the reception process or acknowledgment and attitude steps, the writer should answer the following four questions:

1. How do I anticipate that the reader will react?
2. To whom am I writing?
3. What details—age, rank, sex, attitudes, area of expertise, experience—do I know about the reader?
4. If the reader is unknown to me, what can I fairly guess about him or her?

To reduce unwanted conflict in the transmittal process or action step, the writer should answer the following ten questions:

1. Am I using any dialect variations in my language that the reader may not understand or might misjudge?
2. Am I using any professional jargon that is not absolutely needed?
3. If I am using needed jargon, can the reader understand it?
4. Am I writing in a technically proper manner with good grammar, spelling, punctuation, and mechanics?
5. Can the reader construe what I have written in more than one way?
6. Am I being concrete—that is, am I semantically clear?
7. Am I moderate in tone?

8. Have I avoided patronizing the reader?
9. Have I avoided oversimplification?
10. Have I eliminated any generalizations?

Even if the writer follows these three checklists before composing each written message, miscommunication that leads to pseudoconflict may still occur. Nonetheless a careful review of the answers to the questions in these three checklists should help the writer avoid much of his or her communication-based conflict in writing.

ANALYSIS

As we have just seen, the communication process of writing is complex and requires great care if the writer wishes to avoid nonproductive conflict. Still, it is important to note that although nonproductive conflict is created through writing, conflict is also resolved by writing. Indeed, although the amount one writes admittedly increases the opportunity to miscalculate a step in the writing process and thus increase the chance of causing conflict, frequent communication more often leads to positive behavior and cooperative interaction.

A substantial amount of research indicates that the very existence of some attempt to communicate reduces behavior that causes conflict (Deutsch, 1971a; Swingle, 1976). Brooks and Emmert state that "the presence of a channel in which worded messages can be sent and exchanged, in contrast with the absence of such a channel, clearly increases the amount of cooperative behavior" (1976, p. 228). For all the possible sources of conflict in writing style and communication in general, the failure to write or to communicate is a much greater source of conflict. Rather than not writing to avoid conflict, writers would do better to write carefully to avoid conflict.

SUMMARY

Many individuals are aware that their nonverbal and verbal communication directly affects the way others react to them. This awareness is increased by the fact that the person communicating can *see* the respondent's or listener's reactions.

The act of writing, however, removes the reader from view. Therefore the physical distance often coincides with a lack of adequate concern for how the written message is received and interpreted.

In this chapter we presented the three basic steps of the writing act:

conceptualization, transmittal, and reception. We explored how the lack of attention to any or all of these areas can create nonproductive conflict.

Three key areas exist in which writer error or misperception can lead to potential problems with the reader. These areas are:

1. Analysis of the purpose of the written communication;
2. Accurate analysis and consideration of the reader's capabilities and expectations; and
3. Maintenance of a proper tone and style appropriate for the content and for the reader.

The failure to adhere to these three areas can lead to a pseudo-conflict, which is a conflict caused by a misunderstanding. Equally destructive communication can create an ego conflict, whereby an individual may feel cornered, threatened, or defensive and may respond accordingly.

This chapter presented the ways in which writing can cause or sustain conflict. By attending to these issues, writers can assume their share of the responsibility for effective communication.

SUGGESTED ACTIVITIES

A. FOCUS ON CLARITY

Read the following memo:

To: All Division 5 Employees
From: Charles W. Selrachny
Date: January
Subject: No Smoking

In the near future we will start a new policy of no smoking in hazard areas. Only the cafeteria and some bathrooms are not hazardous. Consequently do not smoke cigarettes except there.

Be prepared to discuss the following questions:
1. How is the ambiguity of the subject line misleading?
2. What are the hazard areas? How could the lack of specificity lead to danger or conflict?

3. When does the new policy begin? What difficulties could the lack of specificity of a starting point for this new policy cause?
4. In the last sentence of the memorandum, only cigarettes (not, for example, cigars or other smoking materials) are forbidden. How could this specificity lead to danger or conflict?

B. FOCUS ON AUDIENCE ANALYSIS: NEUTRAL SUBJECT

Choose or imagine a position at your place of work that you would like to have someone fill. Then write the three following items:

1. A memo asking your boss to permit you to hire someone for that position;
2. An advertisement for the position and accompanying letter to the appropriate newspaper or professional publication; and
3. A memo to the Human Resources or Personnel Department, giving an official job description to place in the new-hire's file.

The way in which one writes changes dramatically, depending on the message's intended reader, even when the general subject of that message remains constant. The three written messages you have just completed have very similar purposes but very different audiences. How do these three audiences differ? How did you adjust your writing of each to adapt to these differences?

C. FOCUS ON AUDIENCE: EMOTIONAL SUBJECT

Consider the following situation: You discover that a colleague from another department in your organization has used *your* ideas in her area. At the directors' meeting, she reports her "new" idea to the vice-president, in front of you. She fails, however, to acknowledge the fact that her unique idea was in fact yours. It is raise and promotion time, and you refuse to sit back and allow her to garner all the credit. You decide to write the two following letters:

1. A letter to your colleague and former friend, indicating your displeasure with the way she handled your confidence;
2. A letter to the vice-president, explaining your concern about the situation.

Analyze both responses. What similarities and differences did you experience when writing about the same situation to the two readers? Explain the conceptualization, transmittal, and reception processes in both cases. Explain how your letter might affect the likelihood of conflict.

D. FOCUS ON DIALECT DIFFERENCES

Read the text of the following complaint letter to a U.S. hotel:

Dear Mr. Lawson:

I wish to inform you that I was very unhappy during my last stay at your establishment, for several reasons.

On my arrival, the lifts were not functioning properly, so I was forced to use the stairs. On the staircase, one of your charwomen refused to let me pass and insulted me. Attempting to step around her, I got a ladder in my stockings and snagged my pullover. Once in my room, I attempted to repair my pullover but found that the sewing repair kit the hotel had provided had no reel of cotton in it. I was so distressed by this that I felt a bit ill, so I went back to your main lobby, only to find the hotel chemist's shop closed.

Thinking it best at this point to relax, I decided to have dinner at the hotel restaurant. However, even there the service was poor. I ordered an underdone undercut with French beans but received a nearly burnt joint with sauteed auberge.

When I returned to my room, I attempted to make a trunk call home, unsuccessfully. Finally, I called the front desk to ask them to knock me up in the morning, and your clerk responded with a rude remark.

I am a solicitor of, if I must say so myself, some note in England. Perhaps this sort of service is acceptable for the average commercial bagman you host at your hotel, but it is not what I would have expected from an establishment of your reputation. I have already shared my views on this with my booking clerk, but I felt that it would only be proper to share my views with you as well.

Sincerely,
Francine Farquhar

1. Although Mr. Lawson and Ms. Farquhar share a common language, Mr. Lawson may have difficulty understanding many of the words Ms. Farquhar uses that reflect her British dialect. How many of the British English words used by Farquhar listed below did you know?

British English	*American English*
lift	elevator
charwoman	cleaning lady
ladder	run in stocking
pullover	sweater
reel of cotton	spool of thread
chemist	pharmacist
undercut	tenderloin
joint	roast
underdone	rare
French bean	string bean
auberge	eggplant
trunk call	long distance telephone call
knock me up	wake me up
commercial bagman	traveling salesperson
booking clerk	ticket agent

2.   The difficulties attendant on the dialect differences in the letter might have been less substantial if Ms. Farquhar had *spoken* her complaint before leaving rather than having *written* her complaint. Why would this be so?

7

CONCLUSION

In his address at American University on June 12, 1963, John F. Kennedy spoke about the importance of confronting differences between people:

> *Let us not be blind to our differences—but let us also direct attention to our common interests and the means by which those differences can be resolved. And if we cannot end now our differences, at least we can help make the world safe from diversity.*

Conflict as it routinely occurs in personal and professional settings can either be regarded as a very negative force or as a source of great potential and productivity. The differences between and among people can readily destroy relationships and hinder personal development or nourish those same relationships and foster personal growth. The outcome rests in how the individuals manage the conflict they face.

In this book we have described an approach for managing conflict productively through directed communication skills. We have discussed the specific verbal and nonverbal communication skills needed to handle conflict-producing behavior effectively. We have considered ways to defuse negative pseudoconflict and to establish a supportive communication environment for managing actual disagreements. Finally, we have described a five-step model of assessment, acknowledgment, attitude, action, and analysis designed to allow the reader systematically and straightforwardly to put into use these communication skills.

In this book we have introduced specific sources of conflict as well. Although it would be impossible to address adequately all possible communication-based sources of conflict, we have applied our communication skills approach to conflict management in the contexts of three important and nearly universal sources of conflict: gender as a factor affecting communication, cross-cultural communication, and writing as a means of communication that is at once interactive and performed in isolation.

We hope that you will be able to apply the five-step communication model presented in this book not only to the specific conflict situations examined in this book but also to other conflict situations you may face. The communication skills approach delineated in this book is designed to encourage people to face rather than to flee from conflict, because for them conflict will represent an opportunity to engage in an open-minded exchange of ideas by which the synergy of different views of a common situation represent the possibility of strengthening relationships and self-development.

At the beginning of this book, we observed that conflict will not go away simply because individuals are reluctant to deal with it. Those who have considered conflict as something to be avoided, we noted, are often ill-equipped to deal with those conflict situations from which they cannot hide. We also noted that those who attempt to deal with conflict solely in a competitive manner in which one side loses and the other wins are often unable to strengthen the interpersonal relationships out of which the conflict arises. Only the ability to develop a flexible and appropriate attitude to conflict can transform a potentially destructive situation into a positive interaction.

It is our hope that the communication skills approach to handling conflict we have described will provide you with the means to view conflict not as a counterproductive and negative encounter to be overcome but as a potentially productive interaction that can be managed effectively and appropriately. In doing so you will open up a future of opportunity that will allow you to participate in and even embrace conflict situations as a source of change and growth.

REFERENCES

Ablamovicz, H. The new context for interpersonal communications in the context of "global village." *The Speech Communication Annual*, Vol. 7, Spring, pp. 7–23, 1993.

Addington, D. W. The relationship of selected vocal characteristics to personality perception. *Speech Monographs* Vol. XXXV, No. 4, pp. 492–503, 1968.

Adler, N. J. *International Dimensions of Organizational Behavior*. Boston: Kent Publishing, 1986.

Almaney, A. J., and Alwan, A. J. *Communicating with the Arabs*. Prospect Heights, IL: Waveland Press, 1982.

Araki, C. T. Dispute management in the schools. *Mediation Quarterly*. Vol. 8, No. 1, pp. 51–62, 1990.

Argyle, M., and Furnham, A. Sources of satisfaction and conflict in long term relationships. *Journal of Marriage and the Family*, No. 45, pp. 418–493, 1983.

Argyle, M., Inghan, R., Alkema, F., and McCallin, M. The different functions of gaze. *Semiotica*, 7, pp. 19–32, 1973.

Aries, E. Gender and communication. In *Sex and Gender*, pp. 149–176. P. Shaver and C. Hendrick, eds., Newbury Park, CA: Sage Publications, 1987.

Arliss, L. P. *Gender Communication*. Englewood Cliffs, NJ: Prentice-Hall, 1991.

Bales, R. *Interpersonal Communication*. Dubuque, IA: William C. Brown, 1970.

Ball, D. A, and McCulloch, W. H., Jr. *International Business: Introduction and Essentials*, 2nd ed. Plano, TX: Business Publications, 1985.

Bandura, A., and Walters, R. H. *Social Learning and Personality Development*. New York: Holt, Rinehart & Winston, 1963.

Barelson, B., and Steiner, G. A. *Human Behavior: An Inventory of Scientific Findings*. New York: Harcourt, Brace & World, 1964.

Barnlund, D. C. *Interpersonal Communication: Survey and Studies*. Boston: Houghton Mifflin, 1968.

Barnlund, D. C. Communication: The context of change. In *Basic Readings in Communication Theory*, 2nd ed., pp. 6–26. C. David Mortensen, ed. New York: Harper & Row, 1979.

Barry, W. A. Marriage research and conflict: An integrative approach. *Psychological Bulletin*, Vol. 73, No. 1, pp. 47–54, 1970.

Bass, B., and Burger, P. C. *Assessment of Managers: An International Comparison*. New York: The Free Press, 1979.

Baxter, L. A. and Shephard, F. L. Sex-role identity, sex of other, and affective relationship as determinants of interpersonal conflict-management style. *Sex Roles*, Vol. 4, No. 6, pp. 813–825, 1978.

de Beauvoir, S. *The Second Sex*. H. M. Parhsley, trans. and ed. New York: Vintage Books, 1952.

Beck, A. T. *Love Is Never Enough*. New York: Harper & Row, 1988.

Beebe, S. Eye contact: A nonverbal determinant of speaker credibility. *Speech Teacher*, Vol. 23, pp. 21–25, 1974.

Bell, D. C., Chafetz, J. S., and Horn, L. J. Marital conflict resolution: A study of strategies and outcomes. *Journal of Family Issues*, Vol. 3, No. 1, pp. 111–132, 1982.

Bem, S. The measurement of psychological androgyny. *Journal of Consulting and Clinical Psychology*, Vol. 42, pp. 155–162, 1974.

Bem, S. L. *The Lenses of Gender: Transforming the Debate on Sexual Inequality*. New Haven, CT: Yale University Press, 1993.

Benedict, R. *Patterns of Culture*. New York: New American Library, 1934.

Berger, C., and Calabrese, R. Some explorations in initial interactions and beyond: Toward a developmental theory of interpersonal communication. *Human Communication Research*, Vol. 1, pp. 99–112, 1975.

Berman, P. Young children's responses to babies: Do they foreshadow differences between maternal and paternal styles? In *Origins of Nurturance: Developmental, Biological, and Cultural Perspectives on Caregiving*. A. Fogel and G. F. Melson, eds. Hillsdale, NJ: Erlbaum, 1986. (Cited in Sadker and Sadker, 1994, p. 204).

Bernard, J. *The Female World*. New York: The Free Press, 1981.

Berry, D. S., and McArthur, L. Z. Perceiving character in faces: The impact of age-related craniofacial changes on social perception. *Psychological Bulletin*, No. 100, pp. 3–18, 1986.

Berryman-Fink, C., and Eman-Wheeless, V. Male and female perceptions of women as managers. In *Communication, Gender, and Sex Roles in Diverse Interaction Contexts*, pp. 85–95. L. P. Stewart and S. Ting-Toomey, eds. Norwood, NJ: Ablex, 1987.

Billingham, R. E., and Sack, A. R. Conflict tactics and the level of emotional commitment among unmarrieds. *Human Relations*, Vol. 40, No. 1, pp. 59–74, 1987.

Birdwhistell, R. L. *Kinesics and Context: Essays on Body Motion Communication*. Philadelphia: University of Pennsylvania Press, 1970.

Black, J. S., and Porter, L. W. Managerial behaviors and job performance: A successful manager in Los Angeles may not succeed in Hong Kong, *Journal of International Business Studies*, Vol. 22, No. 1, pp. 99–113, 1991.

Blake, D. H., and Walters, R. S. *The Politics of Global Economic Relations*. Englewood Cliffs, NJ: Prentice-Hall, 1976.

Blake, R. R., and Mouton, J. S. The intergroup dynamics of win-lose conflict and problem-solving collaboration in union-management relations. In *Intergroup Relations and Leadership*, pp. 94–142. M. Sherif, ed. New York: Wiley, 1962.

Blake, R. R., and Mouton, J. S. *The Managerial Grid*. Houston, TX: Gulf Publishing, 1964.

Blank, R., and Slipp, S. *Voices of Diversity*. New York: American Management Association, 1994.

Blau, P. D., and Ferber, M. A. *The Economics of Women, Men, and Work*. Englewood Cliffs, NJ: Prentice-Hall, 1986.

Bloom, A. H. *The Linguistic Shaping of Thought: A Study in the Impact of Language on Thinking in China and the West*. Hillsdale, NJ: Erlbaum, 1981.

Blumstein, P., and Schwartz, P. *American Couples: Money, Work, Sex*. New York: William Morrow, 1983.

Borisoff, D. Patterns of gender conflict: A closer look at issues. *New Dimensions in Communication*. Proceedings of the New York State Speech Communication Association, Vol. VI, pp. 11–25, 1992.

Borisoff, D. The effect of gender on establishing and maintaining intimate relationships. In *Women and Men Communicating: Challenges and Changes*, pp. 14–28. L. P. Arliss and D. Borisoff, eds. Ft. Worth, TX: Holt, Rinehart & Winston, 1993.

Borisoff, D., and Hahn, D. F. Thinking with the body: Sexual metaphors. *Communication Quarterly*, Vol. 4, No. 3, pp. 253–260, 1993.

Borisoff, D., and Hahn, D. F. Gender power in context: A re-evaluation of communication in professional relationships. *New Dimensions in Communication.* Proceedings of the New York State Speech Communication Association, Vol. VIII, pp. 11–23, 1994.

Borisoff, D., and Hahn, D. F. From research to pedagogy: Teaching gender and communication. *Communication Quarterly*, Vol. 43, No. 4, pp. 381–393, 1995.

Borisoff, D., and Hahn, D. F. Listening and gender: Values revalued. In *Listening in Everyday Life: A Personal and Professional Approach*, 2nd ed, pp. 47–69. M. Purdy and D. Borisoff, eds. Lanham, MD: University Press of America, 1997.

Borisoff, D., and Merrill, L. Teaching the college course on gender differences as barriers to conflict resolution. In *Advances in Gender and Communication Research*, pp. 351–363. L. B. Nadler, M. K. Nadler, and W. R. Todd-Mancillas, eds. Lanham, MD: University Press of America, 1987.

Borisoff, D., and Merrill, L. *The Power to Communicate: Gender Differences and Barriers*, 2nd ed. Prospect Heights, IL: Waveland Press, 1992.

Brief, A. P., Schuler, R. S., and Van Sell, M. *Managing Job Stress.* Boston: Little, Brown, 1981.

Brooks, H. Technology as a factor in U.S. competitiveness. In *U.S. Competitiveness in the World Economy*, pp. 328–356. B. R. Scott and G. C. Lodge, eds. Boston: Harvard Business Press, 1985.

Brooks, W., and Emmert, P. *Personality and Interpersonal Behavior.* New York: Holt, Rinehart & Winston, 1976.

Broverman, I. K. et al. Sex-role stereotypes and clinical judgments of mental health. *Journal of Consulting and Clinical Psychology*, Vol. 34, pp. 1–7, 1970.

Bruner, J. Social psychology and perception. In *Readings in Social Psychology*, 3rd ed., pp. 83–94. E. E. Macoby, T. M. Newcomb, and E. L. Hartley, eds. New York: Holt, Rinehart, & Winston, 1958.

Bugental, D. E., Loug, L. R., and Gianetto, R. M. Perfidious feminine faces. *Journal of Personality and Social Psychology*, Vol. 17, pp. 314–318, 1971.

Burggraf, C. S., and Sillars, A. L. A critical examination of sex differences in marital communication. *Communication Monographs*, Vol. 54, pp. 276–294, 1987.

Burgoon, J. R., Birk, T., and Pfau, M. Nonverbal behaviors, persuasion, and credibility. *Human Communication Research*, Vol. 17, pp. 140–169, 1990.

Burgoon, J., and Saine, T. *The Unspoken Dialogue.* Boston: Houghton Mifflin, 1976.

Burke, R. J. Methods of resolving superior-subordinate conflict: The constructive use of subordinate differences and disagreements. *Organizational Behavior and Human Performance*, Vol. 5, pp. 393–411, 1970.

Burling, R. *Man's Many Voices.* New York: Holt, Rinehart & Winston, 1970.

Cahn, D. D., Jr. *Letting Go: A Practical Theory of Relationship Disengagement and Reengagement.* Albany: State University of New York Press, 1987.

Cash, T. F., Gillen, B., and Burns, S. Sexism and "beautism" in personnel consultant decision-making. *Journal of Applied Psychology*, Vol. 62, pp. 301–310, 1977.

Casmir, F. L. Stereotypes and schemata. In *Communication, Culture, and Organization Process*, pp. 48–67. W. Gudykunst, L. Stewart, and S. Ting-Toomey, eds. Beverly Hills, CA: Sage Publications, 1985.

Cassell, C. *Swept Away: Why Women Confuse Love and Sex.* New York: Fireside Press, 1984.

Caudron, S. Sexual Politics, *Personnel Journal*, pp. 50–61, May 1995.

Chaika, E. *Language: The Social Mirror.* Rowley, MA: Newbury House, 1982.

Chaney, L., and Martin, J. *Intercultural Business Communication.* Englewood Cliffs, NJ: Prentice-Hall, 1995.

Chelune, G. F., Robison, J. T., and Kommor, M. J. A cognitive model of intimate relationships. In *Communication, Intimacy, and Close Relationships,* pp. 11–40. V. J. Derlega, ed. Orlando, FL: Academic Press, 1984.

Chesanow, N. *The World-Class Executive.* New York: Rawson Associates, 1985.

Chikudate, N. Communication network liaisons as cultural interpreters for organizational adaptation in Japan Europe business environments, *Management International Review,* Vol. 35, No. 2, pp. 27–36, 1995.

Chomsky, N. *Language and Mind.* New York: Harcourt Brace Jovanovich, 1968.

Cixous, H. Le sexe ou la tete? Les cahiers du grif. October 1976. Language and Revolution: The Franco-American disconnection. D. S. Stanton, trans. In *The Future of Difference.* H. Eisenstein and A. Jardine, eds., pp. 73–87. New Brunswick, NJ: Rutgers University Press, 1985.

Clark, R. *The Japanese Company.* New Haven: Yale University Press, 1979.

Cohen, R. *Negotiating Across Cultures.* Washington, DC: United States Institute of Peace Press, 1991.

Condon, J. C., Jr. *Semantics and Communication.* New York: Macmillan, 1965.

Condon, J. S. *With Respect to the Japanese: A Guide for Americans.* Yarmouth, ME: Intercultural Press, 1984.

Condon, J. S., and Yousef, F. *An Introduction to Intercultural Communication.* New York: Macmillan, 1985.

Cooper, P. Women and power in the Caldecott and Newbery Winners. Paper presented at the Central States Communication Association Convention, Chicago, April 1991.

Cooper, P. Gender and Communication in the Classroom. In *Women and Men Communicating: Challenges and Changes,* pp. 122–141. L. P. Arliss and D. Borisoff, eds. Fort Worth, TX: Holt, Rinehart and Winston, 1993.

Copeland, L., and Griggs, J. *Going International: How to Make Friends and Deal Effectively in the Global Marketplace.* New York: Random House, 1985.

Cose, E. *The Rage of a Privileged Class.* New York: Harper Perennial, 1995.

Coser, L. A. *The Functions of Social Conflict.* New York: The Free Press, 1956.

Couch, C., and Hintz, R. A. *Constructing Social Life.* Champaign, IL: Stipes Publishing, 1975.

Coulson, R. Labor arbitration—what you need to know. New York: American Arbitration Association, 1973.

Coulson, R. *Fighting Fair: Family Mediation Will Work for You.* New York: The Free Press, 1983.

Cox, T., Jr. *Cultural Diversity in Organizations: Theory, Research & Practice.* San Francisco: Berrett-Koehler Publishers, 1993.

Cross, G. P., Names, J. H., and Beck, D. *Conflict and Human Interaction.* Dubuque, IA: Kendall Hunt, 1979.

Cummings, L. L., Harnett, D. L., and Stevens, O. J. Risk, fate, conciliation, and trust: An international study of attitudinal differences among executives. *Academy of Management Journal,* Vol. 14, No. 3, pp. 285–304, Sept. 1971.

Cupach, W. R. and Canary, D. J. Managing conflict and anger: Investigating the sex stereotype hypothesis. In *Gender, Power, and Communication in Human Relationships,* pp. 233–252, P. J. Kalbfleish, and M. J. Cody, eds. Hillsdale, NJ: Erlbaum, 1995.

Daniels, H. Nine ideas about language. In *Language,* 4th ed., pp. 18–42, V. P. Clark et al., eds. New York: St. Martin's Press, 1985.

Davis, A. M. Mediation: The field of dreams? If we build it, they will come! *Negotiation Journal* Vol. 9, No. 1, pp. 5–12, 1993.

Davis, F. B. *Fashion, Culture, and Identity.* Chicago: University of Chicago Press, 1992.

Davitz, J. R. *The Communication of Emotional Meaning.* New York: McGraw-Hill, 1964.

Deaux, K., and Major, B. A social-psychological model of gender. In *Theoretical Perspectives on Sexual Difference*, pp. 89–99. D. L. Rhode, ed. New Haven, CT: Yale University Press, 1990.

DeMente, B. L. *The Japanese Way of Doing Business: The Psychology of Management in Japan.* Englewood Cliffs, NJ: Prentice-Hall, 1981.

DeMente, B. L. *Korean Etiquette and Ethics in Business.* Lincolnwood, IL: NTC Business Books, 1988.

DeMente, B. L. *Behind the Japanese Bow.* Lincolnwood, IL: Passport Books, 1993.

Derlega, V. J., and Chaikin, A. L. Norms affecting self-disclosure in men and women. *Journal of Consulting and Clinical Psychology*, Vol. 44, pp. 376–380, 1976.

Deutsch, M. Toward an understanding of conflict. *International Journal of Group Tensions*, Vol. 1, pp. 42–54, 1971a.

Deutsch, M. Conflict and its resolution. In *Conflict Resolution: Contributions of the Behavioral Sciences.* pp. 36–57. C. G. Smith, ed. Notre Dame, IN: University of Notre Dame Press, 1971b.

Deutsch, M. Conflicts: productive and destructive. In *Conflict Resolution Through Communication.* F. E. Jandt, ed. New York: Harper & Row, 1973a.

Deutsch, M. *The Resolution of a Conflict: Constructive and Destructive Processes.* New Haven: Yale University Press, 1973b.

Deutsch, M. Subjective features of conflict resolution: Psychological, social, and cultural influences. In *New Directions in Conflict Theory: Conflict Resolution and Conflict Transformation*, pp. 26–86. R. Vayrynen, ed. Newbury Park, CA: Sage Publications, 1991.

DeVito, J. A. *The Communication Handbook: A Dictionary.* New York: Harper & Row, 1986.

DeWine, S. Female leadership in male-dominated organizations. *ACA Bulletin*, Vol. 61, pp. 19–29, 1987.

Dindia, K. The effects of sex of subject and sex of partner on interruptions. *Human Communication Research*, Vol. 3, pp. 345–371, 1987.

Dipboye, R. L., Arvey, R. D., and Terpstra, D. F. Sex and physical attractiveness of raters and applicants as determinants of resume evaluations. *Journal of Applied Psychology*, Vol. 62, pp. 288–294, 1977.

Dodd, C. H. *Dynamics of Intercultural Communications.* Dubuque, IA: William C. Brown, 1982.

Douglas, M. *Implicit Meanings.* London: Routledge & Kegan Paul, 1975.

Dovidio, J. F., et al. The relationship of social power to visual displays of dominance between men and women. *Journal of Personality Social Psychology*, Vol. 54, No. 2, pp. 233–242, 1988.

Duck, S. *Understanding Relationships.* New York: Guilford Press, 1991.

Duffy, K. G., Grosch, J. W. and Olczak, P. V., eds. *Community Mediation: A Handbook for Practitioners.* New York: Guilford Press, 1991.

Eagly, A. H. *Sex Differences in Social Behavior: A Social-Role Interpretation.* Hillsdale, NJ: Erlbaum, 1987.

Eakins, B. W., and Eakins, R. G. *Sex Differences in Human Communication.* Boston: Houghton Mifflin, 1978.

Ekman, P. Movements with precise meanings. *Journal of Communication*, Vol. 26, pp. 14–26, 1976.

Ekman, P., and Friesen, W. V. The repertoire of nonverbal behavior: Categories, origins, usage, and coding. *Semiotica*, Vol. 1, pp. 49–98, 1969.

Ekman, P., and Friesen, W. V. Hand movements. *Journal of Communication*, Vol. 22, pp. 353–354, 1972.

Ekman, P., and Friesen, W. V. Nonverbal behavior and psychotherapy. In *The Psychology of*

Depression: Contemporary Theory and Research. R. J. Friedman and M. M. Katz, eds. Washington, DC: Winston & Sons, 1974.

Ekman, P., and Friesen, W. V. *Unmasking the Face.* Englewood Cliffs, NJ: Prentice-Hall, 1975.

Elkouri, F., and Elkouri, E. A. *How Arbitrators Work.* Washington DC: Bureau of National Affairs, 1960.

Ellsworth, P., and Ludwig, L. Visual behavior in social interaction. *Journal of Communication,* Vol. 22, pp. 378–381, 1972.

Ellul, J. *The Technological Society.* J. Neugroschel, trans. New York: Vintage, 1964.

Evans, G. W., and Howard R. B. Personal space. *Psychological Bulletin,* Vol. 80, pp. 334–344, 1973.

Fagot, B. The influence of sex of child on parental reaction. *Developmental Psychology,* Vol. 10, pp. 554–558, 1978. (Cited in J. Pearson, *Gender and Communication.* Dubuque, IA: William C. Brown, 1985.)

Fagot, B. I., et al. Differential reactions to assertive and communicative acts of toddler boys and girls. *Child Development,* Vol. 56, pp. 1499–1505, 1985.

Fast, J. *Body Language.* New York: M. Evans, 1970.

Feigenbaum, E. A., and McCorduck, P. *The Fifth Generation: Artificial Intelligence and Japan's Computer Challenge to the World.* New York: New American Library, 1983.

Fields, G. *From Bonsai to Levis, When West Meets East: An Insider's Surprising Account of How the Japanese Live.* New York: New American Library, 1983.

Filley, A. C. *Interpersonal Conflict Resolution.* Glenview, IL: Scott, Foresman, 1975.

Filley, A. C. Conflict resolution: The ethic of the good loser. In *Readings in Interpersonal and Organizational Communication,* 3rd ed., pp. 234–252. R. Huseman, C. Logue, and D. Freshley, eds. Boston: Holbrooke Press, 1977.

Fisher, G. *International Negotiation: A Cross-Cultural Perspective.* Chicago: Intercultural Press, 1980.

Fisher, G. *Mindsets: The Role of Culture and Perspective in International Business.* Yarmouth, ME: Intercultural Press, 1988.

Fisher, J. D., and Byrne, D. Too close for comfort: Sex differences in response to invasions of personal space. *Journal of Personal and Social Psychology,* Vol. 32, pp. 15–21, 1975.

Fisher, R., and Ury, W. *Getting to Yes: Negotiating Agreement without Giving In.* Boston: Houghton Mifflin, 1981.

Fitzpatrick, M. A. *Between Husbands and Wives: Communication in Marriage.* Newbury Park, CA: Sage Publications, 1988.

Folberg, J., and Taylor, A. *Mediation: A Comprehensive Guide to Resolving Conflict without Litigation.* San Francisco, CA: Jossey-Bass, 1984.

Folger, J. P., and Poole, M. S. *Working through Conflict: A Communication Perspective.* Glenview, IL: Scott, Foresman, 1984.

Foucault, M. The subject and power. In *Michel Foucault: Beyond Structuralism and Hermeneutics,* pp. 208–226. N. Dreyfuss and P. Rabinow, eds. Chicago: University of Chicago Press, 1982.

Fox, G. L. Nice girls do: Social control of women through value construct. *Signs,* Vol. 3, p. 2, 1977.

Freedman, R. *Beauty Bound.* New York: Basic Books, 1986.

Gahagan, J. P., and Tedeschi, J. T. Strategy and the credibility of promises in the prisoner's dilemma game. *Journal of Conflict Resolution,* Vol. 12, pp. 224–234, 1968.

Gallimore, R., Boggs, J. W., and Jordan, C. *Culture, Behavior and Education: A Study of Hawaiian-Americans.* Beverly Hills, CA: Sage Publications, 1974.

Garvin, G. International English: Some strings attached. In *Communication at Work,* pp. 53–63. H. Smith, ed. Toronto: Proceedings of the Combined Eastern/Canadian ABCA Canadian STC Meeting, 1985.

Gayle-Hackett, B. Do females and males differ in selection of conflict management strategies? A meta-analytic review. Unpublished manuscript, University of Portland, 1986. (Cited in Cupach and Canary, 1995, p. 235.)

Gibb, J. Defensive communication. *Journal of Communication*, Vol. 11, pp. 141–148, 1961.

Gilligan, C. Woman's place in man's life cycle. *Harvard Educational Review*, Vol. 49, No. 4, pp. 431–446, November 1979.

Gilligan, C. *In a Different Voice*. Cambridge, MA: Harvard University Press, 1982.

Goffman, E. *The Presentation of Self in Everyday Life*. Garden City, NY: Doubleday Anchor Books, 1959.

Goffman, E. *Behavior in Public Places*. New York: The Free Press, 1963.

Goldman-Eisler, F. A comparative study of two hesitation phenomena. *Language and Speech*, Vol. 4, pp. 18–26, 1961.

Goldstein, J. R. Trends in teaching technical writing. *Technical Communication*, Vol. 4, pp. 25–34, 1984.

Goodman, E. Processes of conflict resolution. Lecture at New York University, Summer 1983.

Gourley, C. Mediator differences in perception of abuse: A gender problem. In *Conflict and Gender*, pp. 73–91. A Taylor and J. B. Miller, eds. Cresskill, NJ: Hampton Press, 1994.

Graebner, A. Growing Up female. In *Intercultural Communication: A Reader*. L. A. Samovar and R. E. Porter, eds. Belmont, CA: Wadsworth, 1982.

Graf, L. A., et al. Work centrality and work goals: A comparative study of middle managers in Japanese and U.S. banking institutions. *Journal of Asia-Pacific Business*, Vol. 1, No. 2, pp. 87–107, 1995.

Graham, J. A., and Jouhar, A. J. The effects of cosmetics on person perception. *International Journal of Cosmetic Science*, Vol. 3, pp. 199–210, 1982.

Graham, J. L., and Herberger, R. A., Jr. Negotiators abroad: Don't shoot from the hip. In *Toward Internationalism: Readings in Cross-Cultural Communication*, 2nd ed., pp. 73–87. L. F. Luce and E. C. Smith, eds. Cambridge, MA: Newbury House Publishers, 1987.

Gregory, G. Japan: New center of innovation, evolving from imitator to inventor. In *Speaking of Japan*, Vol. 3, No. 18, pp. 2–9. Keizan Koho Center, Japanese Institute for Social and Economic Affairs, June 1986.

Gudykunst, W. B. Uncertainty reduction and predictability of behavior in low-context and high-context culture: An explanatory study. *Communication Quarterly*, Vol. 31, No. 1, pp. 49–55, Winter 1983.

Gudykunst, W. B. and Hammer, M. The influence of social identity and intimacy of interethnic relationships on uncertainty reduction processes, *Human Communication Research*, Vol. 14, pp. 569–601, 1988.

Gudykunst, W. B. and Kim, Y. Y. *Communicating with Strangers: An Approach to Intercultural Communication*, 2nd ed. New York: McGraw-Hill, 1992.

Gumperz, J. J., and Hymes, D. The ethnography of communication. *American Anthropologist*, Vol. 66, No. 6, Part 2, pp. 1–186, December 1964.

Haire, M., Ghiselli, E. E., and Porter, L. W. Cultural patterns in the role of the manager. *Industrial Relations*, Vol. 2, No. 2, pp. 95–117, February 1963.

Halberstadt, A. G., and Saitta, M. B. Gender, nonverbal behavior and perceived dominance: A test of the theory. *Journal of Personality and Social Psychology*, Vol. 53, pp. 257–272, 1987.

Halberstam, D. *The Reckoning*. New York: William Morrow, 1986.

Hall, E. T. *The Silent Language*. New York: Doubleday, 1959; Fawcett Publications, 1961.

Hall, E. T. *The Hidden Dimension*. New York: Doubleday, 1966.

Hall, E. T. *Beyond Culture*. New York: Anchor Press, Doubleday, 1976.

Hall, E. T. *The Dance of Life: The Other Dimensions of Time*. Garden City, NY: Anchor Press, Doubleday, 1983.

Hall, E. T., and Hall, M. R. *Understanding Cultural Differences*. Yarmouth, ME: Intercultural Press, 1990.

Hall, J. *Nonverbal Sex Differences: Communication, Accuracy and Expressive Style*. Baltimore, MD: The Johns Hopkins University Press, 1984.

Hampden-Turner, C., and Trompenaars, F. *The Seven Cultures of Capitalism: Value Systems for Creating Wealth in the United States, Japan, Germany, France, Britain and the Netherlands*. New York: Currency/Doubleday, 1993.

Harrison, R. P. *Beyond Words: An Introduction to Nonverbal Communication*. Englewood Cliffs, NJ: Prentice-Hall, 1974.

Haste, H. *The Sexual Metaphor: Men, Women, and the Thinking that Makes the Difference*. Cambridge, MA: Harvard University Press, 1994.

Hatfield, E., and Rapson, R. *Love, Sex, and Intimacy: Their Psychology, Biology, and History*. New York: HarperCollins, 1993.

Hatfield, E., and Sprecher, S. *Mirror, Mirror. . . .: The Importance of Looks on Everyday Life*. Albany: SUNY Press, 1986.

Hauser, J. *Good Divorces/Bad Divorces: A Case for Divorce Mediation*. Lanham, MD: University Press of America, 1995.

Hauser, J. Mediation and the communication process: An integrated perspective. *Speech Communication Annual*, Vol. X, pp. 61–79, 1996.

Haynes, J. Divorce mediation: A practical guide for therapists and counselors. New York: Springer, 1981.

Heilman, M. E., and Saruwatari, L. F. When beauty is beastly: The effects of appearance and sex on evaluations of job applicants for managerial and non-managerial jobs. *Organizational Behavior and Human Performance*, Vol. 22, pp. 360–372, 1979.

Henley, N. M. *Body Politics: Power, Sex and Non-Verbal Communication*. Englewood Cliffs, NJ: Prentice-Hall, 1977.

Heslin, R. Steps toward a taxonomy of touching. Paper presented to the Midwestern Psychological Association, Chicago, May 1974. (Cited in M. L. Knapp, *Essentials of Nonverbal Behavior*. New York: Holt, Rinehart & Winston, 1980.)

Hilton, C. B. Japanese international business communication: The place of English. *Journal of Business Communication*, Vol. 29, No. 3, pp. 253–265, 1992.

Hoban, P. He said, she said: Couples therapy is the flavor of the month. *New York*, pp. 31–36, June 1, 1992.

Hochschild, A. Smile wars: Counting the casualties of emotional labor. *Mother Jones*, pp. 35–42, December 1983.

Hochschild, A. *The Second Shift*. New York: Avon Books, 1990.

Hocker, J. L., and Wilmot, W. W. *Interpersonal Conflict*, 2nd ed. Dubuque, IA: William C. Brown, 1985.

Hocker, J. L., and Wilmot, W. W. *Interpersonal Conflict*, 3rd ed. Dubuque, IA: William C. Brown, 1991.

Hoecklin, L. *Managing Cultural Differences: Strategies for Competitive Advantage*. Wokingham (UK): The Economist Intelligence Unit/Addison-Wesley, 1995.

Hofheinz, R., Jr., and Calder, K. E. *The Eastasia Edge*. New York: Basic Books, 1982.

Hofstede, G. *Culture's Consequences: International Work-Related Values*, abridged ed. Beverly Hills, CA: Sage Publications, 1984.

Hofstede, G. *Cultures and Organizations: Software of the Mind*. London: McGraw-Hill, 1991.

Hoijer, H. The Sapir-Whorf hypothesis. In *Intercultural Communication: A Reader*, pp. 210–217. L. A. Samovar and R. E. Porter, eds. Belmont, CA: Wadsworth, 1982.

Husted, B. W. A study of negotiations between Mexican and U.S. business executives: A view from Monterrey, Nuevo Leon, Proceedings of the Business Association of Latin American Studies, pp. 223–232, 1993.

Hymes, D. The scope of sociolinguistics. *Social Science Research Council Items*, Vol. 25, pp. 14–18, 1972.

Illich, I. *Toward a History of Needs.* New York: Pantheon, 1977.

James, D. L. *The Executive Guide to Asia-Pacific Communication.* Tokyo: Kodansha International, 1995.

Jamieson, D. W., and Thomas, K. W. Power and conflict in student-teacher relationship. *Journal of Applied Behavioral Science,* Vol. 10, No. 3, pp. 321–336, 1974.

Jamieson, K. H. *Beyond the Double Bind: Women and Leadership.* New York: Oxford University Press, 1995.

Janssens, M. Brett., J. M., and Smith, F. S. Confirmatory cross-cultural research testing the viability of a corporation-wide safety policy, *Academy of Management Journal,* Vol. 38, No. 2, pp. 364–382, 1995.

Jensen, J. V. Communicative functions of silence. *Etcetera,* pp. 249–257, 1973.

Jensen, J. V. Perspective on nonverbal intercultural communication. In *Intercultural Communication: A Reader,* pp. 260–276. L. A. Samovar and R. E. Porter, eds. Belmont, CA: Wadsworth, 1982.

Johnson, F. L. Political and pedagogical implications of attitudes toward women's language. *Communication Quarterly,* Vol. 31, No. 2, pps. 133–138, 1983.

Jones, G. M. Action zone theory, target students and science classroom interaction. *Journal of Research in Science Teaching,* Vol. 27, No. 7, pp. 651–660, 1990.

Jones, G. M., and Wheatley, J. Gender differences in teacher-student interaction science classrooms. *Journal of Research in Science Teaching,* Vol. 27, No. 9, pp. 861–874, 1990.

Jones, S. E. *The Right Touch: Understanding and Using the Language of Physical Contact.* Cresskill, NJ: Hampton Press, 1995.

Kanter, R. M. *Men and Women of the Corporation.* New York: Basic Books, 1977.

Keashly, L. Gender and conflict: What does psychological research tell us? In *Gender and Conflict,* pp. 167–191. A. B. Taylor and J. B. Miller, eds. Cresskill, NJ: Hampton Press, 1994.

Keen, S. Fire in the Belly: On Being a Man. New York: Bantam Books, 1991.

Keltner, J. W. *The Management of Struggle: Elements of Dispute Resolution through Negotiation, Mediation, and Arbitration.* Cresskill, NJ: Hampton Press, 1994.

Kendon, A. Some functions of gaze direction in social interaction. *Acta Psychological,* Vol. 26, pp. 22–63, 1967.

Kennedy, C. W., and Camden, C. T. A new look at interruptions. *Western Journal of Communication,* Vol. 43, pp. 45–48, 1983.

Key, W. B. *Subliminal Seduction.* New York: Thomas Y. Cromwell, 1968.

Kluckhohn, C. *Mirror for Man: A Survey of Human Behavior and Social Attitudes.* Greenwich, CT: Fawcett, 1964.

Knapp, M. L. *Essentials of Nonverbal Communication.* New York: Holt, Rinehart & Winston, 1980.

Knapp, M. L., and Hall, J. A. *Nonverbal Behavior in Human Interaction,* 3rd ed. Fort Worth, TX: Holt, Rinehart, and Winston, 1992.

Kramarae, C. *Women and Men Speaking.* Rowly, MA: Newbury House, 1981.

Kramer, E. The judgment of personal characteristics and emotions from nonverbal properties of speech. *Psychological Bulletin,* Vol. 60, pp. 408–420, 1963.

Kressel, K., and Pruitt, D. G. Themes in the mediation of social conflict. *Journal of Social Issues,* Vol. 41, No. 2, pp. 179–198, 1985.

Kroeber, A. L., and Kluckhohn C. *Culture: A Critical Review of Concepts and Definitions.* New York: Random House, 1954.

LaFrance, M., and Henley, N. M. On oppressing hypotheses: Or differences in nonverbal sensitivity revisited. In *Power/Gender: Social Relations in Theory and Practice,* pp. 287–311. H. L. Radtke and H. J. Stam, eds. Thousand Oaks, CA: Sage Publications, 1994.

Lakoff, R. *Language and Women's Place.* New York: Harper & Row, 1975.

Lalljee, M. C. Disfluencies in normal English speech. Unpublished dissertation, Oxford

University, 1971, quoted in M. L. Knapp, *Essentials of Nonverbal Communication*. New York: Holt, Rinehart & Winston, 1980.

Lander, H. *Language and Culture*. New York: Oxford University Press, 1966.

Lass, N. J., et al. Speaker sex identification from voiced, whispered, and filtered isolated vowels. *Journal of the Acoustical Society of America*, Vol. 59, pp. 361–374, 1976.

Laurent, A. The cultural diversity of western conceptions of management. *International Studies of Management and Organization*, Vol. 13, No. 1–2, pp. 75–96, Spring-Summer 1983.

Lee, J, and Jablin, F. M. A cross-cultural investigation of exit, loyalty and neglect as responses to dissatisfying job conditions. *Journal of Business Communication*, Vol. 29, pp. 203–228, 1992.

Lerner, H. G. *The Dance of Intimacy*. New York: Harper & Row, 1989.

Likert, R., and Likert, J. G. *New Ways of Managing Conflict*. New York: McGraw-Hill, 1976.

Lincoln, J. R. Employee work attitudes and management practice in the U. S. and Japan: Evidence from a large comparative survey, *California Management Review*, Vol. 32, pp. 89–106, Fall 1989.

Lips, H. *Women, Men, and the Psychology of Power*. Englewood Cliffs, NJ: Prentice-Hall, 1981.

Lippitt, G. L. Managing conflict in today's organizations. *Training and Development Journal*, pp. 67–77, July 1982.

Livingstone, J. M. *The International Enterprise*. New York: Wiley, 1975.

Luce, L. F., and Smith, E. C. Cross-cultural literacy: A national priority. In *Toward Internationalism: Readings in Cross-cultural Communication*, 2nd ed. pp. 3–9. L.G. Luce and E. C. Smith, eds. Cambridge, MA: Newbury House Publishers, 1987.

Lulofs, R. S. *Conflict: From Theory to Action*. Scottsdale, AZ: Gorsuch Scarisbrick, 1994.

Lynn, D. B. *Parents and Sex-Role Identification*. Berkeley, CA: McCutchan, 1969.

Macoby, E. E., and Jacklin, C. N. *The Psychology of Sex Differences*. Stanford, CA: Stanford University Press, 1974.

Maier, N. R. F. *Problem Solving Discussions and Conferences: Leadership Methods and Skills*. New York: McGraw-Hill, 1963.

Maier, N., and Sashkin, M. Specific leadership behaviors that promote problem solving. *Personal Psychology*, Vol. 24, pp. 35–44, 1971.

Maier, N., and Solem, A. F. Improving solutions by turning choice situations into problems. *Personal Psychology*, Vol. 15, No. 2, pp. 151–157, 1962.

Maltz, D., and Borker, R. A cultural approach to male-female miscommunications. In *Language and Social Identity*, pp. 196–216. J. J. Gumperz, ed. Cambridge, England: Cambridge University Press, 1982.

Mandelbaum, D., ed. *Edward Sapir: Culture, Language, and Personality*. Berkeley: University of California Press, 1962.

March, R. M. *The Japanese Negotiator*. Tokyo: Kodansha International, 1988.

Martin, L. Eskimo words for snow: A case study in the genesis and decay of an anthropology example, *American Anthropologist*, Vol. 88, 418–423, 1986.

Maruyama, M. Changing dimensions in international business. *The Academy of Management Executive*, Vol vi, No. 3, pp. 88–96. August 1992.

Mathes, E. W., and Kahn, A. Physical attractiveness, happiness, neuroticism and self-esteem. *Journal of Psychology*, Vol. 90, pp. 27–30, 1975.

McClone, R. E., and Hollien, H. Vocal pitch characteristics of aged women. *Journal of Speech and Hearing Research*, Vol. 6, pp. 164–170, 1963.

McConville, D. J. The casual corporation. *Industry Week*, vol. 243, pp. 12–16, June 20, 1994.

Mehrabian, A. *Silent Messages: Implicit Communication of Emotions and Attitudes*, 2nd ed. Belmont, CA: Wadworth, 1981.

Miller, G. R. and Steinberg, M. *Between People: A New Analysis of Interpersonal Communication*. Chicago: Science Research Associates, 1975.

Miller, J. J., and Kilpatrick, J. A. *Issues for Managers: An International Perspective.* Homewood, IL: Richard D. Irwin, 1987.

Miller, N., et al. Speed of speech and persuasion. *Journal of Personality and Social Psychology,* Vol. 34, pp. 615–624, 1976.

Mischel, W. Sex typing and socialization. In *Carmichael's Manual of Child Psychology,* 3rd ed., Vol. 2. P. H. Mussen, ed. New York: Wiley, 1970.

Montagu, A. *Touching: The Human Significance of the Skin.* New York: Columbia University Press, 1971.

Moore, C. W. Have process, will travel: Reflections on democratic decision making and conflict management practices abroad. *National Institute for Dispute Resolution Forum,* pp. 1–12. Winter 1993.

Moore, G. W. *The Mediation Process. Practical Strategies for Resolving Conflict.* San Francisco, CA: Jossey-Bass, 1986.

Morain, G. G. Kinesics and cross-cultural understanding. In *Toward Internationalism: Readings in Cross-Cultural Communication,* 2nd ed. pp. 117–142. L. F. Luce and E. C. Smith, eds. Cambridge, MA: Newbury House Publishers, 1987.

Moran, R. T., and Harris, P. R. *Managing Cultural Synergy.* Houston, TX: Gulf Publishing, 1982.

Morris, D., et al. *Gestures: Their Origins and Distribution.* Briarcliff Manor, NY: Stein & Day, 1979.

Morrison, A. M., White, R. P., Van Velsor, E., and The Center for Creative Leadership. *Breaking the Glass Ceiling: Can Women Reach the Top of America's Largest Corporations?* Reading, MA: Addison-Wesley, 1987.

Mueller, B. D. Steps towards an intercultural methodology for teaching foreign languages. In *Intercultural Competence, Volume I: The Secondary School,* pp. 71–116. L. Sercu, ed. Aalborg, Denmark: Aalborg University Press, 1995.

Mulac, A., et al. Male/female language differences and effects in the same-sex and mixed-sex dyads: The gender-link effect. *Communication Monographs,* Vol. 55, pp. 315–335, 1988.

Mulde, A., Hanley, T. D., and Prigge, D. Y. Effects of phonological speech upon three dimensions of attitudes of selected American listeners. *Quarterly Journal of Speech,* Vol. 60, pp. 11–420, 1974.

Mulder, M. Reduction of power differences in practice: The power distance reduction theory and its applications. In *European Contributions to Organization Theory.* G. Hofstede and M. S. Kassem, eds. Assen, Netherlands: Van Gorcum, 1976.

Mulder, M. *The Daily Power Game.* Leyden: Martinus Nijhoff, 1977.

Munter, M. *Guide to Managerial Communication,* 3rd ed. Englewood Cliffs, NJ: Prentice-Hall, 1992.

Mysak, E. D. Pitch and duration characteristics of older males. *Journal of Speech and Hearing Research,* Vol. 2, pp. 46–54, 1959.

Niyekawa-Howard, A. *A Psycholinguistic Study of the Whorfian Hypothesis Based on the Japanese Passive.* Honolulu: Educational Research & Development Center, University of Hawaii, 1968.

Nostrand, H. W. Describing and teaching the sociocultural context of a foreign language and literature. In *Trends in Foreign Language Teaching,* pp. 1–25. A. Valdman, ed. New York: McGraw-Hill, 1966.

O'Reilly, C. A., and Roberts, K. H. Job satisfaction among whites and non-whites. *Journal of Applied Psychology,* Vol. 19, No. 2, pp. 295–299, 1973.

Osborn, A. F. *Applied Imagination.* New York: Scribners, 1957. In *The Communication Handbook: A Dictionary.* J. DeVito, ed. New York: Harper & Row, 1986.

Ouchi, W. G. *Theory Z.* Reading, MA: Addison-Wesley, 1981.

Page, J. A. *The Brazilians.* Reading, MA: Addison-Wesley, 1995.

Pearson, J. C. *Gender and Communication.* Dubuque, IA: William C. Brown, 1985.

Pearson, J. C., and Cooks, L. Gender and power. In *Gender, Power and Communication in Human Relationships,* pp. 331–349. P. J. Kalbfeisch and M. J. Cody, eds. Hillsdale, NJ: Erlbaum, 1995.

Pearson, J. C., and West, R. An initial investigation of the effects of gender on student questions in the classroom: Developing a descriptive base. *Communication Education,* Vol. 40, pp. 22–32, 1991.

Pearson, J. C., Turner, L. H., and Todd-Mancillas, W. *Gender and Communication,* 2nd ed. Dubuque, IA: William C. Brown, 1991.

Person, E. *Dreams of Love and Fateful Encounters: The Power of Romantic Passion.* New York: Penguin, 1989.

Phatak, A. V. *International Dimensions of Management.* Boston: Kent Publishing, 1983.

Pike, K. L. *Language in Relation to a Unified Theory of the Structure of Human Behavior,* 2nd rev. ed. The Hague: Mouton, 1971.

Pinker, S. *The Language Instinct: How the Mind Creates Language.* New York: William Morrow, 1994.

Polit, D., and LaFrance, M. Sex differences in reaction to spatial invasion. *Journal of Social Psychology,* Vol. 102, pp. 59–70, 1977.

Porter, R. E., and Samovar, L. A. Approaching intercultural communication. In *Intercultural Communication: A Reader,* pp. 26–42. L. A. Samovar and R. E. Porter, eds. Belmont, CA: Wadsworth, 1982.

Powell, G. N. *Women and Men in Management,* 2nd Ed. Newbury Park, CA: Sage Publications, 1993.

Pruitt, D. G. *Negotiation Behavior.* New York: Academic Press, 1981

Pullum, G. K. *The Great Eskimo Vocabulary Hoax and Other Irreverent Essays on the Study of Language.* Chicago: University of Chicago Press, 1991.

Putnam, L. L. Lady you're trapped: Breaking out of conflict cycles. In *Women in Organizations: Barriers and Breakthroughs.* J. J. Pillota, ed. Prospect Heights, IL: Waveland Press, 1983.

Putnam, L. Leadership and conflict management. *ACA Bulletin,* Vol. 61, pp. 42–29, 1987.

Putnam, L. L., and Jones, T. S. Reciprocity in negotiations: An analysis of bargaining interaction. *Communication Monographs,* Vol. 49, No. 3, pp. 171–191, 1982.

Putnam, L. L., and Poole, M. S. Conflict and negotiation. In *Handbook of Organizational Communication,* pp. 549–599. F. M. Jablin, et al. eds. Newbury Park, CA: Sage Publications, 1987.

Reik, T. Men and women speak different languages. *Psychoanalysis,* Vol. 2, No. 3, pp. 13–23, 1954.

Reitz, H. J. The relative importance of five categories of needs among industrial workers in eight countries. *Academy of Management Proceedings,* pp. 270–273, 1975.

Ricks, D. A., Fu, M. Y. C., and Arpan, J. S. *International Business Blunders.* Columbus, OH: Grid, 1974.

Richmond, V. P., and Gorham, J. Language patterns and gender role orientation among students in grades 3–12. *Communication Education,* Vol. 37, pp. 142–149, 1988.

Roberts, J. V., and Herman, C. P. The psychology of height: An empirical review. In *Physical Appearance, Stigma, and Social Behavior: The Ontario Symposium,* pp. 113–140. C. P. Herman, M. P. Zanna, and E. T. Higgins, eds., Vol. 3. Hillsdale, NJ: Erlbaum, 1986

Rogers, C. *Client-Centered Psychotherapy.* Boston: Houghton Mifflin, 1951.

Rogers, C. *On Becoming a Person.* Boston: Houghton Mifflin, 1961.

Rogers, C. Toward a modern approach to values. *Journal of Abnormal and Social Psychology,* Vol. 68, No. 2, pp. 160–167, 1964.

Ronen, S. *Comparative and Multinational Management.* New York: Wiley, 1986.

Rosenthal, R., and DePaulo, B. M. Sex differences in eavesdropping on nonverbal cues. *Journal of Personality and Social Psychology,* Vol 37, pp. 273–285, 1979.

Rosenzweig, P. M. and Singh, J. V. Organizational environments and the multinational enterprise, *Academy of Management Review*, Vol. 15, No. 2, pp. 340–361, 1991

Rothman, E. *Hands and Heart: A History of Courtship in America.* New York: Basic Books, 1984.

Ruben, B. D. Human communication and cross-cultural effectiveness. *International and Intercultural Communication Annual*, Vol. 4, pp. 98–195, December, 1977.

Ruben, B. D., Guidelines for Cross-Cultural effectiveness. In *Toward Internationalism: Readings on Cross-Cultural Communication*, 2nd ed, pp. 36–46.L. F. Luce and E. C. Smith, eds. Cambridge, MA: Newbury House Publications, 1987.

Rubin, L. B. *Worlds of Pain: Life in the Working-Class Family.* New York: Basic Books, 1976.

Rubin, L. B. *Intimate Strangers: Men and Women Together.* New York: Harper & Row, 1983.

Ruesch, J., and Kees, W. *Nonverbal Communication: Notes on the Visual Perception of Human Relations.* Berkeley: University of California Press, 1964.

Rugman, A. M., LeCraw, D. J., and Booth, L. D. *International Business.* New York: McGraw-Hill, 1985.

Ruhly, S. *Orientations to Intercultural Communication.* Palo Alto, CA: SRA, 1976.

Rybczynski, W. *Taming the Tiger: The Struggle to Control Technology.* New York: Viking Penguin, 1983.

Sadker, M., and Sadker, D. Sexism in the schoolroom of the '80s. *Psychology Today*, pp. 54–57, March 1985.

Sadker, M., and Sadker, D. *Failing at Fairness: How America's Schools Cheat Girls.* New York: Charles Scribner's Sons, 1994.

Saint Exupery, A. *Airman's Odessey.* New York: Reynal, 1939.

Sarbaugh, L. E. *Intercultural Communication.* Rochelle Park, NJ: Hayden, 1979.

Scholes, R., and Klaus, C. H. *Elements of Writing.* New York: Oxford University Press, 1972.

Seelye, H., *Teaching Culture: Strategies for Intercultural Communication.* Lincolnwood, IL: National Textbook, 1984.

Shapiro, L. Guns and dolls: Nature or nurturance? *Newsweek*, pp. 56–65, May 28, 1990.

Sheldon, W. H. *The Variation of Human Physique.* New York: Harper & Row, 1940.

Sheldon, W. H. *The Varieties of Temperament.* New York: Harper & Row, 1942.

Siderits, M. A., Johannsen, W. J., and Fadden, T. F. Gender, role, and power: A content analysis of research. *Psychology of Women Quarterly*, Vol. 9, No. 4, pp. 439–450, 1988.

Sieburg, E., and Larson, C. Dimensions of interpersonal repines. Paper presented to the International Communication Association, Phoenix, 1971.

Simmons, G. J., and McCall, J. L. *Identities and Interactions.* New York: The Free Press, 1966.

Singer, M. R. *Intercultural Communication: A Perceptual Approach.* Englewood Cliffs, NJ: Prentice-Hall, 1987.

Slater, J. R. Beyond the Language Barrier: Principles for the Transcoding of Printed Linguistic-Iconic Texts. Unpublished dissertation, New York University, 1987.

Smith, S. W., et al. Self-monitoring, gender, and compliance-gaining goals. In *The Psychology of Tactical Communication*, pp. 91–135. M. J. Cody and M. L. McLaughlin, eds. Clevedon, PA: Multilingual Matters, 1990.

Snowdon, S. *The Global Edge: How Your Company Can Win in the International Marketplace.* New York: Simon & Schuster, 1986.

Spender, D. *Man and Language*, 2nd ed. London: Routledge & Kegan Paul, 1985.

Starkweather, J. A. Vocal communication of personality and human feelings. *Journal of Communication*, Vol. 11, pp. 63–72. 1961.

Stewart, C. J., and Cash, W. B., Jr. *Interviewing: Principles and Practices*, 5th ed. Dubuque, IA: William C. Brown, 1988.

Stewart, E. C. American assumptions and values: Orientation to action. In *Toward Internationalism: Readings in Cross-Cultural Communication*, 2nd ed., pp. 51–72. L. F. Luce and E. C. Smith, eds. Cambridge, MA: Newbury House Publishers, 1987.

Stewart, L. P., et al. *Communication between the Sexes: Sex Differences and Sex-Role Stereotypes,* 2nd ed. Scottsdale, AZ: Gorsuch Scrisbrick, 1990.

Stockard, J., and Johnson, M. M. *Sex Roles: Sex Inequality and Sex Role Development.* Englewood Cliffs, NJ: Prentice-Hall, 1980.

Stuart, R. B. *Helping Couples Change: A Social Learning Approach to Marital Therapy.* New York: Guilford Press, 1980.

Swingle, P. G. *The Management of Power.* New York: Wiley, 1976.

Tannen, D. *You Just Don't Undestand: Women and Men in Conversation.* New York: William Morrow, 1990.

Tannen, D. *Gender and Discourse.* New York: Oxford University Press, 1994.

Tarvis, C. *The Missmeasure of Women.* New York: Simon & Schuster, 1992.

Tedeschi, J. T. Self-presentation and social influence: An interactionist perspective. In *The Psychology of Tactical Communication,* pp. 301–323. M. J. Cody and M. L. McLaughlin, eds. Clevedon, PA: Multilingual Matters, 1990.

Terpstra, V. *International Dimensions of Marketing.* Boston: Kent Publishing, 1982.

Terpstra, V., and David, K. *The Cultural Environment of International Business,* 2nd ed. Cincinnati: South-Western Publishing, 1985.

Thill, J. V. and Bouvee, C. *Excellence in Business Communication,* 3rd ed. New York: McGraw-Hill, 1996.

Thomas, K. W. Conflict and conflict management. In *The Handbook of Industrial and Organizational Psychology,* pp. 889–935. M. D. Dunnette, ed. Chicago: Rand McNally, 1976.

Thomas, K. W., and Kilmann, R. H. *Thomas-Kilmann Conflict Mode Instrument.* Tuxedo, NY: XICOM, 1974.

Thomas, K. W., and Kilmann, R. Developing a forced-choice measure of conflict handling behavior; the 'mode' instrument. *Educational and Psychological Measurement,* Vol. 37, pp. 309–325, 1977.

Thomas, K. W., and Schmidt, W., II. A survey of managerial interests with respect to conflict. *Academy of Management Journal* Vol. 19, No. 2, pp. 315–318, 1976.

Thomas, R. R., Jr. *Beyond Race and Gender.* New York: American Management Association, 1991.

Ting-Toomey, S. An analysis of verbal communication patterns in high and low marital adjustment groups. *Human Communication Research,* Vol. 9, pp. 306–319, 1983.

Ting-Toomey, S. A face negotiation theory. In *Theories in Intercultural Communication.* Y. Kim and W. Gudykunst eds. Newbury Park, CA: Sage Publications.

Ting-Toomey, S. Toward a theory of conflict and culture. In *Communication, Culture, and Organizational Process,* pp. 71–86. W. Gudykunst, L. Stewart, and S. Ting-Toomey, eds. Newbury Park, CA: Sage Publications, 1985.

Triandis, H. C. *Interpersonal Behavior across Cultures: Variations in Black and White Perceptions of the Social Environment.* Urbana: The University of Illinois Press, 1976.

Trudgill, P. *Sociolinguistics: An Introduction to Language and Society.* Harmondworth, Middlesex: Penguin Books, 1974.

Tucker, R. W. *The Inequality of Nations.* New York: Basic Books, 1977.

Varner, I., and Beamer, L. *Intercultural Communication in the Global Workplace.* Chicago: Irwin, 1995.

Vayrynen, R., ed. *New Directions in Conflict Theory: Conflict Resolution and Conflict Transformation.* Newbury Park, CA: Sage Publications, 1991.

Victor, D. A. Stamp: A formula for teaching business communication theory. *The Bulletin of the Association for Business Communication,* Vol. 49, No. 3, pp. 34–35, 1986.

Victor, D. A. *International Business Communication.* New York: HarperCollins, 1992.

Vogel, E. *Japan as Number One.* Cambridge, MA: Harvard University Press, 1979.

Vonsild, S. Intercultural competence in a vocational context, In *Intercultural Competence,*

Volume II: The Adult Learner, pp. 125–140. A. A. Jensen, K. Jaeger, and A. Lorentsen, eds. Aalborg, Denmark: Aalborg University Press, 1995.

Wall, J. A., Jr., and Blum, M. Community mediation in the People's Republic of China. *Journal of Conflict Resolution,* Vol. 35, No. 1, pp. 3–20, 1991.

Watson, C. An examination of the impact of gender and power on managers' negotiation behavior: Implications for ADR practitioners. *Proceedings for the Society for Professionals in Dispute Resolution,* pp. 154–162, Washington, DC: SPIDR, 1991.

Watson, C. Gender differences in negotiating behavior and outcomes: Fact or artifact? *Conflict and Gender.* A. Taylor and J. B. Miller, eds. Cresskill, NJ: Hampton Press, pps. 191–209, 1994.

Watson, G., and Johnson, D. *Social Psychology: Issues and Insights.* Philadelphia: Lippincott, 1972.

Watzlawick, P., Beavin, J. H., and Jackson, D. D. *Pragmatics of Human Communication: A Study of Interactional Patterns, Pathologies, and Paradoxes.* New York: Norton, 1967.

Webster's New Collegiate Dictionary, Springfield, MA: G. & C. Merriam, 1981.

Wehr, P. *Conflict Resolution.* Boulder, CO: Westview Press, 1979.

Wheeless, V., and Dierks-Stewart, K. The psychometric properties of the Bem sex-role inventory. *Communication Quarterly,* Vol. 29, pp. 173–186, 1981.

Whitely, W., and England, G. Managerial values as a reflection of culture and the process of industrialization, *Academy of Management Journal,* Vol. 20, pp. 439–453, 1977.

Whorf, B. L. *Collected Papers on Metalinguistics.* Washington, DC: Department of State, Foreign Service Institute, 1952.

Wierzbicka, A. *Semantics, Culture and Cognition.* New York: Oxford University Press, 1992.

Wilken, L. What is ethnography and how can it be used to raise cultural awareness? In *Intercultural Competence, Volume II: The Adult Learner,* pp. 77–88. A. A. Jensen, K. Jaeger, and A. Lorentsen, eds. Aalborg, Denmark: Aalborg University Press, 1995.

Williams, F. The psychological correlates of speech characteristics: on sounding disadvantaged. *Journal of Speech and Hearing Research,* Vol. 13, pp. 472–488, 1970.

Williams, J. E., and Best, D. L. *Measuring Sex Stereotypes: A Thirty Nation Study.* Beverly Hills, CA: Sage Publications, 1982.

Willis, F. N., Jr. Initial speaking distance as a function of the speaker's relationship. *Psychonomic Science,* Vol. 5, pp. 221–222, 1966.

Wood, J. T. Gender and moral voice: Moving from women's nature to standpoint epistemology. *Women's Studies in Communication,* Vol. 15, No. 1, pp. 1–24, Spring 1992.

Wood, J. T. Naming and interpreting sexual harassment: A conceptual framework. In *Sexual Harassment: Communication Implications,* pp. 9–26. G. L. Kreps, ed. Cresskill, NJ: Hampton Press, 1993.

Wood, J. T., and Inman, C. C. In a different mode: Masculine styles of communicating closeness. *Journal of Applied Communication Research,* Vol. 2, No. 3, pp. 279–295, August 1993.

Wood, J. T. *Gendered Lives.* Belmont, CA: Wadsworth, 1994.

Wolf, N. *The Beauty Myth.* New York: Anchor Books, Doubleday, 1991.

Wolvin, A. D., and Coakley, C. G. *Listening.* Dubuque, IA: William C. Brown, 2nd ed. 1985.

Yli-Jokipii, H. *Request in Professional Discourse: A Cross-Cultural Study of British, American and Finnish Business Writing.* Helsinki: Suomalainen Tiedeakatemia, 1994.

Zack, A. M. *Public Sector Mediation.* Washington, DC: Bureau of National Affairs, 1985.

Zand, D. E. Trust and managerial problem solving. *Administrative Science Quarterly,* Vol. 17, No. 2, pp. 229–239, June 1972.

Zimmerman, D., and West, C. Sex roles, interruptions and silences in conversation. In *Language and Sex: Difference and Dominance.* B. Thorne and N. Henley, eds. Rowley, MA: Newbury House, pps. 105–129, 1975.

AUTHOR INDEX

Ablamovicz, H., 149
Addington, D.W., 94
Adler, N.J., 170, 191, 192, 194
Almaney, A.J.
Alwan, A.J., 182
Araki, C.T., 22
Argyle, M, 63, 88
Aries, E., 105, 109, 111, 115, 131, 136, 142
Arliss, L.P., 105, 111, 132
Arpan, J.S., 160
Arvey, R.D., 80

Bales, R., 206
Ball, D.A., 160
Barnlund, D.C., 4, 17, 18, 39, 42, 46, 48, 50, 53, 58, 67, 112, 113
Barry, W.A., 42, 119
Bass, B., 153, 179
Baxter, L.A., 142
Beamer, L., 150, 153, 176
Beavin, J.H., 6, 17
Beck, A.T., 9, 116, 127, 136
Beck, D., 1
Beebe, S., 187
Bell, D.C., 142
Bem, S.L., 104, 105, 106, 109, 111, 115, 120, 121, 126, 129, 131, 132, 142, 143, 144
Benedict, R., 154, 173
Berger, C., 173
Berman, P., 121
Bernard, J., 9, 67, 104, 115, 120, 121
Berry, D.S., 80
Berryman-Fink, C., 127
Best, D.L., 13, 105, 128, 129
Billingham, R.E., 142
Birdwhistell, R.L., 15, 17, 75, 137
Birk, T., 140
Black, J.S., 153
Blake, D.H., 165
Blake, R.R., 8, 9, 29, 38, 42, 58
Blank, R., 80, 81
Blau, P.D., 109
Bloom, A.H., 157, 209
Blum, M., 21
Blumstein, P., 120
Boggs, J.W., 76

Booth, L.D., 167
Borisoff, D., 24, 59, 104, 105, 107, 108, 111, 115, 121, 127, 131, 132, 182
Borker, R., 111, 140
Bouvee, C., 204
Brett, J.M., 153
Brief, A.P., 8, 64
Brooks, H., 165
Brooks, W., 207, 217
Broverman, I.K., 121, 129
Bruner, J., 127
Bugental, D.E., 138
Burger, P.C., 153, 179
Burggraf, C.S., 142
Burgoon, J.R., 79, 140
Burke, R.J., 206
Burling, R., 158
Burns, S., 80
Byrne, D., 137

Cahn, D.D., Jr., 59
Calabrese, R., 173
Calder, K.E., 165
Camden, C.T., 136, 140
Canary, D.J., 142
Cash, T.F., 80
Cash, W.B., Jr., 56
Casmir, F.L., 44
Cassell, C., 122
Caudron, S., 81
Chafetz, J.S., 142
Chaika, E., 210
Chaikin, A.L., 131, 138
Chaney, L., 151
Chelune, G.F., 127
Chikudate, N., 176
Chomsky, N., 157
Cixous, H., 131
Coakley, C.G., 56
Cohen, R., 151
Condon, J.C., Jr., 17
Condon, J.S., 151, 153, 163, 170
Cooks, L., 111
Cooper, P., 124, 125
Copeland, L., 161, 162, 188
Cose, E., 80

Coser, L.A., 1
Couch, C., 193
Coulson, R., 21, 24
Cox, T., Jr., 151
Cross, G.P., 1
Cummings, L.L., 13
Cupach, W.R., 142

D'Andrade, R.G., 157
Daniels, H., 158
David, K., 153, 162, 166
Davis, A.M., 23
Davis, F.B., 127
Davitz, J.R., 94
Deaux, K., 104
de Beauvoir, S., 122
DeMente, B.L., 164, 171, 175
Derlega, V.J., 131, 138
Deutsch, M., 2, 3, 4, 6, 11, 19, 23, 40, 41, 42, 46, 66, 67, 105, 217
DeVito, J.A., 51, 52, 56, 59, 65, 66
DeWine, S., 67
Dierks-Stewart, K., 129
Dindia, K., 131, 136, 140
Dipboye, R.L., 80
Dodd, C.H., 151, 153, 180, 188
Douglas, M., 159
Dovidio, J.F., 141
Duck, S., 4, 116, 127
Duffy, K.G., 22

Eagly, A.H., 93
Eakins, B.W., 131, 136, 140
Eakins, R.G., 131, 136, 140
Ekman, P., 83, 84, 86, 90
Elkouri, E.A., 24
Elkouri, F., 24
Ellsworth, P., 187
Ellul, J., 165
Eman-Wheeless, V., 127
Emmert, P., 207, 217
Evans, G.W., 137

Fadden, T.F., 141
Fagot, B., 121, 123
Fast, J., 82
Feigenbaum, E.A., 165
Ferber, M.A., 109
Fields, G., 164, 164
Filley, A.C., 9, 10, 38, 40, 51, 64
Fisher, G., 22, 174, 191
Fisher, J.D., 137
Fisher, R., 4, 18, 22, 48
Fitzpatrick, M.A., 116, 142
Folberg, J., 21, 23
Folger, J.P., 38
Foucault, M., 126
Fox, G.L., 122
Friesen, W.V., 83, 84, 86, 90
Fu, M.Y.C., 160
Furnham, A., 63

Gahagan, J.P., 17
Gallimore, R., 76
Gayle-Hackett, B., 142
Ghiselli, E.E., 170
Gianetto, R.M., 138
Gibb, J., 16, 17, 38, 39, 40, 45, 46, 48, 49, 51, 53, 58, 66, 67, 68, 69, 70, 98, 113
Gillen, B., 80
Gilligan, C., 104, 111, 121, 127
Goffman, E., 17, 42, 44, 117
Goldman-Eisler, F., 95, 97
Goldstein, J.R., 152
Goodman, E., 26, 28
Gorham, J., 124
Gourley, C., 22, 24
Graebner, A., 121
Graf, L.A., 171
Graham, J.A., 81
Graham, J.L., 190, 191
Gregory, G., 165
Griggs, J., 161, 162, 188
Grosch, J.W., 22
Gudykunst, W.B., 151, 173, 174, 190, 194
Gumperz, J.J., 157

Hahn, D.F., 24, 105, 111, 115, 121, 131
Haire, M., 170
Halberstadt, A.G., 138
Halberstam, D., 167
Hall, E.T., 12, 13, 42, 92, 93, 120, 153, 163, 173, 182, 183, 184, 185, 186, 187, 188
Hall, J.A., 93, 131, 132, 137, 138, 139, 140
Hall, M.R., 173
Hammer, M., 173
Hampden-Turner, C., 183
Hanley, T.D., 156
Harnett, D.L., 13
Harris, P.R., 194
Harrison, R.P., 78
Haste, H., 104, 109, 132, 142, 145
Hatfield, E., 80, 116, 127, 131
Hauser, J., 22, 23
Haynes, J., 22
Heilman, M.E., 80
Henley, N.M., 9, 92, 93, 104, 131, 132, 137, 138, 139, 140, 187
Herberger, R.A., Jr., 190, 191
Herman, C.P., 80
Heslin, R., 91
Hilton, C.B., 161
Hintz, R.A., 193
Hoban, P., 3, 4
Hochschild, A., 120, 138
Hocker, J.L., 2, 4, 5n, 9, 19, 46, 55, 57, 59, 64
Hoecklin, L., 153
Hofheinz, R., Jr., 165
Hofstede, G., 152, 153, 170, 173, 178, 179, 194
Hoijer, H., 157
Horn, L.J., 142

Howard, R.B., 137
Husted, B.W., 175
Hymes, D., 157

Illich, I., 165
Inman, C.C., 24, 111, 127, 131

Jablin, F.M., 169
Jacklin, C.N., 121
Jackson, D.D., 6, 17
James, D.L., 176
Jamieson, D.W., 10
Jamieson, K.H., 9, 109, 115
Janssens, M., 153
Jensen, J.V., 96, 188
Johannsen, W.J., 141
Johnson, D., 18, 38, 46, 57, 67
Johnson, F.L., 142
Johnson, M.M., 9, 67, 104, 115, 120, 121
Jones, G.M., 125
Jones, S.E., 91, 139
Jones, T.S., 141
Jordan, C., 76
Jouhar, A.J., 81

Kahn, A., 81
Kanter, R.M., 141
Keashly, L., 131, 142
Keen, S., 122, 131
Kees, W., 186
Kelly, G.A., 152
Keltner, J.W., 22, 23, 24, 25
Kendon, A., 88
Kennedy, C.W., 136, 140
Key, W.B., 154
Kilmann, R.H., 8, 9, 11, 14, 39, 46, 64
Kilpatrick, J.A., 153
Kim, Y.Y., 151, 173, 190, 194
Klaus, C.H., 204
Kluckhohn, C., 151
Knapp, M.L., 13, 17, 44, 87, 93, 95, 137, 139
Kommor, J.J., 127
Kramarae, C., 9, 66, 104, 131, 132, 134, 140, 142
Kramer, E., 94
Kressel, K., 21
Kroeber, A.L., 151

LaFrance, M., 104, 137
Lakoff, R., 104, 131, 132, 134, 135
Lalljee, M.C., 95, 97
Lander, H., 157
Larson, C., 59
Laurent, A., 178
LeCraw, D.J., 167
Lee, J., 169
Lerner, H.G., 116
Likert, J.G., 194
Likert, R., 194
Lincoln, J.R., 171
Lippitt, G.L., 4
Lips, H., 132

Livingstone, J.M., 172
Loug, L.R., 138
Luce, L.F., 149
Ludwig, L., 187
Lulofs, R.S., 4

McArthur, L.Z., 80
McCall, J.L., 42, 44, 127
McConville, D.J., 79
McCorduck, P., 165
McCulloch, W.H., Jr., 160
Macoby, E.E., 121
Maier, N.R.F., 18, 49, 50, 51, 53, 68
Major, B., 104
Maltz, D., 111, 140
Mandelbaum, D., 157
March, R.M., 175
Martin, J., 151
Martin, L., 157
Maruyama, M., 150
Mathes, E.W., 81
Mehrabian, A., 17, 40, 41, 43, 44, 45, 78, 97, 137, 188
Merrill, L., 59, 104, 105, 111, 131, 132, 182
Miller, G.R., 148, 208, 209
Miller, J.J., 153
Montagu, A., 91
Moore, C.W., 148
Moore, G.W., 21
Morain, G.G., 186
Moran, R.T., 194
Morris, D., 83
Morrison, A.M., 109
Mouton, J.S., 8, 9, 29, 38, 42, 58
Mueller, B.D., 158
Mulac, A., 136
Mulde, A., 156
Mulder, M., 178
Munter, M., 204

Names, J.H., 1
Niyekama-Howard, A., 157
Nostrand, H.W., 153

Olczak, P.V., 22
O'Reilly, C.A., 170
Osborn, A.F., 52
Ouchi, W.G., 194
Page, J.A., 175
Pearson, J.C., 66, 105, 111, 124, 132, 134
Person, E., 122
Pfau, M., 140
Phatak, A.V., 170
Pike, K.L., 157
Pinker, S., 157
Polit, D., 137
Poole, M.S., 38, 114, 116
Porter, L.W., 153, 170
Porter, R.E., 151, 180
Powell, G.N., 105, 109, 115, 127, 142
Prigge, D.Y., 156
Pruitt, D.G., 21, 50

Pullum, G.K., 157
Putnam, L.L., 68, 114, 116, 131, 141

Rapson, R., 116, 127, 131
Reik, T., 145
Reitz, H.J., 170
Richmond, V.P., 124
Ricks, D.A., 160
Roberts, J.V., 80
Roberts, K.H., 170
Robison, J.T., 127
Rogers, C., 40, 42, 49, 57, 194
Romney, A.K., 157
Ronen, S., 151, 153
Rosenzweig, P.M., 168
Rothman, E., 119
Ruben, B.D., 151, 193
Rubin, L.B., 9, 104, 111, 122, 129
Ruesch, J., 186
Rugman, A.M., 167
Ruhly, S., 153
Rybczynski, W., 165, 166, 167

Sack, A.R., 142
Sadker, D., 123, 124, 125, 126
Sadker, M., 123, 124, 125, 126
Saine, T., 79
Saint-Exupery, A., 1
Saitta, M.B., 138
Samovar, L.A., 151, 180
Sarbaugh, L.E., 193
Saruwatari, L.F., 80
Sashkin, M., 18, 50, 51, 53
Schmidt, W., II, 4
Scholes, R., 204
Schuler, R.S., 8, 64
Schwartz, P., 120
Seelye, H., 153, 162, 169
Shapiro, L., 125
Sheldon, W.H., 79
Shephard, F.L., 142
Siderits, M.A., 141
Sieburg, E., 59
Sillars, A.L., 142
Simmons, G.J., 42, 44, 127
Singer, M.R., 151, 153, 154, 162, 189, 190
Singh, J.V., 168
Slater, J.R., 158
Slipp, S., 80, 81
Smith, E.C., 149
Smith, F.S., 153
Smith, S.W., 111, 112, 117, 118
Snowdon, S., 182
Solem, A.F., 49
Spender, D., 136
Sprecher, S., 80
Starkweather, J.A., 94
Steinberg, M., 148, 208, 209
Stevens, O.J., 13
Stewart, C.J., 56
Stewart, E.C., 190, 194

Stewart, L.P., 136
Stockard, J., 9, 67, 104, 115, 120, 121
Stuart, R.B., 4
Swingle, P.G., 217

Tannen, D., 9, 111, 131, 134, 135, 136, 140
Tarvis, C., 80
Taylor, A., 21, 23
Tedeschi, J.T., 17, 117
Terpstra, B., 153, 162, 166
Terpstra, D.F., 80
Terpstra, V., 169
Thill, J.V., 204
Thomas, K.W., 2, 4, 8, 9, 10, 11, 14, 39, 46, 64
Thomas, R.R., Jr., 80
Ting-Toomey, S., 63, 151, 194
Todd-Mancillas, W., 105, 132
Triandis, H.C., 12, 55, 64, 189
Trompenaars, F., 183
Trudgill, P., 210
Tucker, R.W., 165
Turner, L.H., 105, 132

Ury, W., 4, 18, 22, 48

Van Sell, M., 8, 64
Van Velsor, E., 109
Varner, I., 150, 153, 176
Victor, D.A., 151, 153, 154, 162, 169, 174,
    182, 204
Vogel, E., 165
Vonsild, S., 149

Wall, J.A., Jr., 21
Walters, R.S., 165
Watson, C., 131, 141, 142
Watson, G., 18, 38, 46, 57, 67
Watzlawick, P., 6, 17
Wehr, P., 4, 23
West, C., 134, 135, 136, 140
West, R., 124
Wheatley, J., 125
Wheeless, V., 129
White, R.P., 109
Whorf, B.L., 157, 209
Wierzbicka, A., 158
Wilken, L., 170
Williams, F., 94
Williams, J.E., 13, 105, 128, 129
Willis, F.N., Jr., 137
Wilmot, W.W., 2, 4, 5n, 9, 19, 46, 55, 57, 59,
    64
Wolf, N., 80
Wolvin, A.D., 56
Wood, J.T., 24, 91, 105, 111, 127, 131, 132,
    136, 138
Yli-Jokipii, H., 176
Yousef, F., 151, 153, 163
Zack, A.M., 23
Zand, D.E., 18, 48, 51
Zimmerman, D., 134, 135, 136, 140

SUBJECT INDEX

Accent differences, 155–156
Accommodation, 10–11, 116
Acknowledgment, in conflict management,
    11–13, 119–126, 152–154
Action phase, in conflict management,
    16–18, 37, 131–141, 188–195, 215–217
Adaptability, 193
Adaptors, nonverbal, 86–88
Affect displays, 85
African Americans, 80–81
Ambiguity, 211
Analysis, in conflict management, 19,
    141–143, 195–196, 217
Analyzing the reception and, 207–208
Anger, displaying, 142–143
Apology, rhetoric of, 25–28
Appearance, 14, 79–82
    cross-cultural aspects of, 185–186
Arab world, 180–182, 185, 186, 187–188
Arbitration, 24–25
Articulation, 41
Artifacts, 79
Asia, 194
Asian Americans, 80, 81
Assertions, admitting one's, 40–41
Assertiveness
    gender and, 81
    levels of, 9
Assessment, in conflict management, 5–11,
    104–119, 148–152, 204–207
Attitude, in conflict management, 13–16,
    126–131, 154–188, 208–215
Attribution
    of behavior, 13–14
    of belief, 67–68
Authority conception, 177–180
Automatic phrasing, 43, 44–45
Avoidance behavior, 9, 62, 116

Barriers, to interaction, 40, 45
Belgium, 84
Beliefs, 6
    attribution of, 67–68
Beltlining, 65–66
Blaming, 40–41, 62, 64

Body language. See Kinesics (body language)
Body types, 80
Brainstorming, 51–53
Brazil, 175

Cambodia, 188
Canada, 163
Climate
    cultural, 162–169
    defensive and supportive, 39–40
    examination of, 8, 113–116
    human, 164
    work, 113–114
Clothing, 79, 185–186
Coercive influence, 117
Cognitive oculesics, 88–89
Collaboration, 11, 38–39, 116
Communication environment. See Climate
Communication technology
    cultural influences in, 165, 166, 167
    power and, 165
    second-language users and, 159
Competition, 9, 116, 224
    gender styles of, 141–142
Competitive behavior, 63–68
Compound requests, versus direct, 134–135
Compromise, 10, 116, 117–118
Computer skills, sex differences in, 125. See
    also Communication technology
Confiding in others, 51, 138
Confirming assertions, 59–60
Conflict
    defining, 1–2
    learning to manage, 2–3
Conflict-handling behavior
    five modes of, 116–119
    types of, 38–39
Conflict management
    attributes of, 4
    five step model for, 5–19, 20–21, 116–119
    languages of (oral/verbal), 37–73
    languages of (nonverbal), 75–102
    languages of (written/verbal), 203–223
    styles of, 5n, 8–11
    training for, 2–3

Connotations, 40
Connotative meanings, of words, 42–43
Contexting, 172–177
Cooperation, 59
  levels of, 9, 10
Credibility, establishing, 189
Criticism, avoiding negative, 52
Cross-cultural awareness, 147–201
  acknowledgment, 152–154
  action, 188–195
  analysis, 195–196
  assessment, 148–152
  attitude, 154–188
  pseudoconflicts, 148–151, 152, 157, 163
Cross-cultural differences. *See* Cultural
    differences
Cultural differences
  defining, 148, 151–152
  in emblems, 83–84
  in nonverbal communication, 75–76
  in regulators, 85–86
  see also Cross-cultural awareness
  Cultural diversity, 151
Cultural evaluation, 12–13
Culture
  defining, 148, 151–152
  environment and technology of a, 162

Defensive climates, 39–40, 51, 67
Defensiveness, 50
Definitional side tracking, 63
Denials, excuse making, 60, 64
Denmark, 149–150, 170
Denotative meanings, of words, 42
Descriptive speech, 40–48, 49, 98
Dialectic differences
  in formal writing, 209–210
  within the same language, 160
  in word choice, 156
Disclaimers, use of, 133–134
Disconfirming responses, 59–60
Dominance, 9

Education, sex differences in, 123–126
Ego conflict, 209
E-mail, 160
Emblems, 186
  cultural differences in, 83–84
Emotional expression, 85
Empathy, 53–57, 99
Enunciation, 156
Environment, communication. *See* Climate
Equality, in exchanges, 57–68
Ethnic stereotypes, 80
Ethnocentrism, 153–154
Evaluations, avoiding, 54–55
Exaggerations, 41
Explaining, 25–28
Expressive oculesics, 90–91
Eye contact. *See* Oculesics (eye contact)

Facial expression, 16, 17, 85
Facial stereotypes, 80
Fairness, 63–68
Feedback
  appropriate, 51
  discouraging, 57–58
  fear of, 55
  giving and receiving, 193
  seeking, 18
  oral constructs for, 55–57
Feminine traits, 130–131
Fillers, word, 44–45
First impressions, 79
France, 84, 173

Gender differences, conflicts based on, 82,
    103–146
  acknowledgment, 119–126
  action, 131–141
  analysis, 141–143
  assessment, 104–119
  attitude, 126–131
Gender influences, 24, 104
  on nonverbal communication, 75–76,
    136–141
  on power balance, 132
  on verbal communication, 133–136
Gender polarization, 126
Gender stereotypes, 80, 81
Generalities, employing, 41
Generalizations, 62, 215
Germany, 163, 164
Gestures, 186, 187
"Glass ceiling," 128
Goals
  clarification of, 7, 9, 111–113
  establishment of, 192
Grammatical errors, 211
Gunnysacking, 65–66

Haptics (touching behavior), 17, 91–92
  cultural differences in, 187
  gender differences in, 92, 139–140
  "taboo" touches, 139
Hawaiian, 76
Hostile expressions, 46–47
  joking, 46–47
  questioning, 47–48, 55–56

Illustrators, nonverbal, 84–85
Immoderation, 215
Incongruity, 63
Individual traits, 6, 105–106
Influencing tactics, 117–118
Intercultural communication, 148–151,
    188–195
Interrupting behavior, 61, 135–136
Intimacy, 91, 92
Iran, 166
Issues, stating clearly and specifically, 41–42

Japan, 160, 163–164, 167, 170–171, 175–176, 186, 187, 194
Jargon, 209, 210–211
Jewelry. *See* Artifacts
Joking, 46–47, 60–61, 66
Judging others, 65

Kinesics (body language), 82–88
    cultural differences in, 186
    gender differences in, 137–138
Korea, 175

Language differences, 155–162
Language misuse, 211–212
Language style, 16
Leaders, gender-linked responses to, 138
LESCANT model, 155
Linguistic differences, 157–159

Malayasian, 185–186
Manipulation, 51, 118
Marriage, 3–4
    adjustment to, 119
    Masculine traits, 130
Mediation, 21–25
    process stages of, 22–23
    skills in, 23–24
    voluntary, 24
Message tactics, 117–118
Mexico, 175
Minorities, 80–81
Monitoring oculesics, 89–90
Multinational corporations, 150

Negative sanctions, 67
Negotiation, 50–51, 52
    gender differences in, 141–143
Nepotism, 171
Nonverbal behavior
    assessing, 98
    awareness of, 14–15
    contradictory, 63
    cross-cultural aspects of, 185–188
    self-awareness of, 97
Nonverbal communication
    defining, 77–78
    direct, types of, 78–94
    effect of culture on, 75–76
    effect of gender on, 75–76, 136–141
    reliance on, 75–76
    strategies for conflict management, 97–99
Nonverbal cues, 16–18

Oculesics (eye contact), 86, 88–91
    cognitive, 88–89
    cultural differences in, 187–188
    expressive, 90–91
    gender differences in, 137–138
    monitoring, 89–90
    regulatory, 90
Oral Communication, See Verbal
        Communication
Overlaps, in conversation, 135–136

Paralanguage, 78, 94–97
    gender differences in, 140–141
Paraphrasing, 56
Passivity, 55
Patronizing, 215
Pauses, 95–97
    overuse of, 45
Personal attacks, 65–66
Personal constructs, 54
Personality conflict, 88
Personality traits, 93, 130
Personal space. *See* Proxemics (personal
        space)
Perspective, understanding other's, 54
Philippines, 177
Physical appearance, 79–80, 81–82
Physical attractiveness, 80
Physical contact. *See* Haptics (touching
        behavior)
Physical traits, 79–81, 93
Place
    concept of, 168
    factors of, 162–169
    see also Climate
Power
    legitimate, 126
    perceived, 93, 132, 141
Power balance, 57–58
Power distance, 178–180
Power imbalance, gender-based, 132
Problem solving
    assessing solutions, 50–51
    communication in, 68
    creativity in, 52, 53, 193–194
    identifying the problem, 49, 190
    orientation, 48–51, 98, 190
    proposing solutions, 50
    summarizing decisions, 195
Professional jargon, 209, 210–211
Proposals
    appraising, 53
    combining and integrating, 53
Provisionalism, 68
Provocative terms, 43
Proxemics (personal space), 79, 92–94
    cultural differences in, 163, 188
    gender differences in, 136–137
Pseudoconflict
    cross-cultural, 148–151, 152
    defining, 154
    sources of, 157, 163
    in writing style, 214–215

Qualifiers, use of, 133
Questions
    basic classifications of, 56
    facilitating communication, 56
    hostile, 47–48, 55–56
    tag, 134

Racial stereotypes, 80
Rationality, use of, 117

Reactions, anticipating, 193
Referent influence, 118
Regulators, 135
  nonverbal, 85–86
Regulatory oculesics, 90
Reprisals, 67
Respect, mutual, 58–59
Responsibility, denial of, 64
Role reversal, 56

Sarcasm, 46–47, 60–61, 66
Saudi Arabia, 180–182
Self-absorption, 38
Self-disclosure, 51, 138
Self-esteem, 81
Semantics, 42–48
  cross-cultural difficulties in, 214
  obstacles to communication, 43–45
Semantic unclarity, 212–215
Sex. *See* Sexual behavior
Sex differences. *See* Gender differences; Sex roles
Sex roles, 104, 105
  acculturated, 120–126, 127
  expected, 107, 126, 131
  in the family, 120–122, 126–131
  proxemics and, 93
Sex role stereotypes, 123, 127–131
Sex stratification, 67
Sex-trait stereotypes, 24, 105, 106, 128–131
Sexual behavior
  gender differences in, 122
Sexual discrimination, 109
Sexual harassment, 81, 139
Silence, use of, 176
Silences, 95–96
Silencing strategies, 61
Slang expressions, 44
Social institutions, behavior and, 170
Socialization
  and sex roles, 120–126, 127
Social organization, 169–172
  defined, 169
Societal norms, 104, 121, 129
Sociolinguistics, 156
Soviet Union, former, 187
Spontaneity, versus strategy, 51–53, 99
Status, recognizing, 191–192
Status differences, 58
Stereotypes
  ethnic, 80
  facial, 80
  gender, 80, 81
  racial, 80
  sex role, 123, 127–131
  sex-trait, 24, 105, 106, 128–131
Stereotyping, 14, 44, 62
  consequences of, 128–131
  processes of, 127–128
Strategic behavior, 51, 99
Student-teacher interaction, 123–124
Supportive climates, 39–40, 43, 51, 98

Syntactic selection, 45–48

Tag questions, 134
Tags, word, 45
Temporal conception, 180–185
  monochronic, 182–185
  polychronic, 183, 184
Third-party intervention, 19–25
Thought processing, 169–185
Threats, 46
Time, concept of, 180–185
Tonal error, 214–215
Topic, changing the, 61
Touching behavior. *See* Haptics (touching behavior)
Translation difficulties, 159–162, 191
Trivialization, 60
Trust
  attitude of, 38, 39
  establishing, 189
  mutual, 51

Underresponsiveness, 60

Value systems, 6
  judging other's, 65
Verbal communication
  cross-cultural effects on, 155–162, 190–191
  effects of gender on, 133–136
  effects of writing on, 203–221
  oral strategies, 37–73
Verbal cues, 16–18
Vocabulary variation, 209–211
Vocal cues. *See* Paralanguage
Voice(s)
  production and expressiveness, 94
  tonal error in, 214–215
  of women, 140
  see also Paralanguage

White males, 81
"Win-lose" strategies, 9
"Win-win" mode, 11, 38
Word choice, 42–48
Writing, in conflict management
  acknowledgment, 207–208
  action, 215–217
  analysis, 217
  assessment, 204–207
  attitude, 208–215
Writing styles, 203–221
  basic steps in writing, 204
  choosing, 204
  conceptualization process, 204–207, 216
  inappropriate, 204
  in a potentially explosive situation, 206–207
  problems in reception, 207–208
  problems in transmittal, 208–215, 216
  purpose and, 205, 206
  tonal error in, 214–215